D1601106

The Jewish Radical Right

STUDIES ON ISRAEL

Series Editor

JOEL MIGDAL

The Jewish Radical Right

Revisionist Zionism and Its Ideological Legacy

Eran Kaplan

The University of Wisconsin Press

The University of Wisconsin Press
1930 Monroe Street
Madison, Wisconsin 53711

www.wisc.edu/wisconsinpress/

3 Henrietta Street
London WC2E 8LU, England

1   3   5   4   2

Printed in the United States of America

Library of Congress Cataloging-in-Publication Data
Kaplan, Eran.
The Jewish radical right: Revisionist Zionism and its ideological legacy / Eran Kaplan.
p.   cm.—(Studies on Israel)
Includes bibliographical references.
ISBN 0-299-20380-8 (hardcover: alk. paper)
1. Revisionist Zionism—Israel—History.
2. Israel—Politics and government—20th century.
3. Religious right—Israel.
4. Right and left (Political science)
I. Title.
DS150.R5K37   2005
320.54´095694—dc22´   2004012859

This book was published with the support of
the Koret Foundation Jewish Studies Publications Program.

Contents

Preface

When I arrived at the Jabotinsky Institute in Tel Aviv to begin my re-search on Zionist revisionism, my grandfather, Julius Kaplan, came with me to introduce me to the institute's staff; he was then the head of Misdar Jabotinsky (the Jabotinsky Order), and there was no end to his delight that his grandson had decided to study the history of the movement to which he and my grandmother, Ida Kaplan, have dedi-cated much of their lives. My grandparents on my mother's side, who died long before I began this project, were also active supporters of Jabotinsky's movement. Gutman Rabinovich, my maternal grand-father, was a member of the Irgun; on October 29, 1937, he was se-verely wounded while guarding Jewish worshipers at the Western Wall, and in 1944 the British jailed him and sent him into exile to a camp in Africa. But despite my family's deep roots in the Revisionist movement, this was not what initially drew me to study its history. My initial interest in the history of Zionist revisionism arose from my interest in the reactions, primarily the Jewish reactions, to mod-ernity and its challenges. I found in Zionist revisionism an intriguing, complex, and at times conflicting response to the Zionist attempt to modernize every aspect of Jewish life, an effort that was rooted in the intellectual currents of fin-de-siècle Europe. Unlike the more tradi-tional critics of modernity in the Jewish world, the Revisionists did not reject all aspects of modernity—they embraced modern technol-ogy and its practical as well as its cultural possibilities—yet they viewed it as a potentially dangerous and decadent development in Jewish history, one that could prevent the Zionist movement from fulfilling its political aspirations.

The core of this book is my analysis of the Revisionists' critique of modern culture and of the Labor movement's Zionist vision, and its attempt to formulate an alternative cultural and ideological model. But as this project evolved, I realized that it was also becoming more personal. I was not necessarily writing my family's history—in fact, I am afraid that my grandparents would not be at all happy with many of my conclusions—but I was exploring the ideological origins of the movement, which for my generation has become the central and most influential force in Israeli politics. In 1977 Menachem Begin led the Likud Party to a surprising win in the polls, and decades of Labor dominance of the Zionist movement came to an abrupt end. Today, after years of being marginalized by the Zionist Left, Revisionists have become the leading party in Israel politics. Thus the history of the movement is no longer a secondary, though vocal, chapter in the annals of Jewish nationalism but a critical part of the history of Zionism and modern Israel.

The 1990s were perhaps the most tumultuous in the admittedly short, though highly contentious, history of Zionist and Israeli studies. During that time Zionist historiography experienced some profound changes: It adopted new methodological tools, and it dramatically expanded its scope and viewpoints. And the emergence of New History and the post-Zionist critique (see introduction) have led to some heated debates about the nature, history, and future of the Zionist enterprise. It has been my hope, throughout this process, to add the study of Zionist Revisionist thought, which I believe was the most original and multifaceted of all the Zionist intellectual currents, to this rapidly shifting field.

This book, which originated as a doctoral dissertation at Brandeis University, has been an integral part of my life since 1997, and I am delighted to have the opportunity to thank the people and institutions that supported me along the way. Antony Polonsky, my dissertation adviser, and Jehuda Reinharz of Brandeis University, a leading historian of Zionism, have offered invaluable guidance and encouragement. Anita Shapira of Tel Aviv University read part of the manuscript and supported this project. My colleagues at the University of Cincinnati have been very helpful and gave me great support in the final stages of this project.

Derek Penslar of the University of Toronto has been a true mentor, friend, and constant source of motivation. I revised my dissertation into a book manuscript while I was the Ray D. Wolfe Fellow at the University of Toronto; Derek and his family helped make it a most productive and enjoyable year. My thanks also go to the Wolfe family for its generosity and to the Jewish Studies Program at Toronto for providing me with an intellectually stimulating working environment. My cousin Joe Triebwasser, a doctor and a writer (in an earlier time he would have made a fine Revisionist intellectual), read the manuscript in its various stages. His intelligence, perceptiveness, and mastery of the English language helped me tremendously; without him I would never have finished this project. My friend and colleague Yaron Peleg, now of George Washington University, has, since the inception of this project, read, repeatedly, every version, and his keen intellect and relentless optimism inspired me throughout.

This book has benefited from generous financial support from Brandeis University, the Tauber Institute for the Study of European Jewry, the Dorot Foundation, and the Taft Memorial Fund. Amira Stern, the director of the Jabotinsky Institute, and her staff were extremely accommodating and treated me like a member of the family. I want to thank Yossi Achimeir for inviting me to his house and giving me access to his family archive. Special thanks go out to the editors and staff at the University of Wisconsin Press for all their support and dedication. A revised version of chapter 5 appeared previously as "Decadent Pioneers: Land, Space and Gender in Zionist Revisionist Thought, " *Journal of Israeli History* 20, no. 1 (2002): 1–23.

My family has accompanied and supported me throughout this project. My sister, Moran, and brother, Guy, have been true friends. My parents, Michal and Shmuel, were full partners in this endeavor; they provided encouragement, care, thought-provoking discussions, and acute observations—after all, they both grew up in Revisionist homes. My son, Jonathan, arrived in this world as this book was nearing completion; his smiling eyes have made every day brighter. Last, I dedicate this book to my wife, partner, and friend, Ravit. Her love made all this possible.

Introduction

Revisionism—A Time for Reassessment

> I have tried to learn from all my predecessors, without re-
> peating their failures and without being partisan as they
> were. This book was not written for the sake of defending or
> prosecuting but for the purpose of understanding all sides of
> this complicated phenomenon. . . . I confess that in these
> types of inquiries the writer's basic view of historical pro-
> cesses is very relevant, but maybe I can say here, with great
> caution, that Jewish historiography chose to ignore the fact
> that for the messianic idea the People of Israel have paid
> dearly.
>
> Gershom Scholem, *Shabbetai Zevi*

At the end of 1935 a group of Zionist activists, members of Beitar,
the Revisionist youth movement, traveled to various Jewish communities in Europe to raise money and solicit support. Nothing about
this was extraordinary; Zionist activists often took part in such mis-
sions. Although Zionists tried to portray themselves as a new brand
of Jews who lived off the fruits of their own labor, the pioneers in
Palestine could not do without outside help. But something about
that particular group of Beitarists was unique, for it left a great impression on the different Jewish communities it visited: Its members
rode in on motorcycles and dressed in leather jackets.[1]

Zionism, the Jewish national revival movement, arose at the end of
the nineteenth century in response to two great challenges: assimila-
tion and a newly resurgent anti-Semitism. The Zionists attempted to
address these challenges both politically, by creating an independent

Jewish state in Palestine, and through a national psychological revolution, by creating a new type of Jew to inhabit that future state. Zionists regarded the Diaspora Jew as passive and weak and sought to create the "new Hebrew"—a pioneer who lived off the land and fought for its protection.

Since the time of the second Aliya (the second wave of Jewish emigration to Palestine, 1904–14), and especially after the rise to dominance of the Labor movement in the 1920s, Zionism promoted a clear image of the ideal Zionist *halutz* (pioneer)—a farmer who conquered the Palestinian wilderness and turned it into a healthy and productive environment, thereby staking the claim of a strong and independent Jewish society to its own land.

As the philosopher Martin Buber wrote of the qualities of the Zionist pioneers, "these people bound their own welfare to the welfare of the nation and The Land through labor. This bond was the essence of the change they brought about. By virtue of it they created a new type—of self-realization, of *halutziut* [pioneering]."[2] Similarly, David Ben Gurion, the leader of the Labor movement in Israel, described *halutziut* as "a great and mighty power, an invisible power, the power of the Hebrew nation's will to exist, be free and independent. . . . It is the impetus that made the pioneers get up and take over the labor in the land. It is not by force but by the power of their historical mission that the pioneers took [it] upon themselves to pave the way to the return of the Jewish masses to their country."[3] Zionists portrayed the pioneering spirit as a positive force of building and creating, a force that promised progress and a better future for the entire nation. The young Revisionist motorcycle riders, however, presented an image very different from that of the socialist *halutzim*.

Members of Beitar, who used to march in the streets of Tel Aviv in their brown uniforms and perform martial arts drills, did not see themselves as farmers tied to the land. One of their leaders, Benjamin Lubotzky, wrote in 1933 that the only moral teachings that they should follow were those of power and strength.[4] For the Beitarists the Zionist revolution meant unleashing the violent and destructive forces that Jews had suppressed for nearly two millennia. The young Revisionists saw themselves as warriors, the leaders in the fight for independence. They regarded themselves as the modern-day Biryonim, the zealots of the Second Temple period who rebelled against the Romans. In the Beitarists' eyes they, not the socialists, were the Jewish nation's true avant-garde.

The poet Ya'acov Cohen anticipated the movement in his poem *Biryonim,* which the young Beitarists used as inspiration:

> We rose up, we returned! With a renewed spirit, youthful and potent,
> We rose up, we returned: We are the Biryonim!
> We came to redeem our exploited country—
> We demand our rights by force!
>
> In blood and fire Judah fell
> In blood and fire Judah will rise!
>
> War! War to our country, war for freedom—
> And if freedom is forever lost—long live revenge!
> If there is no law in the land—the sword will serve as judge![5]

As used by the Beitarists the word *Biryonim* gradually shed its historical and religious meaning and came instead to mean hoodlums or thugs—hence their dress and demeanor, which anticipated the image of the outlaw rebel that Marlon Brando would immortalize two decades later in the 1954 movie *The Wild One.*[6] As the link between the fighters of Masada and the fighters of the Jewish national revival, the Beitarists saw themselves both as the messengers of an ancient tradition and as people of the future. They admired modern technology and the new aesthetic possibilities that it offered and tried to present a very modern image of power and violence, of weapons and fire. Beitarist leaders wanted their members to learn boxing, fencing, and sharpshooting and expected them to practice jujitsu as well as the principles of modern military engineering.[7] The Beitarists were the Hebrew messengers of Marinetti's futurist vision of heroes and machines in war.[8] In the Revisionist imagination the Messiah was to arrive in a tank, not astride a white donkey.

The prominent Revisionist leader Abba Achimeir promised the Beitarists that the future was not going to present itself as an idyllic rural utopia but rather as an urban industrialized reality of heroes who would lead the masses.[9] Or as Ze'ev Jabotinsky, the titular head of Beitar and the leader of the Revisionist movement, put it: "For the generation that grows before our eyes and who will be responsible, probably, for the greatest change in our history, the alphabet has a very simple sound: young people learning how to shoot."[10] Jabotinsky told his young followers to ignore the criticism leveled at them by the Zionist establishment, which labeled Beitarists as militarists and nationalists; ultimately, he promised his young followers, they, not the establishment, would be leading the nation in its fight for independence.[11]

The Revisionists embodied the dark side of the Zionist dream, and the violent and militaristic element that they represented has long been ignored and overlooked by both the Zionist (and Israeli) academic and the political leadership. Instead, the history of Zionism has been told primarily from the perspective of the Labor movement, which dominated the Zionist establishment for nearly seventy years. As Myron Aronoff has argued, Labor was able to establish the dominance of its ideological version of Zionism, and the historiographical field has reflected this dominance.[12] The Zionist establishment has for decades tried to portray its movement as a just and positive force, an idealistic quest to save the Jewish people by peaceful means. The Revisionist prophets of war fit into this image poorly, if not at all.

Until the late 1970s studies of revisionism were few, and most were written by members of the movement itself who did not attempt to hide their propagandist intent. Living in a hostile intellectual environment, on the fringes of the academic and literary world, they shunned even the appearance of objective methodology as they strove to preserve the legacy of the founders. Revisionist intellectuals saw their role as providing a voice for what they felt was a persecuted minority, not as exposing that minority's past to rigorous, potentially critical, scrutiny.[13]

Even with the emergence in the late 1980s of the self-described new historians, who attempted to challenge the traditional representations of Zionist history, the intellectual history of revisionism and its contribution to the development of the Zionist ethos have remained largely overlooked.

The first wave of studies by the new historians focused on the 1948 war, offering a radical new portrayal of the Zionist movement as an aggressive power that seized the opportunity to expel the native Palestinian population while rejecting real efforts to achieve peace.[14] Other new historians analyzed, in a very critical way, the Israeli establishment's treatment of the new immigrants—Holocaust survivors and Jews from Muslim countries—who arrived in the early years of statehood.[15]

According to Benny Morris, perhaps the most notable Israeli new historian: "The old historians, who perhaps should more accurately be called chroniclers, offered a simplistic and consciously pro-Israeli interpretation of the past, and generally avoided mention of anything that reflected poorly on Israel. . . . Blackening Israel's name, it was argued, would ultimately weaken Israel in its ongoing struggle for survival. *Raisons d'etat* often took precedence over telling the truth."[16]

However, despite these (considerable) elements of novelty, the new historians, like their traditional counterparts, have focused primarily on the ideology and politics of the Labor movement and the Zionist establishment.[17] While critical of Labor, they are still caught in its historical webbing, reducing the entire Zionist discourse to the words and deeds of Labor's leaders.[18]

Thus there may be room for a new Zionist and Israeli history that attempts to tell the story of the other groups and forces that were part of the history of Zionism. Such a new history might address the roles of Ultra-Orthodox Jews, members of the National Religious movement, Mizrahi Jews, women, and Zionist Revisionists, groups that traditional Zionist historiography has all but ignored. In telling these previously untold stories, we may be able to broaden the Zionist historical discourse, highlight Zionism's many facets and voices, and provide a richer and fuller description of its development.

This book, which focuses on Revisionist Zionism, attempts to add a new dimension to the historical discussion of Zionism by exploring the Revisionists' original and complex ideology, which emerged in the interwar period outside (and in opposition to) the orbit of Labor Zionism. In the shadows of the dominant Zionist ideology of the period, the Revisionists produced a rich corpus of writings on a wide range of topics, in the process creating a radical new vision of the Hebrew national revival. This book focuses on the cultural and intellectual origins of revisionism during the period that began with the disbanding of the Hebrew Legion in 1920 and ended in 1937 with the creation of the Irgun, the paramilitary organization associated with the Revisionist movement, and the shift of power to the leaders of the Revisionist movement's militaristic wing.

With the passage of time and the ascendancy of the Likud (the name of the Revisionist political bloc after 1973) to enormous power and influence, a small number of historians and scholars without an ideological commitment to revisionism have begun to study the history of the movement. The most prominent so far has been the historian Ya'acov Shavit, whose research has provided the most comprehensive analysis to date of the political and institutional history of revisionism in the prestatehood period. (The majority of studies on the Zionist Right have focused on the Likud's recent political history, and they provide a rather limited account of the movement's intellectual and cultural origins.[19])

Shavit's wide-ranging study looks at revisionism as a Zionist political movement that was one of (many) political responses to the overall situation of the Jews before the creation of the State of Israel.[20] For Shavit revisionism was a movement that included a variety of Zionist ideologies, leaders, and groups that were united by their opposition to Labor's Zionist vision but were not defined by a particularly well-delineated ideology of their own. Shavit suggests that the unifying characteristic of the Revisionists seems to have been their alienation from socialism.

It may be that Shavit unnecessarily downplays the Revisionists' achievements in creating a cultural synthesis that was at once a response to the challenges of modern culture and a remedy to the Jewish condition in the Diaspora. In particular, Shavit all but ignores the broader, quintessentially European, intellectual context of revisionism, which, during the period between the two world wars, was as much a literary and intellectual movement as it was an organized political party.

By examining the many Revisionist newspapers and publications that appeared during the period under discussion, as well as the writings (including newly discovered archival materials) of the movement's prominent figures, I am attempting to present Zionist revisionism as a comprehensive national philosophy that sought to refashion every aspect of Jewish national life in its image, a philosophy whose political and cultural imprint is still very much evident in modern-day Israel.

The unique qualities of Revisionist thought in the interwar period lay in how its leaders saw themselves: primarily as intellectuals and visionaries, not as political activists. And from this unusual position they created a unique brand of Jewish radical nationalism, an all-encompassing ideology that attempted to reinvent the Hebrew nation by cultural means.

It is important to note here that not all the movement's followers and supporters were ideologically committed to every aspect of the teachings of Jabotinsky (and the movement's other leaders)—though most were familiar with his writings.[21] In fact, many were middle-class Zionists who sought a social and economic alternative to socialist Zionism. However, in the period under discussion the Revisionists' main contribution to Zionism was as a cultural and intellectual force. This book, then, focuses on the movement's leaders and their ideological formulations and not on the social and political background of the movement's rank-and-file.

Like other radical right-wing movements in Europe, revisionism was a revolt against rationalism, individualism, and materialism, against what Ze'ev Sternhell has called the heritage of the Enlightenment and the French Revolution.[22] In rebelling against rationalism, the Revisionists rejected what they perceived to be the dualistic nature of modern culture in an attempt to find a single force that was the true causative agent in human history. The Revisionists sought to rely on instinct—basic human desires that are not restricted by any false moral or rational categories. The Revisionists wanted to uncover the authentic power that could allow people to realize their true selves and live a virtuous life. However, unlike early romantic Zionists', the Revisionists' was not a romantic revolt against modernity but rather a modernistic movement that sought to mobilize the masses while relying on technology and the forces of modern capitalism.

In this book I am trying to examine how the antirational impetus of Zionist revisionist thought shaped its many facets into a comprehensive ideological plan. Chapters 2 to 4 examine the Revisionists' philosophical, economic, and aesthetic program as a Zionist version of contemporary European ideologies. In chapter 5, I explore the Revisionists' vision of the spatial and physical qualities of the future Hebrew state and examine their view of women and gender relations as an extension of their spatial vision. Chapter 6 explores the Revisionists' perception of ancient Israel as a Mediterranean nation and shows how this historical analysis served to justify their contemporary international orientation, which called on the Zionist movement to cooperate with Italy rather than with Great Britain. Last, this book looks at the legacy of revisionism in modern-day Israel. It examines how some of the more important social and cultural changes that Israel has experienced in recent years can be understood as an expression of the Revisionist criticism of the Labor movement and of its Zionist ethos.

I prefer to use the term *radical Right* rather than *fascism* in discussing the cultural roots of revisionism.[23] In his essay "Power and Strategies" Michel Foucault wrote, "The non-analysis of fascism is one of the important political facts of the past thirty years. It enables fascism to be used as a floating signifier, whose function is essentially that of denunciation."[24] The term *radical Right* allows for a more historicist analysis of the groups that were part of the cultural, intellectual, and political revolt against the values of modernity, an analysis that focuses more on the origins and development of this historical phenomenon than on its horrifying aftermath.

In 1952 Abba Achimeir wrote that in the early 1930s, the Revisionist movement did not achieve one of its main objectives: preventing the association of fascism and anti-Semitism.[25] With these considerations in mind, I hope it will prove possible to examine revisionism without associating it with the anti-Semitic side of radical right-wing thought and instead regard revisionism as a Zionist cultural revolt against the values of modernity. I will attempt to examine it as one of the many ideologies of mass society that developed in the early part of the twentieth century in response to the great challenges posed by the modern age.

The Jewish Radical Right

1

Between Left and Right

Revisionism in Zionist Politics

What is disclosed to us here is not fixed and definite doctrine.
It is, rather, a move-ent of thought that ever renews itself, a
movement of such strength and passion that it seems hardly
possible in its presence to take refuge in the quiet of "objective" historical contemplation.

Ernst Cassirer, *The Question of Jean-Jacques Rousseau*

The history of Revisionist Zionism in its formative years, the institutions it had all over the world, and its thousands of members are
inextricably associated with the life story of one person, its founder
and leader, Ze'ev (Vladimir) Jabotinsky (1880–1940). The evolution
of revisionism mirrored his political and intellectual biography.

Jabotinsky was born to an assimilated middle-class family in
Odessa, Russia, and was exposed from a young age to Jewish intellectual circles in that cosmopolitan city on the Black Sea. In 1898 he
went to Berne, Switzerland, as the foreign correspondent for *Odessky
Listok* and enrolled in the local university's law school. In the fall of
that year he moved to Rome and continued his studies at the University of Rome. Italy, he later wrote, became his spiritual motherland,
the place where his ideological and social outlook was shaped.[1]

Jabotinsky returned to Russia in 1901, and in the years before
World War I, he made a name for himself as a journalist (he wrote
for several Russian newspapers), author, and translator. During this
time he also took his first steps as a Zionist ideologue and activist.[2]
He was selected as a delegate to the sixth Zionist Congress in 1904

and he played a central role in the Helisingfors Conference of Russian Zionists in 1906.[3]

In 1914 Jabotinsky covered the western front for the Russian paper *Russkia Vidomosty,* and he went to Egypt that December. There he met Jewish refugees from Palestine and became involved in the campaign to form a Jewish legion to take part in the British conquest of Palestine from the Ottoman Empire.

The creation of the Jewish legion was Jabotinsky's first major political act as a Zionist leader and a realization of some of his early ideological formulations that set him apart from the increasingly dominant Zionist left wing. In 1912, in an article titled "The Rebel," Jabotinsky attacked the socialist Zionists, who claimed that social and class issues were more important than national ones. He argued that his experience as a student in Italy had taught him that the creation of a national home should be the only objective of a nationalist movement. The Left, he wrote, was obsessed with fighting about the nature of the future state, whereas the only concern of the Zionist movement should be building enough power to establish a Jewish state.[4]

Some socialist Zionists supported the formation of labor legions that would operate under the auspices of the British army but would concentrate on civilian tasks (in other words, national service).[5] Jabotinsky strongly opposed such units, arguing that only active military participation in liberating the land, even with a limited number of soldiers, would grant moral legitimacy to the Jewish claim for a national home in Palestine.

In 1915 the First Zion Mule Corps was established, but Jabotinsky did not join because he did not expect it to see active combat duty in Palestine. (He was correct: The corps was used primarily to transport supplies to the front in the Gallipoli campaign.) Finally, in August 1917, after a long political and propaganda campaign, Zionists established a Jewish legion, and its three battalions participated in the last stages of the war in Palestine. Jabotinsky enlisted as a private and was promoted to lieutenant.

The moral significance that Jabotinsky attributed to the Hebrew regiment was clearly evident in his letter to Gen. Edmund Allenby, the commander of the British forces in Palestine: "The British government recognized the Jews as a nation. The government created two Jewish battalions and sent them to the Land of Israel. It was done for the very purpose of eliminating any false claims that the Land of Israel was liberated by foreigners without Jewish participation."[6]

In 1920 the British authorities jailed Jabotinsky for his involvement in the creation of a Jewish self-defense group formed in response to Arab attacks on the Jewish population. He was sentenced to fifteen years in prison. However, because of his involvement in the Jewish legion, Jabotinsky was by now a public figure with followings both in Palestine and Europe. Jews pressured the British authorities, and they soon released him. In the summer of 1920 he left Palestine for London, never to return on a permanent basis.

After the Jewish legion was officially disbanded in 1921, Jabotinsky continued to champion the cause of Jewish militarism as the only way to advance Zionist goals. In May 1921 he wrote to Winston Churchill, the British colonial secretary: "Both in Jerusalem and in Jaffa British troops failed to prevent loss of Jewish life and destruction of Jewish property. . . . But it is impossible to make the Jewish masses forget the eloquent fact that so long as there were 5,000 Jewish soldiers in Palestine, no riots against Jews took place, whereas after their reduction to 400, six Jews were killed in Jerusalem. . . . But, should this not be obtained, there would be no other course left to Jews but the raising of a strong permanent self-defense organization, adequately armed and supported by its own intelligence service—because we must be protected."[7]

Jabotinsky's positions on such issues as Jewish militarism and the Yishuv's relationship with the British government eventually led to his resignation from the Zionist Executive in 1923.[8] In Paris in 1925 Jabotinsky established Ha-Tzohar, the Zionist Revisionist Organization.

From this point on Jabotinsky continued to formulate his political ideas and win new followers; but even though his movement at times seriously challenged Labor in several election campaigns for World Zionist Organization congresses, he could not translate his ideology into political action in Palestine because his movement was denied access to the Zionist movement's resources and institutions.[9]

Inevitably, the clearer Jabotinsky's ideology became, the further he and his movement were pushed to the fringes of the Zionist political world. In 1935 the Revisionists split from the World Zionist Organization altogether and formed Ha-Tzah (an acronym for New Zionist Organization).[10]

Increasingly, Jabotinsky devoted his attention, time, and energy to his intellectual and cultural projects as he continued to cultivate his literary and journalistic career. In 1923 he was appointed editor of the Zionist publication *Rassvyet* (Dawn), which was published in Berlin. A year later an important collection of translations of his poems into Hebrew was published, and in 1927 his first novel, *Samson the Nazerite*, appeared.

Jabotinsky's cultural endeavors symbolized the nature of the Revisionist movement in general. In London and later in Paris, Jabotinsky regularly moved between two worlds: He was the leader of a political party and involved in its daily operations, but at the same time he was a writer and intellectual living in self-imposed exile (from his homeland, Russia, and from his ideological homeland, Palestine) in a universe inhabited by books and ideas, roving among the many languages (and cultures) that he mastered and detached from everyday reality.[11]

In the prestatehood era Zionism operated within singular historical conditions. It was a national movement without a territorial base and operated in a political vacuum, always at the mercy of other powers. Unlike almost all other national movements of that time, whose efforts consisted largely of waging wars of independence, Zionist activities centered on negotiation, diplomacy, and advocacy in the international arena. Under Jabotinsky's leadership Revisionists were an extreme case of this historical anomaly. On the fringes of Zionism itself, they operated almost entirely as an ideological, cultural, and literary enterprise, lacking, as they did, the institutional means to turn their highly original vision into a reality.

Meanwhile, and in sharp contrast, Labor honed its infinitely more practical brand of political philosophy, focusing on small, relatively achievable, goals that would (its leaders hoped) lead to the creation of a Jewish state. Visionary dreamers though they may have been, the Laborites were also skilled politicians and strategists with a strong, even passionate, interest in economics. Laborites foresaw a gradual process by which the Zionists would take over the land by establishing agricultural settlements and understood the need to inculcate the requisite pioneering spirit—not to mention basic farming techniques—in Jewish immigrants, a people to whom agricultural life was exotic and new.

The Revisionists would have none of this. Despising what they perceived to be the materialism of the Left, they declared that national revolutions were predicated on radical mental transformations. With a flare for drama that perhaps stemmed from his roots in the world of romantic literature, Jabotinsky envisioned a grand revolution, a great spiritual awakening that would result in a mass of Zionist warriors who would take over the land by force.

The Revisionists saw themselves as adventurers and visionaries, not as politicians, and operated in a rarefied ideological sphere far removed from the drab activities that the Laborites embraced. Jabotinsky and his followers established Revisionist publications and newspapers in Palestine and throughout the world, giving themselves forums for their ideological and literary battles. They presented their theoretical and ideological arguments not as earthbound political programs but as novels, poems, literary critiques, and newspaper editorials.[12]

Jabotinsky himself turned to poetry to express some of his most deeply held ideals. In perhaps his most personal poem, "The Hunchback" (1930), he wrote:

> I cling to the wall
> Long-limbed and awkward . . .
>
> Your hustling and loud marketplace frightens me,
> My city is a desert with no roads:
> Among people I am despised
> In cultivating the truth—I am the Son of God.
>
> And in a frightful night,
> a night in which I will have to die on the cross like an ancient brother,
> my student will betray me and renounce me in front of the masses.[13]

This poem shows that Jabotinsky regarded himself as a biblical prophet—burdened by his knowledge of the truth, forced to proclaim God's word to the unbelieving populace, despised, hunted, and eventually crucified for his efforts. After his brief brush with "big tent" politics in the World Zionist Organization, Jabotinsky swore off the political process, with its compromises, negotiations, and coalitions; compromises were for politicians, and Jabotinsky saw himself as both more and less than that: He was a seer.

Eventually, the Revisionist leader's detachment from practical considerations and from participation in the actual daily struggle for national liberation led to the rise of a new generation of Revisionists, who challenged the leadership of Jabotinsky and his contemporaries. This newly ascendant group consisted mainly of young Jews from Poland who had joined Beitar, the Revisionist youth movement, during the 1920s. They embraced Jabotinsky's nationalist ideology of militarism and power, but they wanted to implement it and transform the Revisionist movement from a purely ideological entity into a real army that would fight for national liberation.

The Beitarists took as their model Jozef Pilsudski, who had led the Polish Legion in World War I and who, unlike Jabotinsky, had continued to fight both politically and militarily for his people's goals after the war was over. The young Revisionists saw in Pilsudski a leader who not only wrote eloquently on the importance and implications of militarism but actually used his army to achieve concrete, recognizable goals.

The young Beitarists in Poland regarded themselves as members of a militia, of the Hebrew nation's liberation army, and they sought a leader who could lead them in actual, not just imagined, battle. They were drawn to Beitar by Jabotinsky's ideas and rhetoric, but they came to regard him as a man of words when the Jewish people were yearning for action.

Menachem Begin, the preeminent figure among the young Beitarists, argued at Beitar's World Conference of 1938 that the era of political Zionism had ended and a new era of a military struggle had arrived. Jabotinsky, present in the room while Begin was speaking, did his theatrical best to dismiss criticism by literally turning his back on Begin and saying that the younger man's words sounded like no more than the screeching of a door. To what we may presume was Jabotinsky's surprise, most younger Beitarists sided with Begin.[14]

The younger generation, clamoring for action, found its chance with the consolidation of the Irgun Tzva'i Le'umi (National Military Organization). The Irgun was created in 1937 after Beitar rejected an agreement between the Haganah (the main Labor-controlled Jewish defense organization in Palestine) and Haganah B (which had split from the Haganah in 1931 and included mainly non-Labor members) to reunite in view of the Great Arab Revolt, which had started in 1936.

The members of the Irgun, mostly young Beitarists, announced that they were uninterested in an organization that would only defend Jewish settlements from Arab attacks. They wanted a military organization that would initiate attacks on both Arab and British targets. True to their Polish roots, the founders of the Irgun were inspired by the example of Pilsudski's military organization in Poland.[15] The Irgun's leaders saw their new underground militia—active where Jabotinsky was passive, proactive where the Haganah was purely defensive—as the only means to mobilize the nation in its struggle for independence.

The circumstances that led to the creation of Ha-Tzohar and the Irgun symbolize the important differences between these two Revisionist organizations. Ha-Tzohar was created in Paris in April 1925 at a meeting at the Café de Pantheon (in the Latin Quarter) between Jabotinsky and some of his followers, other Zionist dissidents without a political home. The organization was founded by a man who could not withstand the pressures of operating within a big political organization and who sought to create his own movement in which he and his followers would enjoy greater ideological freedom. Twelve years later the Irgun was established in Palestine as an underground movement at the height of the Arab revolt and at a time when tensions between the Yishuv and British authorities were reaching a boiling point. It was created to address the urgent needs of the Jewish community, which was seriously threatened and fighting for its survival.

By the late 1930s Jabotinsky was losing support among the younger Revisionists. Still officially the head of Beitar, he remained active in certain spheres, for example, in trying (unsuccessfully) to arrange for the massive evacuation to Palestine of Polish Jewry, but in reality power was now in the hands of David Raziel, the head of the Irgun, and Begin, who arrived in Palestine in 1942 and took over command of the Irgun.[16] After Begin got to Palestine, Revisionist leaders also offered him the leadership of Beitar, but he refused, arguing that Beitar had only one leader, Jabotinsky.[17] Begin saw himself as a military commander, not as an ideological leader.

By 1937 the era of revisionism as an ideological and cultural movement under the leadership of Jabotinsky had come to an end. The young Revisionists were no longer interested in theoretical speculations about power, militarism, and national liberation; they were interested in praxis, in applying Jabotinsky's theories of power to political action. As the Revisionist movement entered the critical period that led to the creation of the state, military organizations were leading the way, and the Irgun was at the forefront of the battle.

After 1937 the Revisionists were no longer fighting their ideological wars in the press and in literary and cultural publications but in the streets and out in the fields. Yet in their radicalism, in their celebration of violence, and in their apocalyptic vision of the Jewish-Gentile conflict, they retained the ideology formulated by the first generation of Revisionist thinkers. As Menachem Begin wrote,

> There exists a similar reciprocal influence between poetry and literature in general, and the era. Sometimes, the era produces the poet. Sometimes one creates the other. But the poetry and literary work of Ze'ev Jabotinsky preceded an era—he created it. He wrote of Jewish strength before it came into being; of revolt before it took place; of a Jewish army while its weapons were still a dream; of a Jewish State when many of our contemporaries still derided its very mention and of "Hadar" [honor, respect] while the manners—or lack of manners—of the Ghetto still prevailed in our people.[18]

Between Left and Right

One of the more difficult tasks facing the historian of the Revisionist movement is determining its true ideological character during the interwar period. Judging by the disputes that dominated the discourse between the Revisionists and the socialist parties in the 1920s, and especially the 1930s, the Zionist Revisionists were, from the perspective of their opponents, exemplars of a radical right-wing movement.

In October 1932 the Frumin food factory in Petah-Tikvah hired a worker who was not a member of the Histadrut (Federation of Workers Unions). The Histadrut, which was controlled by Mapai (the Israeli Workers Party), responded by declaring a strike at the factory. In return, the Revisionists, who had long objected to Histadrut's monopoly of the labor market, signed an agreement with Frumin's ownership stipulating that Revisionist workers would replace the striking Histadrut members and that some of these workers would be guaranteed employment after the strike ended. Tensions rose and the Revisionists were drawn into an acrimonious debate with the supporters of organized labor.

The Revisionists maintained that what they regarded as Bolshevik and tyrannical unions would sacrifice the future of the entire Zionist movement in order to protect the interests of a particular class.[19] Socialist publications in Palestine, on the other hand, portrayed the Revisionists as fascists who represented the interests of the oppressive classes. Socialist circles published a special pamphlet titled "The Biscuit Front" (Frumin manufactured baked goods), in which they provided quotes from several Revisionist leaders (including Jabotinsky) that expressed fascist sentiments, including support of Nazism.[20]

Ben Gurion published a book in 1933 that discussed the Frumin affair and other labor disputes; he called the first part of the book "Jabotinsky in the Footsteps of Hitler." In the book Ben Gurion argued, "We must arrive at the conclusion that this Hotontonic morality is at the core of the Revisionist party. . . . From here comes the harsh demagoguery that they employ during election time. . . . From here come all the fascist methods with regard to the Duce on the one hand, and the public on the other."[21]

The struggle between the two camps went beyond the scope of labor disputes. The strongest criticism yet leveled against the Revisionists came during the summer of 1934 at the height of the Arlozoroff murder trial. Three members of the radical revisionist group Brith ha-Biryonim (the Brotherhood of Zealots) were being tried for the murder of Chaim Arlozoroff, a leading socialist activist who was slain on a beach in Tel Aviv on June 16, 1933. The trial of Abba Achimeir, Zvi Rosenblatt, and Avraham Stavsky brought the Yishuv's political tensions to dangerous levels.

In the spring of 1933 Arlozoroff had traveled to Europe, a tour that included a visit to Germany, to facilitate the emigration of young Jews to Palestine during the rise of Nazism. At the same time Jabotinsky and the Revisionists declared a complete ban on all dealings (political and economic) with Germany. The Revisionists took the lead in anti-German activities, in part, to improve their image, which had been tarnished by a string of pro-Nazi and pro-Hitler statements and articles that had appeared in the Revisionist press in years past.[22] Members of Brith ha-Biryonim spearheaded the anti-German activities, which included the removal of the German flag from the German consulate in Jerusalem.

That spring the Revisionists launched a series of attacks on Arlozoroff and his dealings with the German authorities. They portrayed him as a traitor who was willing to betray the Zionist movement out of pure greed. A week before the assassination, the Revisionist daily *Hazit ha-Am* offered the following commentary, "At a time when the entire People of Israel, in the Diaspora and in Israel, are in the midst of a defensive struggle for its honor and existence against Hitler's Germany—a ban on its products—an official of the Jewish Agency [Arlozoroff] offers not only to lift the ban but to guarantee a market for German exports. . . . By this action, Mapai is stabbing our people in the back."[23] In the political climate of the time Arlozoroff was an easy target for Revisionist propaganda. He symbolized the association of socialist Zionism with money and materialism, in contrast to the idealistic self-image that the Revisionists attempted to foster.

After Arlozoroff was slain, socialists immediately accused Revisionists of the crime, and the conflict between the two main political movements in the Yishuv came to a head. Charges against Achimeir were dropped a year later (in April 1934), but Stavsky and Rosenblatt were tried in a proceeding that lasted until June 1934. Rosenblatt was acquitted, and Stavsky, after being convicted and sentenced to death, was acquitted on appeal a month later. Yet, despite the acquittal, the Revisionist movement continued to be associated with the murder.[24]

In a meeting of Mapai's central committee in August 1934, during which members discussed the trial, one member compared Jabotinsky and Achimeir to Hitler and Goering,[25] while in another meeting that summer Eliyahu Golomb, a founding member of the Haganah, argued that the desperation shown by the Revisionists' actions (the murder) was typical of their brand of Jewish fascism.[26]

In 1934 Ben Gurion and Jabotinsky met in London and negotiated an agreement between the two movements that they both hoped would bring peace and stability to the Yishuv's political scene. Mapai's central committee held several deliberations and ultimately rejected the deal,[27] yet what stands out from those discussions is the frequency with which the Laborites characterized the Revisionists as thugs and fascists.

On October 21 Abba Hushi, Mapai's leader in Haifa (and the city's future mayor), described the success of an organization called Antifa that the Labor Party had created in order to fight fascism (the Revisionists) in the northern port city.[28] Hushi's language makes it clear that he viewed his ideological rivals as members of a fascist party. Ten days later, in a telegram that Moshe Shartok sent to Ben Gurion in London, Shartok denounced a proposed agreement between Labor and the Revisionists, arguing that it would legitimize what he called a fascist, hooligan movement that Labor must fight vigorously.[29]

In the same meeting another committee member argued that even if the agreement between the two parties were to be approved, this would not change the fact that the Revisionists were and always would be a fascist party.[30] A month later both Itzhak Tabenkin and Itzhak Ben Aharon, two of the leading ideologues of socialist Zionism, compared the proposed agreement to the way socialists, who had been naive and underestimated their opponents, had been crushed in Germany and Spain by the fascists.[31]

As these examples show, attempts to either characterize the political and ideological nature of Zionist revisionism along the traditional Left-Right axis or to separate the political vitriol of the period from the fundamental differences between the main political camps are fraught with difficulty. At a time when the real political struggle between Labor and revisionism focused not on controlling a nation's ruling institutions but on winning supporters for ideas and a political strategy to achieve statehood, the stakes were relatively low, but the language was untamed. Thus using an analysis of that discourse to determine whether revisionism was a radical right-wing ideology is highly problematic.[32]

While the political discourse of the 1920s and 1930s painted the Revisionist movement as a fascist party, contemporary historiography mainly portrays the party as a nineteenth-century liberal movement. Most current commentators maintain that the Left portrayed revisionism as a fascist movement because the Zionist establishment saw it as a real threat to its control of the Zionist organizations and wanted to delegitimize the Revisionists.

Ya'acov Shavit has summarized this view, claiming that "the emergence of revisionism as a political party, the fact that it presented itself as an alternative to the workers' parties . . . within a short time resulted in its being equated with fascism. . . . The intense rivalry with and the deep-seated hostility toward the workers' parties in essence produced the fascist image of revisionism."[33]

According to Tom Segev, who represents the approach of the Israeli new historians, the Revisionists of the prestatehood era were a classic nineteenth-century liberal party. Segev claims that revisionism was different from socialist Zionism only in its emphasis on a quicker pace in the implementation of Zionist goals in Palestine. In addition, this was a difference with regard to political tactics, not a fundamental ideological difference.[34] Moreover, to Segev, who like other new historians associates what he considers to be the immoral policies of the young State of Israel with the Labor movement, the Revisionists represent a civilized and moral alternative to socialist Zionism. Writing about the failed attempts of Benny Begin, the son of Menachem Begin, to unite the Israeli Right into one political bloc before the 1999 elections, Segev argued that this effort failed because "Begin represents a kind of respected liberalism that was supported by his father and by Ze'ev Jabotinsky before him," and therefore the younger Begin could not join forces with elements of the Israeli Right that support the "Transfer Plan" (a plan to transfer Arabs out of Israel) and who, according to Segev, are the ideological heirs of certain groups within Labor Zionism.[35]

At the heart of the view of Zionist revisionism as a liberal movement is a distinction between the radical maximalist wing of the Revisionist Party, which was led by Abba Achimeir (1897–1962), Yehoshua Heschel Yevin (1891–1970), and Uri Zvi Greenberg (1894–1981), and the movement's mainstream, which was headed by Jabotinsky. The former are depicted as a marginal group that openly embraced fascism, while the latter is portrayed as championing liberal economics and the Jewish middle class.[36]

From Abba Achimeir's series of articles in 1928 that he called "From the Diary of a Fascist" to numerous articles throughout the late 1920s and 1930s that openly supported fascism and renounced socialism, liberalism, and humanism, the maximalists both conceived of themselves and were perceived by others as members of a radical right-wing movement. In a speech before the Revisionists Union Conference in 1932, Achimeir declared that in revisionism now was split into two definite camps (and not a variety of camps, as he had previously thought), and he presented himself as a member of the maximalist faction. At the same meeting Yevin argued that the words of the representatives of the party's mainstream were eloquent, logical, and sensible—but that reality demanded going beyond rational politics to the politics of sacrifice.[37]

Their mission, the maximalists believed, was to free Jabotinsky from the tyranny of Zionist activists and functionaries who prevented him from carrying out his vision. As Achimeir told a group of young followers, "Perhaps Jabotinsky is not to be blamed. At times I think that he is captured by Revisionist activists who only care about their political power in the Zionist Organization. Then, we must release him from their hold."[38]

Jabotinsky, on the other hand, always emphasized his background in the intellectual and cultural climate of the nineteenth century, and he repeatedly pledged his commitment to liberalism, democracy, and parliamentarism. Whereas the maximalists despised the Zionist establishment and wanted the Revisionist movement to assume an independent position, Jabotinsky's attitude toward mainstream Zionism was complicated and ambivalent.

It may be, however, that the differences between Jabotinsky and the maximalists, who by 1932 were the dominant force among the

Revisionists in Palestine, were more apparent than real.[39] The two groups cooperated politically, and the maximalists viewed Jabotinsky as their leader. Certainly, he was their protector within the Revisionist movement and consistently blocked attempts to have the maximalists ousted from the movement.[40] It is possible that rather than merely being strange bedfellows, Jabotinsky and the maximalists had enough in common for them to work as allies despite the clear differences regarding political means and rhetoric. Together, the two camps shaped the ideology of revisionism during the 1920s and 1930s, creating a comprehensive political philosophy based on shared ideas about power and its central role in the fates of individuals and nations.

The Maximalists

In 1934 Abba Achimeir made the following observation with regard to the role of revolutions in the physical and social sciences:

> The science of geology in our time worships Neptune and turns away from Vulcan. This means that geology today deals with water and not with fire. . . . Water is associated with evolution; fire is revolution. . . . The science of geology is still caught in the nineteenth-century view of evolution. The science of the history of the earth is more conservative than the science of the history of human society. In geology and other related sciences the notion of progress is still dominant, whereas in the human sciences today no one takes this notion seriously except for the stupid theologians of the Rousseau and Marx religions. As is the case in the study of history (the annals of humanity), in the study of geology (the history of earth's outer surface) it is Vulcan that reigns supreme, not Neptune. Fire, revolutions, and catastrophes dominate the earth upon which we stand. . . . Wars and revolutions also dominate human history.[41]

When they arrived in Palestine from Europe in the middle of the 1920s, the historian and writer Achimeir, the poet Greenberg, and the physician, essayist, and editor Yevin moved in socialist circles, and their work appeared in socialist publications. They were attracted to the revolutionary aspect of socialism as manifested by the Bolshevik

Revolution, and they believed that the *halutzim* (male pioneers), most of whom belonged to the socialist group, epitomized the vitality of the Zionist movement.

In 1924 Yevin described Zionism as the triumph of pioneering and Jewish manual labor: "For the first time the people of Israel have stopped being preoccupied with learning and returned to man's original role—to work the land and turn it into a blooming garden, to be the earth's gardener."[42] Greenberg wrote in the same year that the Hebrew proletariat on the "Hebrew Island" should turn toward Moscow and salute Lenin's funeral.[43]

However, even if in their early political careers the maximalists shared the revolutionary fervor of the Left, at no point did they subscribe to its full socialist agenda. They shared with the socialists the desire for change and the rejection of the values of bourgeois liberalism, but they did not view the materialistic message of socialism as the optimal means to mobilize the Jewish people.

Like Greenberg and Yevin (and Jabotinsky), Achimeir divided his energy between political activism and the life of an intellectual. As a doctoral candidate at the University of Vienna, he submitted his 1924 dissertation on Oswald Spengler's *The Decline of the West* (1918–22) and the question of Russia; it provides an insight into the political philosophy of one of the men who would be accused of a political murder a decade later.

According to Spengler's model of world history, human cultures are like living organisms that go through a biological cycle of birth, growth, and decay. Cultures are born as a spiritual force that decay over time as materialism overtakes spirituality. This organic, cultural cycle, according to Spengler, is the dominant force in human history—not material and economic factors as the Marxists would have it—and it explains the rise and decline of the world's dominant cultures such as Judaism, classical Greece and Rome, and the West. Cultural decline, in Spengler's conceptual framework, occurs when money and materialism dominate politics, the city becomes more important than the countryside, morals decline, quantity takes precedence over quality, and social hierarchies, especially the dominance of the gentleman-noble class and its civic virtues, are challenged.[44]

According to Spengler, this was the state of the West at the end of the nineteenth and the beginning of the twentieth century, as materialism, mass culture (democracy), and socialism, with its materialistic analysis of history and rejection of idealism and spiritualism, became the leading ideologies. Russia, in Spengler's analysis, was an especially tragic case, because it was a backward son of the West that had not even enjoyed the fruits of the West's growth and prosperity but had been culturally invaded by the West and therefore was partaking in the West's cultural decline. The rise of the Russian cities, Dostoyevsky and his cultural decadence, and finally the Bolshevik Revolution all marked the transformation of Russia into a Western culture on the verge of destruction.

Achimeir accepted Spengler's view of history as consisting of repeated cycles of growth and decline, but he rejected Spengler's analysis of Russian culture. Spengler had compared Russia's interaction with the West to that of Arab culture with the dying classical worlds of Greece and Rome. But Russia, Achimeir maintained, was a unique historical case, because it had developed in a hermetically sealed cultural environment.[45] The Russian Revolution, while influenced by Western ideals, was a distinctly Russian phenomenon that had been influenced as much by Tolstoy's unique brand of Russian nationalism as it was by Dostoyevsky and his European decadence.[46] For Achimeir the Bolshevik Revolution was not necessarily a mark of the decline of the West and the rise to dominance of materialistic ideologies but rather a sign of Russia's evolution as a nation. The force of the revolution did not stem from its social vision but from its nationalistic power and its ability to bring historical processes to a powerful conclusion.

According to Achimeir, revolutions tend to follow ideologies that are not necessarily the most elaborate or developed but those that have the greatest ability to unite people. The strength of Russia's socialist revolution lay not in its founding ideology but in its ability to draw on Russian roots, on the Russian anarchism of Tolstoy rather than on the Western decadence of Dostoyevsky.

Achimeir argued that from a historical perspective, the Bolshevik Revolution was similar to Muhammad's Islamic revolution in the Middle East. Islam, like Bolshevism in the Russian case, offered a monistic theme that unified the people from Persia to Morocco under one dominant ideology, which was more simplistic than some religions that had flourished in the area before (especially in Persia and Egypt) but had the power to unite the Arabs into a single entity.[47]

The "Marxism" of the young Achimeir was thus not a commitment to class war and the dictatorship of the proletariat. It was an infatuation with the antiestablishment nature of socialism, with its resolve to fight the existing order and hierarchies and to mobilize the masses.

In a 1928 article Achimeir differentiated between socialism, which he argued was Western and democratic, and communism, which flourished in the East and was revolutionary and dictatorial in nature. The West, Achimeir maintained, was static and conservative, and socialism there was part of the parliamentary process; it represented the masses as an opposition party but one that accepted the rules of the political game and was not committed to real change. The East, on the other hand, was in a state of constant change, and communism there had evolved as a revolutionary force.[48] Achimeir, as he had shown in his dissertation a few years earlier, was not interested in the substance of Marxist ideology but in its revolutionary qualities and its promise of radical change. Marxism's appeal did not lie in its ability to predict social and economic changes but in its explosive political potential.

Achimeir and the maximalists were not alone in the evolution of their political thought. Such leading and diverse figures of the European radical Right as Georges Sorel, Robert Michels, and Sergio Pannunzio also had begun their political journeys in the nonconformist Left but realized that the proletariat had ceased to be a revolutionary force and that only the nation as a whole could bring about a revolution against democracy, liberalism, and the bourgeoisie. As Ze'ev Sternhell has shown, groups that were originally part of the nonconformist Left have often joined forces with traditional conservative nationalists to form the core of the European radical Right.[49]

The Revisionist maximalists, who admired the revolutionary fervor of the Left but not its materialistic message, concluded that socialist Zionism could not bring about true social and political change. In 1929 Yevin wrote that salvation would not come to

the Jewish people from the socialists' efforts to build and create
but rather from focusing solely on uncovering the basis of the nation's true revolutionary impetus: Jewish force.[50] Or, as Achimeir put
it, "These men continue to live in a world of concepts that are no
longer relevant. At the heart of the twentieth century, the century of
dictatorship, enthusiasm, and the cult of the fist that was formed
amid the fumes of tanks—they want to address the needs of my
people with the liberal rubbish of the middle of the nineteenth
century."[51]

Thus imbued with antiliberal and antisocialist fervor, the maximalists joined the socialists' main opposition within Zionism, revisionism, and its leader, Ze'ev Jabotinsky, whom they believed
possessed the revolutionary spirit that the Zionist movement so des-
perately needed.

The Question of Jabotinsky

In certain ways the alliance between Jabotinsky and the maximalists
represents an uneasy blend of personalities and styles. Jabotinsky
was very different in his public demeanor from the maximalists, who
officially joined his movement in 1928. The Revisionist leader, who
was heavily influenced in his formative years by the liberal attitudes
of Russian literature, made every effort to present himself as a product of nineteenth-century ideologies, especially liberalism. He always tried to portray his movement as part of the legitimate Zionist
camp and to present himself as the protector of Herzl's Zionist vision. When a critic accused Jabotinsky's movement of placing the
state above the individual, as the fascists did, Jabotinsky replied,
"Like the majority of our board members, I completely reject the notion that 'the State is everything.' Be it fascist or communist, I believe
only in 'old-fashioned' parliamentarism, even if it seems inconvenient or futile."[52]

In a 1932 letter, in which he responded to Yevin's suggestions that
he leave the politics of mainstream Zionism and adopt the ways of
the new force in his movement, Jabotinsky said that he would not
find in the Zionist movement two better and more able individuals
than Yevin and Achimeir. He added that, while he admired their willingness to sacrifice themselves for their Zionist beliefs, he feared that

their policies could damage the very foundations of the movement that he had built. Jabotinsky wrote that "Ha-Tzohar is a movement based on nineteenth-century democracy. . . . Even its revolutionary and military character is based on these principles."[53]

Jabotinsky's letter to Yevin expressed his mixed feelings toward the maximalists—on the one hand admiration for their commitment to the Zionist cause but on the other hand fear that their reckless public behavior might further marginalize the Revisionist movement. The language he used also serves as a prime example of Jabotinsky's main rhetorical (and political) strategy. Regardless of the substance of the arguments that he made or the enthusiasm that he showed toward new and radical notions, he always presented himself as a man of the nineteenth century, who followed the liberal and democratic principles of that era.

Even when he discussed matters that were far from the Zionist political agenda, he used these stylistic tactics. In an article on American culture, for example, Jabotinsky described jazz as a revolutionary artistic genre that breaks the strict rules of traditional harmonies and allows the individual to escape the boundaries imposed by culture. But after he finished extolling the virtues of improvisational music, he declared that his personal musical taste tended to be more classical and that it was rooted in nineteenth-century musical styles.[54]

Similarly, when he wrote about Italian fascism in 1936, Jabotinsky claimed that fascist Italy was a true ally of the Jewish people and that under fascism Jews in Italy did not experience outbreaks of anti-Semitism. At the end of this remarkable assessment, however, he declared that he himself was not a supporter of fascism, adding that this dislike had more to do with matters of fashion and personal taste rather than with substantive issues.[55]

As a professional writer, poet, translator, and journalist, Jabotinsky earned his living through words and was well aware of their power and importance. Not surprisingly, he was one of the first Zionist leaders to emphasize Hebrew language and education as the cornerstone of the Zionist enterprise.[56] In his political activities this master of many languages—he seemed to have working knowledge of at least nine—was always conscious of the words and terms that he used and carefully calculated the image that they would convey to the general public.

One case that best exemplified Jabotinsky's understanding of the link between language and politics was the debate about the role of the leader in the Revisionist movement. In one of the articles published under the headline "From the Diary of a Fascist," Achimeir wrote in 1928 about the impending visit of Jabotinsky, the "Duce," to Israel.[57] Achimeir argued that Jabotinsky possessed the unique qualities of a leader who could withstand the pressures of the majority and hold true to his convictions. During the Revisionist World Conference in Vienna in 1932, the maximalists called on Jabotinsky to do away with the movement's democratic institutions and assume full control of the movement as a dictatorial leader. In an article published just before the conference, Yevin wrote, "We are striving toward a radical transformation in the Jewish psyche, toward creating the Zealous race, which will protect the well-being of his homeland and the honor of his people. . . . In conferences, it is always the majority that wins, but in life, it is not always that case; on the contrary, often it is the persecuted minority that wins."[58]

In his speech before the conference Achimeir seconded Yevin's arguments, saying, "Everywhere democracy was defeated, moreover, it has reached a state of bankruptcy. What other proofs do you need? People believed that after the Great War, after so much blood was shed, the younger generation would gain its rights by democratic means. But reality is different, and therefore this century belongs to the youth and dictatorship."[59] Tempers flared as some delegates wanted to eject the maximalists from the party, while the maximalists, undeterred, cheered as Leone Carpi, the Italian delegate, greeted Jabotinsky and the other delegates with a fascist salute.[60] Jabotinsky, for his part, vowed during the conference to preserve the movement's democratic institutions. However, the following year Jabotinsky in effect adopted the maximalist agenda. He issued a statement in which he declared that he assumed full dictatorial control of the party and that instead of democratically elected institutions, a committee appointed by him would run the entire movement.[61]

Rhetorically, then, Jabotinsky opposed the idea of a dictatorship, while in reality he turned his movement into one. A few months after he took full control of the party, Jabotinsky wrote to a Revisionist activist that democracy had been an "idée fixe" for him since childhood and that his "putsch" was in fact a restoration of the democratic principle, representing as it did the will of the majority. Reassuringly, he added that he lacked the qualifications to be a dictator and that he saw himself as no more than an organizer.[62]

In a 1934 article titled "The Leader," he made similar claims against dictatorship:

> What is especially difficult to understand is the mentality of those who yearn for "leaders." In my youth, matters were completely different for the better. We thought, then, that each movement was made of people who were of equal worth: each member a prince, each member a king. When election time came, they chose programs, not people. The people elected were but the implementers of those programs. . . . And here, this doctrine of my youth might have been a fiction (like any other human doctrine) but I like it more. It possesses more splendor and glory despite bearing a name that has lost its eminence—"democracy."[63]

Apparently unaware of the incompatibility of these sentiments with his putsch of the previous year, Jabotinsky continued to publicly express an unwavering commitment to democracy. In a formula that became familiar to his readers over the years, he invariably linked his democratic principles to his youth, his formative years in the nineteenth century, and his loyalty to the popular principles of that era. But if Jabotinsky was influenced by the past, he was a formidable politician and intellectual of what was then the present. Extremely well informed about the political and intellectual climate of his day, he grounded his actions as well as his intellectual arguments in twentieth-century terms. Jabotinsky was very careful to place the word *democracy* in quotation marks to differentiate between the sign "democracy" and its meaning in the real (political) world.

Jabotinsky, always careful of his public persona, attempted to associate himself only with signs and names (democracy, majority rule) that contributed to his image as a traditional liberal. However, he seems to have been fully aware that this was only an outward manifestation, a play of words and that in the realm of human affairs (both politically and intellectually) other doctrines were more efficient and achieved better results. As he perceptively pointed out,

"Democracy is the perfect form of political expression of the people's will; therefore all the prejudices that the people hold are also fully expressed in their actions under the auspices of a democratic regime. That prejudices would disappear by the grace of democracy—this, I believe, no sensible person would argue."[64] And in 1934 he wrote that democracy was a cultural matter and not an absolute ideal.[65] "Democracy" was useful as a political symbol, but when he examined it in the harsh light of reality, Jabotinsky questioned its practicality, exposed its fundamental limitations, and embraced alternative programs.

In his discussion of the qualities of democracy, Jabotinsky frequently alluded to the Hebrew term *hadar,* which can be translated as 'glory' or 'splendor.' Jabotinsky regarded *hadar* as an essential Revisionist virtue, and he wanted it to be the principal tenet of Beitar. In a letter to the cadets of the Beitar naval academy in Civitavecchia, Italy, Jabotinsky instructed them to follow the principal of *hadar,* because it was the only way to fulfill the goals of Zionist revisionism.[66] He explained that by *hadar* he meant that, at all times, the cadets had to be courteous and well dressed, mind their table manners, and respect all school rules. They should also, he wrote, become fluent in Italian and in the local customs and refrain from getting involved in disputes with the local population on either political or personal matters.

In his emphasis on external decorum Jabotinsky was attempting to project his own personal traits onto the youth of his movement. He wanted the Beitarist youth to understand the importance of both the internal and the external, of both the ideals that could mobilize the nation and the manners by which these ideals were manifested in public. Achimeir argued that Jabotinsky was Herzl's true heir, because Jabotinsky possessed Herzl's Zionist drive and, more important, because Jabotinsky represented Herzl's glory and *hadar.* Herzl, Achimeir argued, was the master of external appearances, and so was Jabotinsky, who understood the importance of image in politics.[67]

For Jabotinsky, however, the external was only a means to prepare the people for the critical stage in the Zionist revolution. In a letter addressed to Hebrew youth, Jabotinsky wrote:

The Diaspora has weakened our bodies, and crept deep under the essence of our vital strength—and if this generation does not heal our
race, who would? And if before our people, there appears a real
threat of destruction—as it happened in the past on more than one
occasion—who will protect the old, the women, and the children?
Every young Hebrew, man or woman, is a soldier of our nation, soldier who is ready for the call, the language of our past and future in
his mouth, his arms strong for the battles ahead, and his heart knows
no fear.[68]

Beitarist youth, who had to mind their manners and public appearance, had at the same time to prepare themselves for the physical
battles ahead.[69] While Jabotinsky wanted the youth of his movement
to publicly display mildness and follow conventional social norms, at
the same time he wanted them to revolutionize the Jewish national
psyche, embrace violence and power, and be willing to sacrifice
themselves on the battlefield. In Beitar's anthem he instructed the
youth always to maintain their *hadar:*

> A Hebrew, if poor, if noble,
> if a slave if a simple man,
> was created the son of a king,
> crowned in David's glory.
> In light and in dark, remember the crown—
> the wreath of the nobleman and the peddler.[70]

Yet the ultimate destiny of Hebrew youth, the anthem stipu-
lated, was "to die or conquer the mountain." Beyond the image lay
the substance—the call on Beitarist youth to sacrifice, to die, and to
give up everything in the fight for the nation. At the end, however,
the image and substance were one: To prepare themselves for battle,
Revisionist youth would have to acquire the discipline of the soldier
that, with its emphasis on order and ceremony, was the ultimate expression of *hadar.*

In his autobiography Jabotinsky wrote about his days as a student
in turn-of-the-century Italy. Writing in the 1930s after the rise of fascism, he argued that the Italy of his youth had been in a transitional
phase from liberalism to fascism. In retrospect, Jabotinsky felt that

certain ideas and attitudes that his fellow Italian students expressed were early signs of the radical changes that would occur in Italy in the very near future: "The new Italian is organized, punctilious, and meticulous in his affairs—he builds and conquers, he is stubborn and cruel: these are the origins of fascism."[71]

In the 1930s Jabotinsky preached these very values to Revisionist youth. The discipline of which his fellow Italian students spoke contained the same principles that he demanded of the Revisionist cadets. Jabotinsky underscored the causal relationship between the cultural revolution that started brewing among his fellow Italian students and the rise of the radical Right. Thus *hadar*, while ostensibly the mark of a nineteenth-century gentleman, was also a means to transform the Hebrew nation from a passive victim to a disciplined fighting machine.[72]

Civility, dignity, and adherence to social norms were but the first steps in a national revolution that would liberate the Jews from the mentality of the Diaspora and turn them into a proud nation. In 1932 Jabotinsky defined the goals of Beitar thusly: "Beitar, as we think of it, is a school based on three levels in which the youth will learn how to box, to use a stick, and other self-defense disciplines; the youth will learn the principles of military order; it will learn how to work; it will learn how to cultivate external beauty and ceremony; it will learn to scorn all forms of negligence, or as we call them, poverty or ghetto-life; they will learn to respect older people, women, prayer (even that of a foreigner), democracy—and many other things whose time has passed but are immortal."[73]

To Jabotinsky, maintaining *hadar* and presenting the Beitarists as followers of traditional values would protect the Revisionist movement from its detractors and help legitimize it, but, more important, it was an essential phase in the (militaristic) education of Zionist youth.

Jabotinsky viewed militaristic education as the only way to build a healthy nation or, as he told the Revisionist youth, "Teach your muscles heroism, heroic games today, heroic projects tomorrow."[74] He claimed that the ability of a group of people to show discipline and sacrifice their individual interests for the good of the group was the greatest human attribute. Moreover, he stated that without ceremony there was no liberty. True liberty, to Jabotinsky, was the ability of individuals to give up their own subjectivity and realize themselves as part of a greater subject, the nation.

This was also his view of the true merits of democracy, a tool to channel the wills of the masses into one national will. But, he maintained, true democracy could work only in a utopian world where no real differences (prejudices) existed among individuals. In the absence of such conditions, other, totalitarian forms of government were more desirable to achieve the goals of the collective. In the "Idea of Beitar," Jabotinsky wrote:

> The greatest achievement of a free mass of people is the ability to operate together, all as one, with the absolute precision of a machine. . . . The greatest attribute of the human race is this ability bring into perfect harmony an individual's personality with the personalities of others for a common purpose. . . . Israel's salvation will come when the Jewish people will learn to act together as one as a machine. . . . We all have one will, we all build the same building, therefore we follow the orders of one architect. . . . The "commander," "conductor," "architect" can be one person or a collective— for example, a committee. The two systems are equally democratic.[75]

Jabotinsky's hope was to turn the Jewish masses into a machine that operated harmoniously according to the collective will of the group. This was also the rationale behind the notion of *hadar;* he called upon the young Revisionists to give up their individual traits, desires. and inclinations and, like true soldiers, become part of the general will. The ability to exhibit self-control in public, to restrain individual quirks and notions, was a characteristic not only of nineteenth-century gentlemen but also of soldiers who devote their life to the service of the nation. Jabotinsky hoped that "a day will come when a Jew who wants to express the highest appreciation of human honesty, manners, and honor will not say, 'This is a true gentleman!'—but rather 'This is a true Beitarist!'"[76] For Jabotinsky liberalism, freedom, and democracy, the terms that defined nineteenth-century liberal thought, were all means to advance the one true cause—the defense and betterment of the nation. Freedom meant the ability to renounce one's own will for the good of the collective, and democracy meant the expression of the will as manifested by the will of the leader.

In 1933 Jabotinsky wrote that he followed in the footsteps of Max Nordau and the Italian social criminologists who had shattered naive beliefs of the nineteenth century that had been based on false assumptions about universal values, morals, and rights. The twentieth century, he claimed, was the century of wars and struggles. It might not be as beautiful as the previous century, but it was perhaps more real.[77] In the constant tension between image and substance, between external appearances and the core of the issues, Jabotinsky's decision was clear. He was on the side of the new century and its ideals.

In 1939, a year before his death, Jabotinsky wrote that the world of his youth had been dominated by a rationalist worldview but that as he matured he realized that rationalism could not provide him with answers to life's fundamental questions.[78] His entire adult life was a struggle between the values of the world of his youth and the realities that he encountered as an adult. Ultimately, Jabotinsky chose violence and power over peace, liberalism, and democracy.

Late in life Jabotinsky wrote that in Rome, where he spent his formative student days, the professor who had the most profound influence on him was the father of the modern science of criminology, Enrico Ferri. Ferri was a leader of the radical unorthodox branch of Italian Marxism that made the conceptual leap that paved the way for the emergence of Italian fascism.[79] This group of positivist Marxists accepted the antimaterialistic revision of Marxism and preached the need for a continuing revolution that would destroy the cultural heritage of bourgeois society. However, this group advocated a revolution that was based on the will and enthusiasm of the people, not on materialistic parameters.

As Michael Stanislawski has shown, the young Jabotinsky did not show much interest in Marxist ideology; his cultural preferences were more in tune with fin-de-siècle decadence.[80] However, the mature Jabotinsky did write considerably about Marxism, and while he did not believe in the materialistic message of Marxism, he was captivated by its revolutionary force, its ability to mobilize people, and certain aspects of Marxist terminology, and he certainly sought to present an image of himself as a supporter, from a young age, of certain aspects of Marxist thought.

In an article titled "A Lecture on Israeli History," Jabotinsky wrote, "Even without being a Marxist, a person can accept the Marxist principle that the predominant factor in history is the state of the means of production. But for the ordinary Marxist, means of production means only material means. . . . Truthfully, these are not the important means of production. . . . The most important means of production is thought. Of all the means of production, the greatest one is our spiritual mechanism."[81]

Jabotinsky then went on to argue that each race develops a unique form of thought that distinguishes it from other races. Jabotinsky, the nationalist ideologue, accepted the Marxist notion that a single factor shapes human history. However, like Ferri more than two decades earlier, he rejected the materialistic and universal qualities of this principle and instead maintained that race and national culture were the prime determinants of the course of history.

For the maximalists who were frustrated with the Zionist establishment, which they felt misused the potent enthusiasm of Hebrew youth, Jabotinsky's brand of militaristic, antimaterialistic Zionism was a perfect fit. Like Jabotinsky, the maximalists claimed that the mission of Zionism was to prepare Jewish youngsters for a life of suffering and violence by cultivating their mental strength so that they could withstand the challenges that awaited them. The maximalists regarded Jabotinsky as the ideal leader for such an educational mission. [82] The poet Ya'acov Cohen, who was close to the maximalists, sang Jabotinsky's praises:

> Everybody knows, friend and foe: Jabotinsky is one of this generation's greatest men, if not the greatest of them all.
> Everybody knows: this is a man of national pride, of an ancient spirit of heroism and valor . . .
>
> Here is the New Hebrew man, head of the Biryonim . . .
>
> Jabotinsky's soul derives from that source of pure power, from which men of action throughout history have drawn their strength.[83]

Despite the differences in their demeanor and rhetoric, the maximalists saw in Jabotinsky the champion of militarism, discipline, and Jewish nationalism, the perfect Zionist leader and educator of Zionist youth. And together the fiery revolutionists and the mild-mannered intellectual would formulate a radical right-wing ideology that sought to revolutionize every aspect of the Jewish nation.

2

Monism

Revisionism's Ontological Philosophy

> What is Truth?—Truth is not things that have to be known. It
> means finding a certain spot, a single spot, that is the only
> one, and not any other, from which all things are viewed in
> their true proportions. . . . I must position myself in the
> exact spot that eyes demand, the same eyes that were shaped
> over the generations, in the same spot from which all things
> are arranged according to the proportions of the French. . . .
> True nationalism is realizing the existence of this spot,
> searching for it, and upon finding it, remaining in it in order
> to derive from it all our actions, beliefs and politics.
> Maurice Barrès, *Scenes et Doctrines du Nationalisme*

In his compelling study, *Haeckel's Monism and the Birth of Fascist Ideology,* Daniel Gasman has suggested that the evolutionary monist theory of the German zoologist Ernst Haeckel, one of the most popular scientific theories in Europe in the second half of the nineteenth century, was the one intellectual foundation that united all the different variations of radical Right thought at the beginning of the twentieth century. Gasman contends that fascist ideology was largely the result of the transformation of a scientific system, the post-Darwinian school of natural philosophy known as monism, into a political, philosophical, and religious ideology.[1]

According to Gasman, monism, the belief in a single principle, was an intellectual effort to create a secular faith that would unite science and religion and draw on the human instincts and sentiments usually found in art and myth. Monism drew on the oldest of philosophical traditions, the one that posited that a single force unifies every-thing in the cosmos (including human beings). Evolutionary monism was an attempt to overcome the alienation of modern humans, the consequence, the monists claimed, of the Cartesian separation of matter and spirit and of the Western belief in transcendental truths. Evolutionary monism was an intellectual rebellion against the cultural attempt to impose on people's consciousnesses powers and authorities—such as universal morality, rationality, and equality—that were alien to nature. According to Gasman, the essence of evolutionary monism was the destruction of the systems of thought that had been shaped by transcendental religious and moral teachings. Humans, monist theory claimed, were not free to construct society on the basis of a utopian moral system, as the Judeo-Christian tradition demands: Deeper natural forces determine human existence, and a transcendental system that suppresses humans' true nature should not restrain those forces.[2]

According to Gasman, the logical political outcome of evolutionary monism was inevitable: "Since life is meaningless, man and society would achieve liberation not in freedom from, or domination over nature, but in willing submission to the irrational force and will of nature, or as interpreted by Italian fascism, by adherence to the naturally based spiritual and cultural forces that determine the historical destination of a nation—forces that might be harnessed by the national community for periods of time in order to carry out heroic action, but in the end could lead nowhere except to the realization of the irrational glory of action itself."[3]

Life, according to the evolutionary monist paradigm, had no transcendental meaning, and teleology could not explain the history of human beings. Life was part of nature; it was random and irrational. Any theory, be it religious, moral, political, or social, that tried to account for the ways that human affairs are or should be organized, would remove humans from their true nature and cause a sense of alienation. The only way to live life authentically is to embrace the irrational brute forces of nature and denounce any teachings that try to limit and control those powers.

Monism was one of the fundamental principles of Zionist revisionism during the 1920s and 1930s. The sociologist Erik Cohen has argued that one main characteristic of mainstream Zionism was "universalistic particularism," by which he means that Zionism was a national ideology but one based on universal principles. Zionism sought to reconcile the particularistic national character of the Jewish state with enlightened universal values, most notably, civil equality.[4] Zionism addressed the need of the Jewish people to define themselves as a distinct national group, but it combined that need with universal theories such as socialism in the tradition of modern enlightened movements, or, as Ben Gurion maintained: "Two basic aspirations underlie all our work in this country: to be like all nations, and to be different from all nations."[5] The Revisionists, on the other hand, rejected the idea that Zionism could be based on a multitude of ideas and declared that the time had come to resurrect the nation of Israel, which was to be driven by a single (monist) national force.[6]

Monism gave the Revisionists a philosophical framework for their single-minded pursuit of statehood and their wish to purge the Zionist agenda of all other aspirations. Following Herzl's assertion that only a national home would solve the "Jewish problem," the Revisionists maintained that a national home should be the sole objective of the Zionist movement. They accused the Zionist establishment of neglecting the movement's true calling and of liquidating the Zionist dream for a socialist agenda.

According to the Revisionists, a nation-building movement could not have more than one ideal. Only by adhering to a monist philosophy, they argued, could the Zionist movement realize its true ambitions, or, as Jabotinsky formulated it: "It is an iron law and irreversible principle—that man cannot truly aspire after something if he is not willing to sacrifice some views of his when needed. This is the essence of the great and sacred zeal, the purity of every ideal. Ideal is a creature that does not tolerate any competition. Different views can reside side by side without any limitation. But man can only be committed to one view, and reject all others; regardless of how beautiful and enchanting he might find them to be, he must desert them."[7]

Yet for the Revisionists monism was not only a political plan of action. It was a means to cure the Jewish spirit after two millennia of the Diaspora. Jabotinsky maintained that "a perfect soul is only a monist soul. By its content the word *ideal* can have only a single meaning. In a healthy soul there is only one ideal."[8] The Revisionists contended that by adhering to socialist (and other universal) ideals, mainstream Zionism was not only delaying the realization of the Jewish national home but depriving Zionism of its reparative essence and in fact bringing the Diaspora to Zion. In hindsight the monist component of revisionism makes the rift between the movement and the Zionist establishment seem not only understandable but, perhaps, unavoidable.

Revisionist Monism

In the Zionist perception of Jewish history the destruction of the Second Temple and the Diaspora signaled not only the end of the Jewish national home but also—and what is more important—the loss of Jewish national identity. Once a nation whose heroes had been the great judges and kings who fought for Jewish independence and sovereignty, the Jews became dominated by prophets and rabbis, and their existence as a unique group of people depended solely on the observance of the 613 commandments of the Torah.

According to the Revisionists, following the loss of the Jews' geographical unity, Judaism changed from a national movement to a set of moral and universal teachings.[9] A nation that had once controlled its destiny through its army and great leaders became a passive religion whose essence was a belief in a transcendental savior, a Messiah who would lead the Jews back to their homeland.

In the Diaspora, the Revisionists maintained, the Jews relinquished the hope of winning back their national independence and instead turned themselves into the carriers of a universal vision that would save all humanity. An editorial in the Revisionist daily *Hazit ha-Am* about the role of the shofar in Jewish life said that when the Jews were in their national home, they used the shofar to call Jewish men to arms, whereas after two thousand years of exile it had become a religious tool held by the trembling hands of men who feared judgment, not the foes of the nation.[10]

The Jews in the Diaspora had become, in short, the people of the book. As Dov Chomsky claimed in *Madrich Beitar,* "The term 'The People of the Book' is the result of the dangerous and weakening belief that Israel is different from all other nations. It is the result of the prevailing notion that the Jews were scattered all over the world in order to advance humanity and spread the humanistic teachings of the prophets. It is the result of the distortion of nationalism and the nullification of the historical subject, the rights of the nation."[11]

For the Revisionists universalism and internationalism were emblematic of a people without a land.[12] Jews in the Diaspora had become the leaders of movements (Christianity, Marxism) in search of universal justice that would benefit all peoples—including the Jews—who in return would have to give up their unique national identities. Away from its natural home, Judaism was now a cosmopolitan movement. Jewry had become an extraterritorial entity, and Jewish nationalism was but a distant memory.[13]

The Revisionists contended that beyond the persecutions and the hardships that the Jews had endured over the centuries, the Diaspora had caused a deep psychological schism in the Jewish soul. The Jewish self became torn between its universal mission and the knowledge that it was part of a group that shared a common religion and history and a common language of prayer and study. The natural human ambition to actualize a true self by being part of a national collective was, in the Jews' case, thwarted by historical circumstance, forcing the Jews to become a "chosen people" with a message for all humanity. This dichotomy, between an innate national urge and an international existence, was the cause of the much discussed "Jewish problem." Only a return to monist nationalism could cure the ruptured Jewish soul.

Abba Achimeir provided a powerful analysis of the torn Jewish soul in the portion of his doctoral dissertation on Spengler's *Decline of the West* that is dedicated to Jewish history. Spengler, Achimeir wrote, saw history as the inevitable organic process of the rise and decline of cultural units, and the Jews figured prominently in his writings. Spengler made a clear distinction between the Israelites, who dwelled in the Land of Israel until the destruction of the First Temple, and Judaism, which, as he perceived it, emerged after the Babylonian exile. Post-exilic Jewry, according to Spengler, was a landless nation dispersed through the ancient world that spread its religion by means of conversion of other groups.[14]

Spengler included Judaism in what he called the Magian world—a group of cultures and civilizations that in addition to the Jews included Persia, Paul's Christianity, and Muhammad's Arabian world—which developed in the Near East and emphasized the international qualities of salvation (a Messiah) and the victory of good over evil.[15] The Magian worldview was not tied to a specific locale and could be practiced anywhere. Spengler argued that Paul's assertion—that "the nation of the redeemer was identical with mankind"—typified the Magian ethos.[16] This was the reason, he claimed, that the destruction of Jerusalem by the Romans did not destroy Judaism; Jerusalem was not a national but a religious center for the Jews, who, since their first exile, already were spread throughout the world.

According to Spengler, a young vibrant nation is bound to the land and draws its inspiration and vitality from nature. Decadent nations, on the other hand, are predominantly urban. They are alienated from nature and perceive the world through rational disciplines like science, which offer a representation of reality rather than a true experience of nature. The springtime of Judaism, Spengler argued, occurred during the first five centuries of Christianity. At that time the Jews, wherever they lived, were predominantly farmers who worked the land. Culturally, that was the period when the Talmud, the work that epitomizes the Jewish spirit, was written. The height of Jewish culture, its baroque period, Spengler maintained, came during the Jewish golden age in Spain. With their Magian brethren, the Arabs, the Jews achieved greatness in the realms of philosophy, literature, and politics. The decline of Jewish culture, on the other hand, occurred in the Christian West. There the Jews became a wandering nation, detached from the land and repeatedly forced to move according to the vagaries of political and economic life.

With their long intellectual tradition the Jews served the emerging West as its economic and administrative class, even as the ruling Christians forced the Jews into the city and often into a ghetto. Spengler argued that these are typical signs of a declining culture (Jewish culture was urban, and socially and culturally Jews were restricted to materialistic occupations), and he predicted that Jewry's future was gloom: "Detached from any land-footing since, centuries ago, it saved its life by shutting itself off in the ghetto, it is fragmented and faced with dissolution."[17] The predicament of the Jews, Spengler contended, was caused by their being a Magian nation caught in a Faustian (Western) world in which the dominant culture would always regard Jews as strangers and intruders, because Jews are so fundamentally different from the dominant society. In times of crisis the Jew as outsider would always serve as a convenient scapegoat for societies that could not cope with their internal problems.

As we have seen, Achimeir accepted Spengler's overall historiographical approach, but he rejected Spengler's analysis of Jewish history (just as he rejected Spengler's analysis of Russian history). Achimeir questioned Spengler's characterization of Judaism as a Magian culture. Whereas Spengler viewed Jerusalem solely as the spiritual center of world Jewry and argued that its loss did not, by itself, alter the course of Jewish history, Achimeir of course believed otherwise. Jerusalem and the historical Land of Israel were the political center that defined the Jewish nation, and their decline and the rise of the Jewish Diaspora marked the destruction of Jewish culture, not its birth. According to Achimeir, ancient Israel underwent a process similar to that of Hellenic colonization when Greece's Asian colonies overshadowed Greece itself, yet the homeland remained the (declining) cultural heart of the Hellenic world.[18]

While Spengler viewed the biblical prophets and Ezra as the fathers of Judaism, Achimeir saw the prophets as the reformers of Judaism; the true fathers of the Jewish nation, according to Achimeir, were the biblical political heroes of the pre-exilic period such as Joshua and David. Achimeir claimed that Isaiah, who ushered in the era of the prophets, was the Jewish equivalent of Luther, a reformer whose message marked a fundamental change in the history of Jewish culture but not its beginning. Judaism became a landless culture only after the destruction of the Second Temple, and as such Judaism's history was similar to that of other cultures, which, like Judaism, had lost their territorial base over time .

Achimeir pegged the beginning of the Jewish decline to the appearance of Ezra, the great reformer, and not, as Spengler would have it, to the emergence of the Jewish ghetto in Christian Europe.[19] Unlike Spengler, Achimeir did not view Judaism as a historical anomaly, a Magian nation trapped in the Faustian world, but rather as a (once) normal nation that experienced a decline as a result of the loss of its national home.[20] The Jewish tragedy was that as a result of the loss of its territorial and political base, Judaism reinvented itself as an international entity: Yavneh, a strictly religious center, overtook Jerusalem—as both religious center and political capital—whereas the Talmud, a product of the Diaspora, superseded the Bible, which tells the story of a sovereign nation living on its own land.[21]

Achimeir provided what is perhaps the most introspective depiction of the Jewish predicament in a short story titled "Raskolnikov in the Central Jail."[22] Achimeir's Raskolnikov is a young prisoner in Jerusalem's central jail, who, like the protagonist of *Crime and Punishment,* has a tormented soul. But unlike Dostoyevsky's Raskolnikov, the predicament of Achimeir's is strictly the result of his unique national condition and history, not the consequence of a crime that he has committed.

Achimeir described the inmate as a young Christian Arab who has been convicted of murder. He is part of the jail's Arab population, but he is an outsider in this group because of his religion. His name, Jesus—originally a Jewish name, Achimeir points out—further separates the inmate from his fellow Arab prisoners.

After his conviction Achimeir's Raskolnikov chooses to wear a red jail outfit, which symbolizes his interests in socialism and Marxism. At the same time he is popular among the jail's Catholic population because he was convicted by Protestant (English) authorities. As a murderer he is admired by the other prisoners, because killers occupy the top of the jail's criminal hierarchy. But at the same time the jail's administrators like him because he is a productive worker in the jail's printing shop (Achimeir claimed that printer is a historically Jewish occupation).

Achimeir offered a detailed description of the sexual habits of the jail's male population. He argued that the European prisoners tend to act as both males and females in their sexual relationships. The Eastern prisoners, on the other hand, assume only one role, as either man or woman. According to Achimeir, his Raskolnikov should have been a male in his sexual relations with other inmates because of his great stature among the prisoners. However, the prisoner was once a prostitute who performed the feminine role in his relations with male clients, so in jail he becomes the "female" partner of the most dominant prisoners. Achimeir also described the inmate's manner of dress on Sundays, writing that when his protagonist goes to pray in church, he wears an Arab robe as well as Western pants, emphasizing his dual identity as a man of both East and West.

Achimeir published "Raskolnikov in the Central Jail" in August 1935, not long after he himself was released from this facility. The writer had been arrested because of his alleged involvement in the assassination of Chaim Arlozoroff and in other illegal activities of Brith ha-Biryonim, and the story reflects Achimeir's experiences in jail. But the story also provides a unique analysis of the plight of Judaism.

Achimeir's Raskolnikov is a tormented soul, because he lacks true identity. He is at once part of the Occident and the Orient. He is dominant yet feminine and a Marxist who is a practicing Catholic. Raskolnikov represents the condition of the Diaspora Jews, even those physically living in Palestine—torn between opposing identities, between their own national needs and their extraterritorial international condition, unable to uncover and realize their true nature.

According to Achimeir, the schism in the Jewish soul is manifested in the two main religious and philosophical movements that Jews founded: Christianity and Marxism.[23] (His Raskolnikov practices both.) These two movements advocate universal messages that transcend national boundaries, and, for Jews who had lost their national identity, they offered a framework that promised salvation. This promise, however, was false because universalistic ambitions only suppressed humans' true nature, which for Achimeir could be expressed only through the nation. Thus, like Raskolnikov in Jerusalem's central jail, the Jews were torn between their knowledge that they had a unique identity and the universal role that they had assumed in the Diaspora.

According to Achimeir, the Zionist movement fell into the same trap of oppositions as his Raskolnikov did in its futile attempts to resurrect the Jewish national home. Instead of focusing on reviving the Jewish national urge, the movement attempted to justify its nationalist goals by declaring itself part of a universalistic movement, socialism. Revisionist monism was a fight against socialism. But, according to Achimeir, it was also a fight against self-hatred. When Jews were willing to go to jail for foreign ideals and values, they were acting *against* themselves, against their national nature. They were wasting their historic opportunity to return to their golden age. As Achimeir put it elsewhere, "A war against socialism is a war against anti-Semitism. From this the conclusion is that the war against socialism is not only a war for monism but also against anti-Semitism."[24]

In Spengler's cyclical view of human history, all cultures go through an initial phase of growth, which is marked by faith and spirituality. Cultural vitality, according to Spengler, is characterized by national independence and unity and by an unrestrained will to power. A culture's decline, on the other hand, is marked by a preoccupation with matter and by the rise of sciences that deal with the material world and eliminate the religious and spiritual. While Spengler's scheme is pessimistic, because cultures cannot escape their impending doom, it also leaves room for optimism, because by understanding history, people can understand which factors could create a thriving new culture.

Spengler argued that war is part of nature, whereas peace is the result of the preaching of intellectuals. Pacifism is but an illusion, a mark of senility and decay. Whoever adopts pacifism abandons the future. Strong and vital races are not pacifistic; they embrace war, and war and violence are the marks of an emerging culture.[25] Achimeir wholeheartedly adopted Spengler's stance on this point. In a letter addressed to Hebrew youth, Achimeir wrote: "It seems that Spengler's prophecy about the declining West in light of the degeneration of the socialist and liberal worldviews saved Europe from the parliamentary rule of chattering politicians, and, more important, national dictatorship saved the people of central Europe from civil war and Marxist utopias."[26]

The only way for the Hebrew nation to revitalize itself, Achimeir maintained, was by rejecting the dominant ideologies of the West, which preached pacifism and other universal ideals, and by returning to the pre-exilic Israelite ethos of the warrior judges who had roamed the ancient land. The Jews should not emulate the declining West but return to their own national values. The West, Achimeir argued, had become a culture of science and rationality and had lost its vitality. Zionism should not follow in this path. It should not give up its national interests in the name of false ideals but instead should seek spiritual unity. True Zionists would have to be true monists.[27]

Achimeir's fellow maximalist, Y. H. Yevin, had trained as a physician, but once in Palestine he diagnosed and prescribed remedies only for society's ills, not those of individuals. Like Achimeir, Yevin focused on the conflicting demands of universalistic humanism and the more instinctive calls of nationalism. Jews, he maintained, should not follow the example of Stephan Zweig (and other European Jewish intellectuals), who gazed back longingly at the age of Erasmus and the birth of modern humanism: Jews should live in the present and accept the truth that nationalism is the only viable course of action.[28]

Yevin lamented that Zionism had been conceived during the heyday of one of the West's most superficial ideas—progressive liberalism. The First World War, he argued, had destroyed progressive liberalism's credibility, and Jews had to acknowledge this. Zionism could not be constituted on the liberal principles of universal justice and moral truths; the time had come for the monist Zionism of power and revolt.[29]

Yevin attacked the traditional division of the Zionist movement into spiritual and political Zionism.[30] He maintained that the only true spiritual form of Zionism was political Zionism, because only as an independent nation could the Jews fully explore their spiritual potential. Mainstream Zionism, which adhered to socialist principles, claimed to be a political movement. Yet because it put universal values before the national needs of the Jewish people, the Zionist movement was in fact derived from the spiritual Zionism of Ahad ha-Am, the turn-of-the-twentieth-century thinker who had rejected political Zionism in favor of a purely cultural movement. Ahad Ha-Am's Zionism, Yevin claimed, had hindered the attempt to create a national political home for the Jews. It had emphasized Judaism's special, even unique, status rather than the Jews' viability as a nation: Judaism was to be a purely cultural entity, Israel a purely spiritual center. Yevin argued, "Ahad Ha-Am fought Herzl not in the name of the real Hebrew spirit but in the name of his perception of the Hebrew spirit—in the tradition of the Diaspora—the unique spirit that is different from any other national spirit."[31]

Yevin drew an analogy between Ahad Ha-Am's hope that Zionism would provide broad spiritual benefits to society and mainstream Zionism's emphasis on the influence of a socialist Jewish state as part of a worldwide socialist movement. To Yevin, then, mainstream Zionism was but another chapter in the history of the Jewish Diaspora, in which false values tended to replace true national and political needs. Only by ridding the Zionist movement of its universalistic characteristics could Zionism revolutionize Jewish history. The monism of nationalism, Yevin argued, was the sole spiritual cure for the divided Jewish identity of the Diaspora: "Returning political mastery to the people includes a return to spiritual mastery."[32] Monism, then, was not just a political and strategic choice but, rather, the only way to realize what was, after all, the main objective of Zionism: to re-create the Jewish soul.

Jabotinsky's Monist Philosophy

In 1932 Jabotinsky eulogized Boris Shatz, the founder of Bezalel, the first Hebrew art academy, as "a unique kind of man who followed one concept and one love: a narrow field—practical art— and combined in it all his dreams about beauty, Judaism, and Eretz-Yisrael."[33]

As a young man Jabotinsky had spent three years as a student in Rome, where he came under the influence of Enrico Ferri. Ferri was one of the leading figures in the Italian Marxist-Syndicalist movement at the turn of the century, which, as Gasman has shown, was influenced by Haeckel's scientific positivism and his insistence on violence as a natural factor in human history.[34]

Ferri, a noted criminologist, tried to create a synthesis of Marxism and scientific determinism that would explain human history through a scientific approach predicated on natural laws. He made a clear distinction between the metaphysical worldview and the modern evolutionary approach to science, which he espoused: "The generations, which preceded us, have all been imbued with this notion of the absoluteness of natural laws, the conflicting laws of dual universe of matter and spirit. Modern science, on the contrary, starts from the magnificent synthetic conception of *monism,* that is to say, of a *single substance* underlying all phenomena—matter and force being recognized as inseparable and indestructible, continuously evolving in a succession of forms—forms relative to their respective times and places. It has radically changed the direction of modern thought and directed it toward the grand idea of universal evolution."[35] Ferri maintained that, in contrast to the traditional metaphysical view that had dominated Western culture for centuries, the future of science was positivistic evolution that rejected any duality or transcendental forces and explained everything as being the result of a single scientific principle.

Like Ferri, Jabotinsky attacked the old philosophical division between body and spirit. He maintained that one's spiritual nature is a reflection of one's physical circumstances and that one natural factor determines everything in human affairs.[36] The only way to understand human history, according to Jabotinsky, is to understand the psychology of the different races. The unique physical attributes of each race determines its psychological makeup, as well as its economic, cultural, and political behavior.

Ferri had criticized the utopian brand of socialism (Marxism!) that wanted to fashion society after some utopian (transcendental) model and lead a revolution that would alter the natural course of history. Applying a similar revisionist critique, Jabotinsky rejected the notion that economic conditions alone account for differences among various societies and that the way to change society is by means of a social revolution. Jabotinsky maintained that even if two different races are given identical economic conditions, they will still develop different social, cultural, and political institutions. The only factor that plots a race's history is its psychological characteristics, which are not affected by social or cultural factors but develop according to natural principles.[37]

To Jabotinsky (as well as Ferri) the role of ideology, then, is to create the most favorable conditions for a race to explore its natural tendencies as an independent unit, and to combat other ideologies that suppress those tendencies in the name of alienating utopian or transcendental ideals.

The strand of anti-Semitism that runs through Haeckel's work claimed that Jews are primarily responsible for the introduction of the transcendental dualism that had come to dominate the West. According to the evolutionary monists, the Jews are responsible for the dualistic beliefs that distort the natural course of history, which is predicated on the constant struggle between races and the inevitable survival of the stronger ones. Haeckel regarded the Jews, as the inventors of the transcendental deity, as the perpetrators of the rebellion against the natural order of things, which is at the heart of the morbidity of Western culture.[38]

Jabotinsky, while presumably no anti-Semite, also identified the search for a universal salvation based on transcendental truths as a central characteristic of the Jews and as one of the main contributing factors to the plight of the Jewish nation. He maintained that as long as Jews focused their attention on saving the whole world and preferred universal over national ideals, they could never truly save themselves.

The Jews, Jabotinsky argued, had to realize that they were a single race that had to return to the characteristics that had led them to greatness as an independent nation: "A superior race must first possess a self-consciousness; it must have great pride, not boastfulness, but a strong will, and respect for its spiritual values. For such a race, the mere thought of a foreign element's dominating it physically or spiritually is unacceptable."[39]

The Jewish race (nation) could no longer be dominated by foreign elements, whether they were other governments or ideologies. The spirit of the nation had to remain pure; it could not be diverted from its true organic nature. Real Zionism was, according to Jabotinsky, "the realization of honor and a sovereign self-respect that cannot accept the fact that the Jewish national problem is less important than other problems that have a universal nature."[40] Moreover, the world could not consider itself morally just as long as a Jewish national home did not exist; the fulfillment of the objectives of Zionism as a national movement was a necessary condition for global redemption.

Jabotinsky predicted that language would play a key role in the process of national revival. He perceived the Jewish Diaspora as a world based on a multitude of languages. Jews communicated, interacted, and lived in either Yiddish or the local languages of the Gentiles around them, whereas the use of Hebrew was restricted to the realm of prayers and the study of Judaism.[41] Thus Hebrew, historically the national language of the people of Israel, was reduced to a non-spoken language that dealt solely with religious matters, denying Jews the ability of other nations to use language as a means to manifest power and sovereignty.

Moreover, with the advent of the Haskalah (Jewish Enlightenment), the corpus of Western thought became accessible to educated Jews, and Hebrew suffered another blow: New generations of Jews would conduct all intellectual and spiritual inquiries in other languages, removing from Hebrew still more relevance and vitality.[42] As Uri Zvi Greenberg, the Revisionist poet, described the state of the Hebrew language, "There is no god in Hebrew literature, no godly tremble. There is no elation. This literature, presumably written in a universal language, shows that you can live without a pulse and a heart. There is no impulsive egoistic process of creativity."[43]

Language, Jabotinsky claimed, was a national phenomenon, part of every individual's national instinct. Because of the circumstances of the Diaspora, which led Jews from all over the world to communicate in Yiddish, Jews had come to view language as being disconnected from national boundaries, thereby strengthening Jewish tendencies toward internationalism. The Jewish soul was torn between its authentic spirit of unity and separateness (which it had all but forgotten), and false cosmopolitanism. The remedy to the torn Jewish self was a return to monism, where soul, language, and nation could become one.

Jews, Jabotinsky argued, should be educated in Hebrew from infancy, in a manner true to Hebrew's real nature as a national tongue: "National culture, pure national consciousness, is possible only in that language by which the child receives his first impressions from the world that surrounds him. If he is to receive them in a foreign language, his entire thought process ties in with foreign contents, with foreign forms."[44]

Jabotinsky lamented that Hebrew scholars associated Hebrew with a history of suffering and persecution. Children brought up this way would assume the traditional passive Jewish nature, he argued. They would never be able to find their true identity. Jewish education therefore had to stress the incredible power that the Hebrew language possesses. Students, he claimed, would find comfort in the sense of power that the letters of the aleph bet instilled in them.[45]

Jabotinsky emphasized the need to recover the original sound of the language—the authentic ancient accent—in Hebrew education.[46] He argued that away from Israel and under the influence of foreign languages, Hebrew had lost its true sound. "The curse of the Diaspora is upon us, and on our language and accent. . . . The sound of the language, its accent, and its ring have weakened so much that they are all but forgotten, and we no longer feel the necessity and importance of such things."[47]

Each language has unique sounds (accent) that are part of the language's unique character. In the Diaspora, Hebrew had become strictly a written language, a series of texts that people interpreted over the years. While the words and sounds of a live language had a very definite meaning that an entire nation understood, the meaning of a dead language changed constantly. A dead tongue could not mobilize people; only readily recognizable sounds and symbols could trigger a nation's hidden instincts. Over the years Hebrew had assumed an international sound as it began to resemble the many languages that Jews spoke. The role of Hebrew education, then, was to recover the original national sounds of the language of the great biblical warriors and judges. To be a national language Hebrew would first have to become a living language.

The letters of the Hebrew alphabet, when heard repeatedly from an early age, would instill the proper pronunciation in the new Jewish generation, and Jabotinsky knew what the letters would teach: "For the generation that grows before our eyes and who will be responsible, probably, for the greatest change in our history, the aleph bet has a very simple sound: young people learn how to shoot. . . . For one to be a true person, he must study 'culture' in general. To be Jewish, he must know the language and history of his people. . . . But if you will learn how to shoot, there might be hope. This is the language in which the historical reality of our generation and the next generation speaks to us."[48]

Typically, Jabotinsky managed to express here a profound truth through a particularized image. For Jabotinsky, as for the rest of the Revisionists, truth was to be found less in abstract universal principles than in concrete, specific reality. Monism was the search for unity and wholeness. While Revisionist monism had political implications (focusing on achieving immediate political goals), it also was a philosophical approach rooted in the tradition of evolutionary monism. Revisionist monism was a call to rid the Jewish psyche of its false belief in universal truths in an attempt recover the authentic powers that are at the core of a healthy national movement.[49]

Monism and the Arab Question

The Revisionist brand of Zionist monism played an important role in shaping the Revisionists' attitudes toward the Arab population in Palestine. For the maximalist faction the position regarding the Arabs was clear. The Arabs were Gentiles, one in a succession of nations that had been persecuting the Jews for centuries. The Arabs were an enemy that posed a real threat to the Zionist cause and were to be treated by force in order to establish Jewish domination over the land.

To Yevin the local Arab population was just like the Christian population in Europe, a force that oppressed the Jewish nation and turned it into an agent of the local national economy.[50] Greenberg, similarly, did not see the Arabs as a Semitic people who might be natural allies of the Jews but as another foreign nation that, like the European nations, would seek to destroy the Jewish people. In the "Speech of a Bleeding Man/On Arabia," Uri Zvi Greenberg wrote:

> Amen, for we were wrong; upon our return home;
> Great in wisdom but weak in heart.
>
> We did not find a sister to our race that speaks Arabic;
> And she even belongs to the house of Shem.
>
> We have found a sister and mistress to the Edomite race.[51]

Jabotinsky's view of the Arab question was far more complex that that of the maximalists. He realized that "they [Arabs] look upon

Palestine with the same instinctive love and true fervor that any Aztec looked upon Mexico or any Sioux upon the prairie. Palestine will remain for the Palestinians not a borderland, but their birthplace, the center and basis of their national existence."[52] But his view of the Arabs too rested on the monist principle of national unity and a perception of the Arabs as Other.

Jabotinsky opposed the notion that the Jews would have to expel the Arabs from Israel and maintained that, ultimately, the two sides could live together peacefully: "The writer of these words is considered as the enemy of the Arabs, as a person who wants to push the Arabs out of the land of Israel. There is no truth in that. My emotional disposition toward the Arabs is the same as it is with regard to any other nation: polite indifference."[53] But such a solution would have to be based on Jewish power and an Arab realization that on both sides of the Jordan River that Israel must serve as the Jewish national homeland.

Jabotinsky's thinking about the Arabs was embedded in his monist vision of an ideal unity of race, language, and history: "The ideal type of an absolute nation must have a particular racial composition that separates it from surrounding races. It must occupy, from an early age, one specific territory, one that is devoid of foreign minorities that weaken the national unity. It must have an independent language that is not borrowed from other nations. . . . This means a language whose characteristics reflect the intellectual and emotional character of the nation. It must have an original national religion. And lastly it must have a historical heritage that is common to the nation's different elements."[54] While Jabotinsky conceded that such a nation could not exist in reality, this was the model that any national movement should strive for.

For Jabotinsky human rights, civil equality, and even political equality could not create harmony among individuals. Only the common ties of blood, history, and language could bring people together. In a speech before the 17th Zionist Congress in Basel, Switzerland, Jabotinsky asserted, "We were never guilty of confusing concepts—as the English and French tend to—in arguing that nationalism is by any means related to citizenship."[55]

To Jabotinsky humans were not defined by their political or legal status but by their national and racial affiliation. One of the main demands that the Revisionists made of the Zionist establishment was that it focus all its efforts on creating a Jewish majority in Israel. Jabotinsky wrote: "The creation of a Jewish majority was, is, and always will be the fundamental objective of Zionism, of any form of Zionism, be it political or spiritual."[56] However, this majority was not intended to win over the country democratically but to create such a formidable majority that, as Jabotinsky claimed in his speech before the Zionist Congress, "it would imprint on the land its national character."[57]

Jabotinsky envisioned an "iron wall" as the barrier between Jews and Arabs in Israel. However, he did not advocate a transfer of Arabs out of Israel or preventing them from living in the Jewish state. Jabotinsky claimed that in the Jewish nation, the sons of Ishmael would enjoy full civil rights and would live in peace with their Jewish brethren: "We do not want to expel any Arab from the left or right bank of the Jordan. We want them to prosper both economically and culturally."[58] Yet they would have to do so under Jewish rule, in a state that would be formed in order to accommodate the needs of the Jewish people, because of the indestructible relationship between the nation and the land. "Every distinctive race aspires to become a nation, to create a separate society, in which everything must be in this race's image—everything must accommodate the tastes, habits, and unique attributes of this specific race. This includes every aspect of social life: language, economy, politics, in short—culture. A national culture cannot be limited to music or books as many argue. A national culture is the sum of all customs, institutions, and life forms of the nation."[59]

According to the Revisionist leader, legalistic (or any universally applied) criteria should not determine one's nationality. Thus, while the Arabs might achieve civic equality in the land, they could never be part of the Israeli nation. They could not become one with the dominant force that would determine the nature of the country and would allow individual members of the nation to fulfill their greatest human potential. The iron wall therefore would not physically separate the Jews and the Arabs. It would serve as a spiritual barrier to maintain the distinction between the members of the Hebrew nation, who ruled the country (and determined its character), and the Arabs, whom the Hebrews denied any access to real centers of power.

Mainstream Zionism, with its legacy of the French Revolution, regarded the establishment of a Jewish majority in Palestine as the only means to ensure Jewish political domination. In 1946 Moshe Sharett assured his Arab counterparts before the Anglo-American Commission that the Jewish state would provide for complete equality of rights for all inhabitants, regardless of their race or creed, as well as full eligibility for all political posts.[60] For mainstream Zionists the creation of a Jewish majority was a political necessity, and because legal and political equality for them entailed national equality, they had to adopt political plans that would ensure such a majority—partitioning the land into a Jewish and an Arab state[61]—or, as some Zionist leaders suggested, transferring the Arab population outside the boundaries of the future Hebrew state.[62]

To the Revisionists, however, such plans were unacceptable. In their monist worldview the land of Zion was one with the nation and with the race and therefore could not be partitioned.[63] As for the transfer of Arabs, such an act would not be necessary, because as long as the Jews maintained their iron wall of will and strength, the land would retain its essential Jewishness.

While Jabotinsky's world had room for individual civil rights, they were not the dominant factor in his political program. A state could not be constructed on the principles of political equality and simple majority rule; it drew its legitimacy from the nation, from the collective will of the people. A state was not simply a political vehicle that facilitated the relations between individuals; it was, to paraphrase Haeckel's monist principle, a sacred force that united every (human) phenomenon.

Monism placed the nation and the state above the individual and submitted everything to their authority.[64] When a person is one with the nation, there is no room for individuality. Jabotinsky maintained that only this monist harmony could provide for the healing of the Hebrew soul. And in this monist scheme the native Arab population could achieve certain civil rights, but Arabs could not become part of the monist Jewish nation.

3

A Mobilized Society
Revisionist Economics

> This is politics proper: the moment in which a particular de-
> mand is not simply part of the negotiation of interests but
> aims at something more, and starts to function as the meta-
> phoric condensation of the global restructuring of the entire
> social space.
>
> Slavoj Žižek, *The Ticklish Subject*

In 1938 Y. Kellerman, a Revisionist activist, published in *Metzuda*, a
publication affiliated with Beitar, an article that outlined, for the benefit of Revisionist youth, the principles of Italy's economic system.
According to Kellerman, the Italian economic system was predicated
on six tenets: The nation comes before anything else; the ends and
interests of the state are sacred; each individual must surrender to
those interests; class war is destructive and does not solve any social
problems; all national resources must be concentrated through centralized planning; and private property and private enterprise are the
most efficient ways to achieve national economic goals.[1] The essence
of this economic system lay in the combination of capitalistic modes
of production (private ownership) and a political system that defined
the goals and interests of the national economy and regulated it.

Kellerman was providing for his young Revisionist readers an
introduction to the Italian economic model, but he could have just
as well have been discussing the economic principles of the Zionist
Revisionists that were rooted in the radical right-wing ideologies of
the time.

The radical Right appeared on the European scene at the beginning of the twentieth century as a reaction against liberalism and capitalism on one hand and against Marxism and materialism on the other. The rightists opposed the liberal perception of society as a gathering of individuals who share nothing in common but their rational capabilities as human beings. Liberalism, the radical Right claimed, deprived individuals of their unique features and characteristics, treating them as absolute equals who interacted with one another in a purely rational manner that served their individual needs. As for Marxism, the Right claimed that it was internationalist in nature; it divided the nation along class lines and reduced human history to material factors.

In contrast to these two models, the radical Right viewed people as spiritual beings who were members of a nation and a race. The will, desires, and beliefs of people, the rightists maintained, did not depend on their rational reasoning or their material status alone but rather on their cultural, national, and racial heritage. Yet in formulating its economic and social program, the radical Right drew on capitalism and the revolutionary spirit of Marxism to envision what can be described as a state-controlled capitalist market.[2]

The Zionist Revisionists, who shared the anti–Marxist and anti-liberal sentiments of the European Rightists, created a similar economic plan that suited their perception of the reality and of the needs of the Yishuv. Although the Revisionists were never in a position of power to implement their economic model, this model was an integral part of their overall Zionist vision for the revival of the Hebrew nation.

Statist Capitalism

Capitalism, according to the radical Right critique, fundamentally deprived humanity of its moral foundations. As Ezra Pound phrased it, "The doctrine of Capital has shown itself as little else than the idea that unprincipled thieves and anti-social groups should be allowed to gnaw into the rights of ownership."[3]

According to the writer Jean-Joseph Goux, in his 1990 study of the relationship between economics and symbolism, historically the appearance of money as an economic tool marked the cultural shift from nature and imagination to convention and reason.[4] When the ancient Greeks developed the monetary system in the polis, they moved away from barter economics, which relied on the natural qualities of goods, to a rational economic system that judged all goods according to a single criterion (money) and arranged the exchange market along rational rules (a manipulation of numbers). The development of monetary economics also marked the passage from mythology to philosophy, from the instinctual bonds that united society to a rational system that transcended the particular in people and treated them as generic abstract beings.

The monetary system, according to Goux, developed historically in connection with the evolution of language as a representational medium. He sees a definite correlation between the development of the alphabet and the transition from barter to monetary economics, noting that the one tended to accompany the other.[5] As language ceased to be a series of noises and graphical symbols that imitated natural objects, it developed into a system of arbitrary signs that could be arranged in an infinite number of ways and could ostensibly represent all reality—mental experiences as well as material objects.

According to this "representational" model of language, arbitrary linguistic signs represent real objects, and these signs are constructed (as linguistic statements) in a rational manner, so as to represent the way the real world is arranged. In the realm of economics the representational model sees the transformation of exchange into a flurry of paper notes, credit and bank transactions, as, in effect, the removal of the object, the commodity, from daily human experience. Economic power, which in the barter system consisted entirely of the ownership of actual things, increasingly means the control of capitalist signs that represent monetary value.

The Marxist paradigm extended the representational model to view capitalism as a veritable fetishism of money and other economic symbols in which capital, a mere representation of the real world, became the sole source of economic value and control. All economic interactions became part of the (philosophically) idealistic world of signs, thus becoming alienated from real thought and ignoring the real nature of humans.[6]

Idealism benefits the dominant classes; it is, according to the Marxist doctrine, reactionary in nature. Signs and symbols are easier to accumulate and manipulate than commodities, and they quicken the process by which a limited number of individuals gain access to the centers of social power. Idealism creates ideologies (political, social, and artistic) that justify the dominance of a certain class under the guise of rationality and efficiency. The more rational and efficient the economy of signs, the more power is amassed by those who have access to capital.

To address the inequities of capitalist idealism, Marx propounded his theory of economic materialism. Whereas capitalism focuses on exchange and distribution, Marx focused on production, the material basis of all economic activity, seeking to rearrange the means of production as a means to reinvent society.

Many ideologues of the radical Right came from Marxist circles and shared with the revolutionary Left its antiliberal and antidemocratic sentiments. Much like their counterparts on the Left, the ideologues of the Right felt a need to address the plight of the working masses in an age of industry and mass production, but theirs was a nationalist solution that sought to create harmony between the working classes and the rest of society.

The radical Right accepted the Marxist argument that the economics of monetary representation, which reached its apex with capitalism, reduced culture to a set of abstract symbols. In *The Decline of the West,* which became enormously influential among the radical Right, Spengler decried the evolution of knowledge from pure sensation of the world to a series of abstract symbols, which, he argued, implied a false sense of the mind's liberation from the grip of true reality. The growing reliance of human knowledge on abstraction, he wrote, "gives rise to a stock of signs for communication-speech which are much more than identification-marks—they are names bound up with a sense of meaning, whereby man has the secret numina (deities, nature-forces) in his power, and number (formulae, simple laws), whereby the inner form of the actual is abstracted from the accidental-sensuous . . . by way of abstraction as a piece of waking consciousness uncommitted to activity."[7]

In the realm of economics and social interactions, representation manifested itself in the form of money: "Abstract money corresponds exactly to abstract number. Both are entirely inorganic. The economic picture is reduced exclusively to quantities, whereas the important point about 'goods' had been their quality."[8] Money, then, was fictional, far removed from the essence of real life.

Ezra Pound gave poetic form to the Right's criticism of the culture of money, writing:

> Usura slayeth the child in the womb
> It slayeth the young man's courting
> It hath brought palsey to bed, layeth
> between the young bride and her bridegroom.
>
> (Canto XLV)

For Pound, as for Spengler, usury was the epitome of the culture of money, which turned everything away from the natural and essential and toward speculative representation. As Spengler wrote, "Money is not a product of nature but an invention of man. . . . The nations have forgotten the differences between animal, vegetable, and mineral; or rather, finance has chosen to represent all three of the natural categories by a single means of exchange."[9]

Pound longed nostalgically for a purer world, where men were not manipulated by symbols but were motivated by real things.[10] He rejected the modern world, where empty formulas ruled, and claimed, "For when words cease to cling close to things, kingdoms fall, empires wane and diminish."[11] The radical Right wanted to reverse the effects of the transition from barter to a monetary economy; it wanted to move away from the abstract to the natural, from the historical to the mythic. The rightists wanted to revolt against the liberal bourgeois order and return to the (perceived) values of barter economics.

Although the radical Right wanted to restore the spiritual qualities of the premonetary life, it did not advocate a romantic return to the technological realities of barter culture. As the political scientist Mark Neocleous has pointed out, the Right's attacks on modern capitalism were directed against markets and banking rather than against capitalist modes of production.[12] The Right challenged the manner in which capitalism removed older, more natural qualities from culture and replaced them with arbitrary signs that had no intrinsic meaning to the nation or the race. Capitalism, according to the rightist critique, removed spirituality and real values from human life. It turned people into consumers, into products of the marketplace.

But the radical Right did not want to reverse the material and technological achievements of modern civilization. The Right admired technology; it was fascinated by its speed and power and by its ability to concentrate and amplify violence. While the Right saw in liberal and socialist ideologies attempts to circumvent the natural order, it regarded technology as a pure extension of nature. In its capacity as a revolutionary force, it sought to use the new means afforded by modern technology to mobilize the masses in the struggle against the old bourgeois order.

In order to achieve its economic vision, which promoted the technological achievements of modernity while restoring (what rightists saw as) society's spiritual values, the radical Right created an economic model that combined the Marxist revolutionary spirit with a belief in the capitalist basis of modern society.[13]

Although the radical Right rejected the capitalist culture of money and wealth and advocated an alternative culture of virtues and spirituality, it refrained from interfering with the material basis of society. According to Walter Benjamin, the Right was not concerned with rearranging the social order in a just and equal way but, rather, in developing social harmony by way of distributing symbolic capital to the growing working class.[14]

By objecting to any interference with society's material basis, the radical Right sought to keep the capitalistic infrastructure of private ownership of means of production intact. Instead it focused all its prescriptions for social change on the political, ideological, and cultural realms—on the superstructure, in the Marxist model; the rightists advocated a spiritual and symbolic revolution, not a class-oriented one. Ze'ev Sternhell termed it a new conservative form of socialism, which attacked the moral and cultural deficiencies of capitalism but left private property alone and spoke not for one (oppressed) class but for society as a whole.[15] In contrast to what they perceived as the Marxist call for internal strife and the destruction of one class for the benefit of another, the rightists strove to unite society around positive qualities such as authority, discipline, solidarity, and self-sacrifice. And this unity would find its highest form of expression in the state.

The state, the embodiment of the people's will and spirit, had a dual role—both political and cultural—in the radical Right's economic model. Politically, the state would ensure that the market operated smoothly by prohibiting strikes or any other manifestations of class war and, in contrast to the free-market economy that capitalism advocated, the state would use protective tariffs to safeguard the national economy from foreign goods and capital. The state would not take over private property, but it would become a corporate mechanism, organizing the market in a manner that best served national goals. Culturally, the state would provide the masses with myths, national symbols, and a sense of pride that appealed to the collective unconscious, those basic primordial urges that transcend any economic and social divisions and unite the entire nation despite economic inequalities.

The logical outcome of the rightist economic plan, according to Benjamin, would be war. The call to revolution of the Marxist Left became, in the radical Right's social vision, a call to arms in the name of the state. As Neocleous argues, "Instead of class war, revolutionary social change would be brought about through the war of nations."[16] For the radical Right violence possessed a positive and therapeutic value and would improve the health of the national society. War, by its very irrationality and the totality of its violence, would allow humans to transcend their material condition and logical consciousness and confront their subconscious, the very foundations of their being.[17]

The radical Right, which objected to materialistic ideology as demeaning and corrupting, found in war a distillation of politics, a pure economy (politics) of signs, where symbols and ideas clashed in the most authentic way. Thus, unlike the liberal model, which looked for the most efficient and rational symbolic order, the Right embraced the irrational, the subconscious, the primordial—the images that led people to give up their subjective selves to become part of a greater entity, the state.

Spengler conveyed this message in no uncertain terms: "Money [highly rational, materialistic society] is overthrown and abolished only by blood. . . . Ever in History it is life and life only—race-quality, the triumph of the will-to-power—and not the victory of truths, discoveries, or money that signifies."[18]

Revisionist Statist Capitalism

It was clear to the Revisionists that two distinct camps were engaged in the struggle about the character and nature of the future Hebrew state. An editorial in *Hazit ha-Am,* the Revisionist daily, declared that war had broken out in the Yishuv between the socialist Labor Party and the Revisionist Party, between an internationalist party and a truly nationalist movement.[19]

For the Revisionists socialism was a materialistic ideology that deprived people of their natural qualities as human beings. Marxism, declared *Avukah* (a Revisionist publication), promoted internal strife and turned brothers against one another. Marxism in the Land of Israel turned youth away from the needs of the nation and instead asked Zionists to worry about proletariats in China or Africa.[20]

Socialism was decadent and marked the overall decline of the West, Achimeir argued. Just as Spengler had predicted, the rise of socialism as a materialistic ideology, marked the end of the life cycle of Western culture, Achimeir claimed. Socialism was constructed on false ideals and offered empty values that should not be the basis of an emerging nation. Achimeir promised the Revisionist public that the ideas of escaping the vanities of materialism and of returning to the life of the spirit were gaining strength among Jewish youth, who were beginning to learn the great merits of Jabotinsky's brand of heroic Zionism.[21]

The Revisionist activist A. Asaar claimed that historical materialism was a form of religiosity that forgot about human beings. He argued that undue attention to necessity and material conditions

suppressed free will.[22] Jabotinsky, characteristically more under-
stated than his followers, claimed that socialism diverted Zionist
youth from their true calling, the creation of a Hebrew state.[23]

The Revisionists acknowledged that the twentieth century was the
era of the masses and that the needs of working people had to be addressed. But the Revisionists argued that it had to be done from a national perspective. Aharon Spivak, a Revisionist close to maximalist
circles, suggested that only a national workers' party could relieve
the plight of the proletariat.[24] Human beings, he argued, were not
economic entities. They lived in an environment populated by other
people who shared the same interests and needs. Abstract concepts
that people could not identify with, such as "humanity" or "international proletariat," could not satisfy those needs. Only the nation, the
union of people who share real characteristics, could create solidarity among humans, he maintained.[25]

For the Revisionists the nation was the only social factor that
could provide a complete economic framework that would benefit
all its members. As Abba Achimeir put it, only the nation and its
different organs were responsible for the economic well-being of its
members. And, according to Achimeir, the most efficient way to run
a national economy was to use protective tariffs to encourage local
production while refraining from any intervention in internal economic and social relations.[26]

Achimeir thus invoked the familiar dichotomy between the socioeconomic infrastructure, which should be free from intervention
from above, and the political and legal superstructures, which the
state should control because it is responsible for setting the goals and
guidelines of the national economy.

In a 1933 article Abba Achimeir analyzed the causes of the international financial crisis that followed the 1929 stock market crash.[27] He
argued that neither the Great War nor any other international conflict had caused the crisis, as most economists had claimed. The crisis was the logical outcome of the demise of liberal and free-market
economics. It marked the collapse of the international system, which
suppressed the needs of nations in favor of abstract concepts that
people could not relate to.

People, Achimeir claimed, were national, not economic, beings.

Human society therefore should not be analyzed and constructed according to some abstract economic rationale. An economic model that was developed according to purely economic considerations led inevitably to an international system, whereas a nationalist approach, Achimeir maintained, always led to an active economic reality, where the nation found itself in a constant state of war (to protect its own market and overtake other markets).

In describing the organizational principles of the Revisionist youth movement Beitar, Ze'ev Jabotinsky stated, "The structure of Beitar and its sense of discipline are a successful and healthy combination between freedom on the one hand and a monistic harmony on the other."[28] The Revisionist economic model similarly combined the freedom of capitalist private ownership with the discipline of active state involvement in the operation of the national market.

Critics suggested that this proposed synthesis of capitalism and statism was the result of ideological discrepancies within revisionism. Yoseph Heller, for example, has claimed, "We perceive Jabotinsky as a liberal romanticist but also as populist, whose outlook contained materialistic and anti-materialistic elements at one and the same time . . . [a] confrontation which might have blown up the delicate structure whose credibility and internal logic were getting weaker in the eyes of his supporters."[29]

Heller analyzes Jabotinsky's blend of capitalism and statism as an (awkward) attempt to create a Jewish social and economic system that combined liberalism with ideas advocated by the radical Right.[30] Following Sternhell, however, it perhaps would be more accurate to describe Jabotinsky's and the Revisionists' social and economic worldviews as influenced by the Sorelian synthesis of free-market capitalism with state-controlled social programs and policies. Jabotinsky's synthesis was not a compromise but a direct (and logical) outcome of the radical Right's critique of both liberalism and Marxism.

In contrast to mainstream Zionism, with its socialist orientation, Jabotinsky was a champion of free-market economics and private property, as witnessed by his description of the flow of capital to Palestine in the form of investments. "If it were possible to build the Hebrew majority in Palestine on the basis of 'national funds,' we would all be very happy; but it is impossible, and the success of our enterprise depends, as we all know, on private property. The nature of private property is known to all: It will flow to those areas where it has a chance to yield, and it will not go to a place where it has no hope. This nature, it might be terrible, and I will not argue about it, but it is nature, period."[31]

Under capitalism, the Revisionist leader claimed, the marketplace became a battlefield where people fought to protect their property and to increase it. Capitalism therefore kept people constantly alert and active and did not let them (or the market) stagnate.[32] To Jabotinsky and his fellow Revisionists war was the quintessential human condition, and the national economy should strive to achieve this state.

In 1922 Jabotinsky, perhaps for the only time in his career, wrote about the world of fashion, remarking on the huge boom that the British fashion industry had experienced in the aftermath of World War I: "War and all the phenomena that accompany it testify not only to a clash of interests between groups of people, but they also reflect a strange rise of all appetites and possibilities that are concealed in the living soul of every human being. This animal stood immobile for a long time, and all of a sudden now, all of its organs and faculties started to operate, even those that are not needed for the act of war."[33]

War stimulated people to act and discover their full potential. The ideal society for the Revisionists was a society of warriors that found itself in a constant state of war. In the economic realm this ideal could be realized through the unruly workings of a free market, with its hordes of merchants, bankers, and capitalists fighting for victory over the competition.[34]

In a 1946 article about Jabotinsky's social philosophy, H. S. Halevi wrote that, to Jabotinsky, socialism was dangerous because it removed competition from society and turned it into a sterile environment, one that was immune from social illnesses but that suppressed the human spirit. He quoted Jabotinsky as having said, "If we were able to immunize man from any possible disease in the world, he would become an idiot. The war of life is the essence of life, it gives life its meaning and in it man can fully fulfill his true potential."[35]

While the Revisionists encouraged individuals to compete on the economic front, they maintained that internal competition should continue only so long as it did not jeopardize the people's strength when competing against other nations. At such times the entire nation had to act as one organism and suppress internal tensions and conflicts. As Jabotinsky put it to the Beitarist youth, "We all have one will."[36]

The Revisionists' economic liberalism, then, was applied vigorously but exclusively to the issue of private ownership: The struggle of individuals to amass private capital was beneficial to the state in that it attracted capital from abroad and was psychologically healthy for the citizenry. But on national questions, which had the potential of pitting large groups of people against one another, the state, not individuals, would take the dominant role.[37] According to Jabotinsky, "The variety of relations between capital and labor, on the different branches of capital and the different forms of labor, must submit to the same principle. The issue of salaries and the acceptable profit on capital cannot be left to the 'free play of social forces.' . . . Since this 'free play' is but a synonym for class struggle, this fighting leads to strikes and work stoppages and the inevitable failure of the effort to build our nation."[38]

The primary factor in any economic activity, according to Jabotinsky, was psychology. Only by creating trust among consumers could producers sell their products, thereby setting all other economic activity in motion. The private companies of the world, he wrote in the 1930s, were beginning to invest the bulk of their budgets in advertising, precisely to build up such consumer trust in their products. In order to promote the local economy, Jabotinsky wrote, the state had to follow the lead of the world's major corporations and engage in economic propaganda for the benefit of its national market: "In many countries the governments themselves publicly run propaganda, which is based on ideological factors: Buy national products! What does this mean? In simple terms that means that 'even if you know that foreign goods are better and cheaper and under normal circumstances you would probably purchase it, you must buy our goods.' And this is effective!"[39]

In economics, as in many other parts of Jabotinsky's worldview, the most exciting, most inspiring, most vibrant element was the nation-state. And because he regarded the world economy as a battlefield between national markets, national symbols, and myths, he saw the nation-state as the most efficient means to mobilize the people to make the necessary sacrifices.

Jabotinsky's embrace of classical capitalism, fervent though it may have been, went only so far, and as he was principally a political visionary and not a practical politician, his interest in the workings of fundamental economic forces was finite. Certainly, an example of this was his belief that the quality and costs of goods and services would be less important than patriotism in shaping consumer behavior.[40] According to the Revisionist model, true salvation would not come as the result of too narrow a concern with material progress but would be a spiritual experience on a national scale. Thus, when the nation-state asked individuals to subordinate their material interests to the greater good, they would ultimately be helping themselves: Only as members of the nation, the true expression of the people's will, could individuals' needs fully be served.

The Revisionists expected the Zionist settlers, as both consumers and salaried workers, to put the interest of the state first. In a memorandum to the party's branches in Palestine from 1932, the Revisionist workers' organization stated, "In light of the current situation concerning the Labor party in the Land of Israel, our organization calls on all the Hebrew workers in the Land of Israel to unite and create a national workers union, which will be based on the principle that the nation precedes any class or party considerations."[41]

In the 1930s, at a time when the Histadrut was using strikes as its main tool in fighting for the rights of its members, the Revisionists claimed that creating a harmonious market was more important than achieving temporary economic relief for Hebrew workers. The Revisionists viewed strikes as a divisive tool that turned members of the nation against one another in the name of material values. They regarded strikes as immoral acts that prevented the nation from achieving its true goals. In his 1930 biography of Jabotinsky, Ya'acov Ya'ari described how, as early as 1906, following a strike at the Rishon le-Tzion winery, "Jabotinsky came out vehemently against the 'strike system,' at a time when Jewish history in the Land of Israel was very fragile; and he proved in a logical manner, with examples from pioneering movements from other nations, that when building a new state, a national state, a young state, as you lay its foundations, the building pioneers must place the great national interests above class interests."[42]

The strike might address the needs of certain workers, but the nation as a whole, which included both the employers and the employees, suffers and therefore the very workers who might get temporary relief as a result of the strike would languish in the long run.

The Revisionist solution for addressing labor disputes was the creation of a national labor bureau. In 1929 the Revisionist central committee called for the creation of such a chamber, one that would replace the politics of class struggle with a national arbitration system.[43] Jabotinsky, writing on this issue, argued that "the principle of arbitration must become so 'holy' in our perception that next to it all other 'holy' social and economic matters would disappear— because in it, the holiness of the national Zionist idea is revealed. The notion of social dispute must be regarded as impurity, strike and work stoppage—a national betrayal, an act that excludes an individual or group from the Israeli collective; it turns them into criminals that one must not talk or deal with, and we must say to them one thing: Get away!"[44]

In accordance with the Italian notion of corporatism, Jabotinsky argued that the state, not economic or material factors, should be the ultimate judge of labor disputes—a claim that led his rivals to describe his movement as dictatorial. David Ben Gurion argued that "the institution of mandatory state arbitration, in the sense of coerced arbitration, that by the power of the state determines the labor conditions and labor relations, indeed exists in dictatorial countries (Russia and Italy)." The Labor Party and the Histadrut opposed this institution, because, as Ben Gurion claimed, "in our reality this is a false slogan devoid of any real substance, which is intended only to deprive the workers of the last weapon they possess for defending their interests, the strike."[45] And Mapai's daily, *Davar,* claimed, "The ambition to break the labor organizations is not Jabotinsky's invention. The creator of Revisionism received this

'idea'—along with the brown uniform of the national youth movement and the notion of 'integral nationalism' and the pose of dictator and national liberator—from the patriotic German movement
headed by Hitler."[46]

Undaunted, Jabotinsky argued that the economy, though useful as
a field that prepared individuals for life's real struggles (like the fight
for political independence), should never be allowed to hinder the
national agenda. As long as individuals accepted and understood the
nation's overall goals, the economy should be left alone and allowed
to operate independently. However, whenever the political and economic spheres clashed, as could occur during strikes, work stoppages,
or massive rises in poverty, the political had to take precedence.

One of the foremost obligations of the state, according to Jabotinsky, was to fight and eliminate poverty. He stated that the war on
poverty was to be one of the main battles that the nation as whole
should engage in.[47] Jabotinsky argued that the Left made a fundamental error in judgment: "The socialist dreamers have always made
the same mistake: They sought to alter the entire economic infrastructure, instead of focusing on the most important thing: the elimination of poverty . . . because the only thing society cannot allow itself is hunger; it must provide people with the basic necessities that
ensure their physical survival."[48]

This message was at the heart of Jabotinsky's "biblical socialism,"
and in his articles about it he peppered his economic vision with Jewish motifs. Jabotinsky believed that human nature required an arena
where it could compete and play freely. Humans, Jabotinsky argued,
were naturally inclined to dominate other people, and the economic
arena was one field where this competitive nature properly expressed
itself. Jabotinsky advocated a national marketplace where individuals
could compete with one another, where they could excel, outgain
other people, and accumulate more property. However, society
should not reach a state in which some members reach levels of poverty so desperate that they would do anything to survive, even hurt
other members of society.

It was imperative, Jabotinsky maintained, for the state to create
programs that would prevent any potential for social unrest, but he
opposed the socialist paradigm, which sought to restructure society

and divide all economic and social assets equally—preventing, according to Jabotinsky, any healthy rivalry between individuals and suppressing their natural desire to excel. The "biblical socialist" approach, while accepting the need to eliminate radical social injustices, did not seek to alter the fundamental basis of society. As Jabotinsky described it, "The biblical program has nothing in common with this prophylactic system [socialism] that prevents—a priori—any possibility of social inequality, exploitation, competition, and economic struggle. The Bible seeks to preserve economic freedom, but it sets out to mend it with different regulations and antidotes."[49]

The Bible laid out a set of social rules that provide the people with protection—for example, the Sabbath, when all members of society are entitled to a day of rest; the laws that require landowners to leave a certain percentage of their crops to the poor; and the Jubilee year, when all individual debts are erased and slaves are set free. In contrast to the socialist scenario, in which a single revolution would alter the economic landscape forever and prevent further economic competition, the biblical system, Jabotinsky maintained, did not seek to change the basic social structure. Through cyclical interventions (every seventh or fiftieth year) it ensured that the individuals at the bottom of the economic ladder could remain active in the marketplace and compete in the economic game.

In his analysis of the social message of the Bible, Jabotinsky alluded to the story of Cain, who killed his brother out of envy. Yet, Jabotinsky claimed, God did not punish Cain but protected him from other killers, allowing Cain, the first killer, to go on to excel socially and economically and create the world's first city. The biblical message here was clear, according to Jabotinsky: Jewish tradition supported the notion of economic struggle, even if it involved the loss of life. Individuals were called upon to compete economically, because this was the only way to continue to improve the nation's social conditions.[50]

The crisis of the twentieth century, Jabotinsky maintained, was not that of capitalism (as Marxism claimed) but rather the plight of the proletariat.[51] The solution therefore lay not in a revolution that would bring an end to the capitalist spirit of economic competition but in addressing the social needs of the working masses on a regular basis by way of periodic relief.

Play and Necessity and the Desire to Rule

The ideal "new Hebrew," according to the Revisionist vision, was to be a member of the nation's most vital institution, the Hebrew army. However, for a nation that had not had an independent country for centuries and did not have a military tradition, the task of spawning a new generation of warriors would be a formidable one. The Hebrew national revival movement, then, had to create optimal conditions for the younger generation to overcome these historic barriers in their path.

First, the new generation of Zionists had to be trained and educated as fighters from a young age. They would have to be brought up with the ideals of sacrifice and national pride as their basic credo. They had, from an early age, to learn to play and compete and develop the natural human urge to dominate. n this national vision the economy was to be part of the social training ground. It was a field where individuals could play and compete and develop these spiritual traits.

In contrast to the Marxist doctrine, which, Jabotinsky argued, reduced history to material factors, he analyzed social history through what he referred to as "psychohistorical" categories.[52] In his writings on economics Jabotinsky made a clear distinction between two psychological principles that were at the heart of his social worldview: necessity and play. By *necessity* Jabotinsky meant the basic physical things that each individual needs, such as food and shelter. *Play,* on the other hand, included all the things that human beings desire and possess but are not necessary for their survival. Animals and primitive societies are preoccupied with necessity and with ensuring their physical survival; necessity is the sole factor in their lives. But in more advanced societies, play, the urge to realize the full potential for joy and creativity that each human being possesses, became the dominant human desire, according to Jabotinsky.[53]

Socialism, Jabotinsky maintained, dealt only with necessity, with the biological and beastly side of humanity. It reduced people to biological organisms motivated strictly by their base physical needs. Jabotinsky was well aware that the modern era could lead people to poverty, an existence that revolved entirely around necessity, and this was where his social program entered the picture, ensuring that members of society did not reach the lowest existential level (at least not for an extended period of time) and allowed them to "play." But it also ensured that the economic basis of society did not limit people to a life of necessity. His social program sought to maintain society as an open field of play, where people could give ultimate expression to their true selves.

Jabotinsky's Revisionist notion of play certainly resembled Schiller's formulation of this concept in his aesthetic theory.[54] Schiller regarded play as a state that allowed people the absolute freedom that they needed to discover their true selves through art and beauty, "for, to declare once and for all, Man plays only when he is in the full sense of the word a man, and *he is only wholly Man when he is playing*."[55] Play is a state in which a human's subjectivity overcomes objective limitations and experiences pure beauty. However, to Schiller, an eighteenth-century philosopher in the tradition of the Enlightenment, the search for beauty meant the realization of an absolute truth.[56] To Jabotinsky, on the other hand, play was an offensive and aggressive cause that inspired people to expand the boundaries of their experiences and to extend their domains.[57]

Jabotinsky also referred to play as the "royal factor" and argued, "Each play, be it our scientific understanding of the concept, or the popular conception of it, is an aspiration for rule, for 'royalty.' Analyze any way of satisfying a man's will: It always comes down to 'control.' . . . Pushkin's stingy knight, who does not chase any concrete satisfaction—'I am sufficed with this knowledge'—expresses the consciousness that underlies the power of ruling: 'I reign,' the play factor in its many appearances, is nothing but the desire to rule!"[58]

This desire to rule, to expand one's domain, is the basic tenet of human history (and not the rationalist attempt to uncover objective harmony). The economy therefore has to accommodate this basic human trait. It has to allow individuals to explore fully their desire to reign but at the same time guarantee that all members of society can participate in this historical game and thereby escape a life of necessity.

Shlomo Zemach, the noted Israeli literary critic who gave a philosophic (in the tradition of Western rationalism) voice to mainstream Zionism, wrote in 1939 that the desire to rule is a beastly tendency that suits horses and goats.[59] Zemach claimed that the obsession to rule and master is a senseless waste of human energy. To the Revisionist leader, on the other hand, it was the highest human state.

As a philosophical doctrine, Marxism evolved out of Hegelian dialectics, but it reversed the principal course of Hegelian dialectics. Hegelian philosophy viewed history as a transition from material culture to idealism, a move by which humanity would overcome nature and its physical limitations and discover its idealistic (human) essence. History, in the Hegelian model, has one objective purpose: It is a process by which the human spirit discovers itself and progresses toward an absolute understanding of reality as a spiritual experience. Marxism accepted the notion that human history has an objective end, but it maintained that human history is motivated by material factors. The dialectical progression in history is that of the material and economic basis of humanity, not of abstract thought.

Jabotinsky accepted the Marxist notion that humanity progresses socially and that economic relations evolve in a manner that allows individuals greater freedom. In a letter to Ben Gurion, Jabotinsky wrote: "Since my early days, I remembered the winning charm of the Marxist doctrine, the chain of logic that can only be broken by means of violence."[60] But, he argued, idealistic spiritual factors dominate this historical process.

In fact, Jabotinsky suggested that his approach combined Marxism and Hegelianism, for, he argued, both material and spiritual factors figured into what he termed as play. Domination, he claimed, could be achieved either by material means (accumulating capital) or spiritual, legal, and political means.[61] But, in contrast to both the Hegelian and Marxist models, Jabotinsky proposed that the purpose of history was not to achieve some static objective goal (social equality or rational consciousness) but was, rather, to continue to play.

Jabotinsky's was a Nietzschean world, where no objective, absolute hierarchy of values exists. Human reality is but a struggle for control, for victory, where the weak perish and make way for the heroic and strong. In his novel *Samson* Jabotinsky depicted the quality of life as play: "The world is but a big children's room, full of different plays: kisses, wealth, honor, health, life. We must learn from children; if one play breaks, cry for a moment and replace it with another and relax. . . . When night comes you go to bed. Sleep is death; it is also a play."[62]

History is a game—it is a play between life and death, day and night, change and stagnation; the hero is the one who chooses change, action, and creation over the stability of the material world. The warrior, who constantly fights and expresses his authentic desire to rule, is the true historical hero. The economic order therefore could not be fashioned after some abstract rational or social model. Reality should be in a constant state of flux; it should accommodate the human being's subjective will to reign.

Humans, according to Jabotinsky, seek to play and operate freely. Therefore, an objective reality that is predicated on objective rules contradicts humans' true nature. In Jabotinsky's historical novel, Samson had to go to the land of the Philistines, away from his own culture and its legal restrictions, so that he could play all day and fight.[63] Human beings, the creators, needed constantly to re-create reality in order to fit their needs as rulers.

In Jabotinsky's view all the greatest achievements in world history are the result of play, not "labor." By labor Jabotinsky meant the human activities that satisfy humans' necessities and provide for their basic material needs. Play, however, is a completely spiritual experience. The origins of religion, Jabotinsky claimed, are in play as expressed in dance and song. The greatest technological discoveries are the result of play, the desire of the human mind to transcend its known boundaries. Material wealth and its accumulation are also the result of the human desire to play, Jabotinsky argued, because wealth is a pure spiritual gratification, and its materiality (money, gold) is a mere representation of a spiritual desire.[64]

Here Jabotinsky completely reversed the Marxist scheme, instead enshrining the human spirit as the sole cause of change in human history. Life, according to the Revisionist paradigm, transcends the boundaries of materiality; the world is a battleground of wills. Therefore, the purposes of human history are to change reality, to fight, and to create the proper conditions for spiritual self-expression.

Material reality, for Jabotinsky and the Revisionists, was but a false necessity that needed to be overcome. The study of economics was secondary in Jabotinsky's Revisionist vision. It belonged to the realm of necessities. Moreover, just like the ideologues of the European radical Right, the Revisionists criticized the culture that celebrated money and materialism. Yevin wrote in 1933 that "the worship of money and Marxism are identical. They are similar in their worship of the practical and in their utter rejection of all that is sublime, spiritual, and indivisible by hard cash." [65]

Uri Zvi Greenberg expressed this criticism in his poetry. In "It Is All a Grocery Store," he wrote:

> But it is so: these are grocers.
> And as their father the peddler weighed . . .
>
> The store of poetry
> The store of engineering
> The store of every art and science
> All according to the right account and the laws of interest. . . .
> Therefore my poems are not a poetic commodity
> In the store of new Jerusalem. [66]

According to the Revisionists, instead of creating a new culture of warriors and heroes who would alter the Jewish condition and lead it on a new path, the Zionist establishment adhered to the principles of materialism. In the poem "Jewish Bankers" Greenberg described this ethos of the Jewish Diaspora that Labor Zionists could not overcome:

> And Jewish bankers I saw in foreign countries
> Usurers of great kings
> To build ships, trains and bridges
> And to maintain an army, to feed and arm. [67]

According to Greenberg, this is the ethos of money that dominated life in the Diaspora. Greenberg adopted here the classical anti-Semitic position that regards Diaspora Jewry as a band of usurers devoid of any substantive value to society. According to Ezra Pound, "The Hebraic monetary system is a most tremendous instrument of usury," and "usury is the cancer of the world, which only the surgeon's knife of history can cut out of the life of the nations." [68] Similarly, the

Revisionists called on the emerging Jewish nation to detach itself from materialism and the culture of money, and to adopt nationalism as a means for salvation,[69] because only the development of national power, not wealth, would bring about the true goals of Zionism.

Yevin wrote that in the Diaspora, Jews had always played an important part in the economy and had made critical contributions to the markets in the lands in which they lived but had not themselves benefited from these contributions. Therefore, he argued, if Zionists continued to concentrate on liberating the land by means of building and developing it economically, they would ultimately serve the interests of only the local population (the Arabs). In order truly to build Israel up as an independent nation, the Jews would have to undergo a radical mental and moral transformation that would change the Hebrew nation from an economic entity to a nation that was ready to fight and make sacrifices on life's true battlefields.[70]

The historical mission of the people of Israel, wrote the Revisionist activist M. A. Perlmutter, was to escape slavery and embrace freedom.[71] Socialism as well as liberalism, he argued, turned the world into an international market, and modern technology has turned the worker into an international being, in that his labor produced the same products everywhere. But humans, Perlmutter maintained, by their nature could feel comfortable and enjoy total freedom only within the confines of their own nation and race.

Perlmutter accepted the Aristotelian distinction between a citizen of a nation, who is free to participate in all the great variety that life offers, and a slave, whose life is reduced to producing material goods. The yearning for freedom, which was the basic trait of the Jewish people since their formative experience in Egypt, mandates that Zionism renounce the internationalism that turns people into slaves of the international market and reduces them to material commodities. Instead of conceiving of themselves as mere laborers and producers, the Jews in their own land should perceive themselves as free and proud members of their nation.

Random fluctuations of the market or the economics of material factors should not determine the national agenda, the Revisionists maintained. This agenda should be dominated by the economy of signs, by using as part of national myths those very symbols that would lead people to acts of heroism on the true battlefield of life, where matter (life) is secondary to spirit (the nation, the collective will of the people).

The historian Anita Shapira has argued that from a political point of view the Revisionists took this ideological stance ad absurdum, disregarding reality completely and choosing symbolic achievements over realistic goals.[72] But this choice, impractical and unrealizable as it was, was at the heart of the Revisionist critique. The socialist-dominated Zionist establishment saw the realization of concrete economic and colonization goals as the way to accomplish the overall Zionist mission.

Ben Gurion said, "If there is one thing the summarizes the basic meaning of Zionism—it is Hebrew labor. Creating work opportunities for Jews, for the Israeli masses, for the Hebrew nation in the land—this is what the Zionist doctrine is all about."[73] The Revisionists, on the other hand, believed that the only way to achieve ideological goals—in the economic and social as well as in the political realm—is by way uniting the masses around collective symbols that would drive them to fight under the auspices of the nation.

The Beitarist publication *Avukah* delivered the Revisionist Zionist message to its young readers with simple clarity: "A homeland is not built by money or small deeds but by self-sacrifice of the people for this purpose."[74] The object of Zionism, Jabotinsky and his followers claimed, was to create a new breed of Jews.[75] This meant that Zionism was a revolutionary movement that had to prepare the Hebrew nation for its national independence. As such, it had to change habits and traits that had developed during nearly two thousand years of national homelessness. Ideologues from all spectrums of the Zionist world acknowledged the need for such a far-reaching revolution. However, for the Zionists on the Left, the revolution meant creating material possibilities in the new land to turn the Jewish people into a society of producers.[76] As A. D. Gordon claimed, what the Zionist enterprise lacked was true Hebrew labor, which would link the people to the land.[77]

For the Revisionists, by contrast, the revolution meant transcending labor and necessity and altering the spiritual makeup of the

nation. What made humans different from beasts, what distinguished between civilized and uncivilized human beings, was not
any material factor (which was beastly by nature) but ceremony.

As we have seen, Jabotinsky argued that ceremony dominated
every aspect of human life—legal, political, and cultural. Therefore,
the natural realm for a revolution in human affairs is not a material
but a ceremonial one.[78] The Revisionist revolution was supposed to
be a symbolic revolution, a spiritual endeavor that would alter the
nation's psychological framework. It would be the process by which
the people awakened to the symbols and myths that would unleash
the great powers that they possessed as members of a nation. It
would be, in material terms, a conservative revolution that does not
affect society's economic order. But it would be a profound spiritual
rebellion against the past, against the established order, and against
the ideologies that, the Right felt, suppressed the nation's true nature.

4

The State of Pleasure

Revisionist Aesthetics

> The State unites the two phases, the Subjective and the Objec-
> tive Work of Art. In the State, Spirit is not a mere Object, like
> the deities, nor, on the other hand, is it merely subjectively
> developed to a beautiful physique. It is here a living, universal
> Spirit, but which is at the same time the self-conscious Spirit
> of the individuals composing the community.
> Georg Friedrich Wilhelm Hegel, *The Philosophy of History*

In 1935 Aharon Propes, a leading Revisionist activist, wrote an editorial in the Revisionist newspaper *Ha-Yarden* about the role of public
singing in the development of a national ethos and consciousness.
He argued that singing in public offers not only great aesthetic value
but also serves as a productive tool for expressing the common will.
Hebrew song, he claimed, provided great strength; it invoked in the
Hebrew people a wave of belief and longing. The words of songs
have the ability to enter the human spirit and draw out of it unlimited enthusiasm.[1]

Propes regarded the words of Hebrew songs as forceful means for
evoking the most potent human powers. He did not interpret the
songs' meaning or content but judged them by their ability to reveal
to people the hidden powers that culture suppresses and to channel
people into a collective national effort.

Such questions about representation, or the relationship between
signs and objects, were a critical element of the Revisionist critique
of modernity (and its expression through mainstream Zionism) and

its values. The Revisionists rejected modern Western culture's reliance on a rational approach to reality that separates the linguistic,
artistic, and other representational media from the objective and political world; instead, they followed the European radical Right in ad-
vocating a purely aesthetic approach to life.

In an essay about the work of the great painter Reuven Rubin, titled "In the Grip of Divine Form—Revisionist Impressions in Italy
of the Painter Rubin," the art critic of *Ha-Tzafon,* a Revisionist publication, examined Rubin as a futurist artist.[2] The futurist artistic
ideal, the critic argued, is to escape the constant need to deconstruct
and reconstruct reality. Art should not be consumed with the attempt to produce the ultimate representation of reality, he claimed.
It should elude the limits of reality and reach a state where it can
create an alternative reality that transcends traditional limitations.

Traditional art (and representation), *Ha-Tzafon*'s art critic maintained, accepted the basic opposition between core and decoration,
between center and periphery, between the essential and the conse-
quential. Traditional Western art relied on the external world as its
source of inspiration and as a reference point to validate it. Futurist
art, however, transcended the limits of representation. It turned the
decorative into its central theme, thereby creating an aesthetic experience that did not depend on any subject outside itself.

Art, the *Ha-Tzafon*'s critic wrote, in its purest (futurist) form of
existing for its own sake, is the ultimate expression of humanity.
True art, and Rubin's was such, reveals humans' inability to comprehend the world, exposing the limitations of rationality and leading
us to a different, more exalted plane. Rubin's painting became a form
of Revisionist art, because it broke the duality of representation, and
that, the Revisionist critic argued, is the true aim of art.

M. Shamir, writing in *Ha-Yarden* in 1935 about the role of a national
theater in the development of the national ethos, asked,

> What good is there in pure and beautiful art that is governed by an
> idea that is foreign to us and hated by us? We need a national theater
> that will be a pioneer in the service of the Kingdom of Israel. Such a
> theater will have an enormous influence. It could light a fire in the

people of Israel and turn them into dreamers and warriors in the service of the Kingdom of David. It could uproot the landless exilic ethos and instill a new ethos rooted in the Land of Israel. . . . A culture that plays a critical role in the creation of the Kingdom of Israel is a national culture. It shapes not only the image of the nation but also the national contours; it is the reality in potential, and it will turn it into the actual reality.[3]

The Revisionists sought to aesthetize reality and create a culture that would escape the limits of rationality and confront life through artistic and aesthetic categories. In their writings on aesthetics the Revisionists found an ideal forum for denouncing what they felt to be the repressive qualities of rational morality and for urging people to express their true will, which to the Revisionists was synonymous with the national will.

The Aesthetization of Politics

In "Judiciousness in Dispute, Kant after Marx," the postmodern philosopher Jean-François Lyotard has argued that, according to Kant, in the symbolic realm, in the domain of representation, a constant struggle between imagination and reason exists.[4]

According to Lyotard, in case of a conflict between rational and anthropological regimes, between universal rules and laws that are set by people and are in a state of constant flux, Kant (and modernity) always sided with the transcendental, with the objective, with that which ensures the validity of our conception of the world. However, Lyotard has maintained that if we follow Kant's own reasoning, we must conclude that we have no immediate connection with the thing itself, with the object that supposedly determines the truth value of our statements. All we have access to is our subjective and human experience. And when the "subjective" experience clashes with the "objective," all that we are left with is an exhilarating uneasiness, what Kant referred to as the experience of the sublime. The disputes between reason and imagination, between signified and signifier, between what is supposedly objective and what are considered our subjective impressions of this object, cannot be solved by seeking a transcendental referent that lies outside the conflict and decides it objectively (as Kant would argue).

Epistemological conflicts, Lyotard argues, are decided by cultural or social (anthropological) factors, by debates among people (discourses and narratives) who rely on their varied subjective perceptions.[5] In the postmodern condition no absolute arbitrator exists to determine the truth or moral value of linguistic (or artistic) representations. Choosing to rely on "rationality," "ethics," "science," or any other "objective" system is an arbitrary choice that represents only the primacy of a certain culture that accepts these "objective" ideologies. For the postmodernist, the critic and theorist Terry Eagleton argued, "it would seem that the truth value of a proposition is entirely a matter of its social function, a reflex of the power interests it promotes."[6]

Lyotard denies that any difference exists between signs and object, and he questions the primacy of an objective examination of language. All there are, in Lyotard's postmodern analysis, are signs, a limitless play of signifiers (to paraphrase Derrida), and culture is not bound by any objective criteria but is instead an arena of power struggles among groups and individuals.

At the beginning of the twentieth century the radical Right attacked modern semantics on the very grounds that Lyotard does. The Rightists attempted to break away from what modernity viewed as a necessary difference between the subjective and the objective. Instead, the Rightists wanted to mold reality solely on the subjective experience, which unleashes power—the authentic subjective condition—from the grip of rationality.

Liberating signs and language from the tyranny of rationality entail creating systems of representation (ideology, myth) that are not judged by their ability to provide a true depiction of the world but by their ability to maximize the human spirit and carry it to greater heights. In contrast to objective sciences and theories, which the radical Right considered weak and feminine because such sciences and theories adhere to ethical rules that suppress humans' true nature, the radical Right sought to organize and use signs in a manner that would transcend accepted morality and reveal the true masculine force of humanity.[7]

In the introduction to his *Reflections on Violence*, Georges Sorel wrote, "We enjoy the greatest freedom, when we attempt to create within ourselves a new man, in an attempt to break down the historical borders that limit us."[8] The way to escape the constraints of society and its morals, according to Sorel, is by renouncing the Western ethical teachings that developed out of a narrow social perspective that failed to realize humans' true nature. Only the true human self, the one that is motivated by creative consciousness, can transcend the limits of culture and express the true will of the people.

As part of its overall attack on the values and principles of modern Western culture, the radical Right rejected the modern semantic model.[9] The rightists objected to the modernist view of language and signs as being mere representations of the material world that interact in a logical fashion, as the Rightists sought to escape what they perceived as the "subject-object trap" that restricts human thought and culture to the limits of its ability to analyze the material world.

Maurice Barrés, a founder of the French radical Right, described in his novel *Les Déracinés* the importance of words as a way to return to the true human values that modernity eliminated: "One is right to listen to his voice as a primitive voice. Words, as his prodigious verbal genius knew how to arrange them, made perceptible innumerable secret threads, which linked each of us with nature in its entirety. A word is the murmur of the race fixed throughout the centuries in several syllables."[10]

Barrés challenged the modern semantic model, wanting instead to return to a culture where words were not hollow representations of objects but were powerful entities that could invoke great powers. To Barrés, words are not separate from nature. They do not signify objects but are part of nature, part of the whole.

Barrés wanted people to perceive themselves as part of a race, a culture, and an ancient tradition. People are part of the present life, but at the same time they are an integral part of the past. They are humans who are capable of great deeds, but they are also part of the natural world and its great potential. He wanted individuals to become one with the world, with no boundaries of time or space, the false categories that (Kantian) modernity imposed on people's consciousness.

The radical rightists did not see any value in a rational morality based on the concept of natural rights. Instead, they sought to provide myths, symbols, and signs that would allow society to express its desires and wants without regard to rational or moral limitations. Walter Benjamin argued that the radical Right saw its salvation in giving the masses a chance to express themselves instead of giving them rights.[11]

The radical Right saw history, science, or art that aimed to represent the true order of the world, or to support social structures that adhered to basic moral principles, as an expression of a decadent culture that represses the true destiny of human beings. Such a culture glorifies weakness and promotes differences that turn members of the same nation and race against one another. Instead, the Right emphasized symbols and values that promote harmony within a given society and use the force of a mass of people to overcome objective limitations.

The radical Right sought to use language and signs not as a tool to understand and represent reality but as a way to surpass it, to replace human values with aesthetic considerations that glorify violence and power. The rightists wanted to turn life itself into an artistic experience, one that would not be limited by rational or moral considerations but would allow individuals the greatest freedom possible. Should this come to pass, argued Benjamin, it would mean the end of the Western cultural tradition that began with classical Greece.[12] The radical Right would signal the end of the dualistic principle of separation of subject and object, a separation that, according to Benjamin, ensures that culture, science, and politics follow rational criteria.

The Right, according to Benjamin, wanted to fashion the human experience according to aesthetic values, devoid of rational morality or objectivity, by destroying the accepted boundaries between art and life. The radical Right judged signs, symbols, and language solely by their ability to inspire society to maximize its will to power, without any regard to disciplines, conventions, or judgments grounded in material objectivity. And the ultimate aesthetic experience of the Right was war. War epitomized the idea of art for art's sake. This, according to Benjamin, was the climax of a process of alienation by which humanity had come to see its own self-destruction as a supreme aesthetic pleasure.[13]

Benjamin's response to the radical Right's attack on Western culture was to politicize art, to bolster the relations between signs and the objects they represent.[14] Benjamin wrote, "In eliminating the unutterable of language, in making it pure like a crystal, one obtains a truly neuter and a sober style of writing. . . . This style and writing, is neuter and at the same time highly political."[15] He implored society to harness the aesthetic realm, the most liberated form of representation, where an artist has the absolute freedom to create new worlds that are grounded in morality and justice.

According to Benjamin, "Every artistic thing that is beautiful has semblance because it is alive in one sense or another."[16] Benjamin maintained that in art, as opposed to life, a rupture exists, an expressionless discontinuity that is an integral part of the artistic expression. A picture or a photograph resembles life but is limited by a frame that separates it from life. In a novel characters resemble real people and use language in a manner that resembles real conversations, but their discourse is limited to the pages of the book. As Benjamin phrased it, "The expressionless is the critical violence that, while unable to separate semblance from truth in art, prevents them from mingling. But it possesses this violence as a moral dictum. In the expressionless, the sublime violence of the true appears as it determines the symbolism of the existing universe according to the laws of the moral universe."[17]

Life, Benjamin argued, should not become a work of art where every willful act is permissible. He wanted art to challenge oppressive institutions and lead society on the road to progress. Unlike Lyotard, with his random epistemological view, Benjamin sought to legitimize the authority of rationality and morality. By maintaining the difference between art and politics, he wanted to protect the very foundation that the radical Right attempted to invalidate. He thereby hoped to ensure that art that is free from any moral restrictions does not define the borders of politics and that the political reality, the interaction among people, is predicated on moral principles rather than on aesthetic considerations, as the radical rightists would have it.

In 1946 the Revisionist activist Y. Triush wrote about a conversation he had held with Jabotinsky fifteen years earlier about the merits of art. In that conversation, Triush recalled, Jabotinsky had argued that human spirituality was revealed in two basic forms: logic, which is expressed mainly in the sciences, and creativity, which is expressed primarily in art. With regard to logic, Jabotinsky maintained that "what people call the logic that rules their lives is false logic; it is a walk on a logical rope that leads our thoughts into a maze that has no exit and wherein hypocrisy and deceit reign."[18] However, when discussing the qualities of art, Jabotinsky claimed: "All that is included in the concept of art belongs to the virtuous side of man's soul. . . . If I were pretentious enough to even try and define what art is, I would say that it is the act of giving form to all that surrounds man and clarifies his consciousness; art is a reflection of life, the sum of life's virtues; it exposes life's fundamentals and preserves it for future generations."[19]

In the Zionist Revisionist discourse on aesthetics and the relation between art and politics, we encounter a critical stance similar to that of the European radical Right. The Revisionists rejected the representative (logical) model and sought to free signs and symbols from the grip of the objective world and to use them as political and ideological tools. The Revisionists maintained that, to complete their national revolution, the Jewish people had to appeal to the greatest spiritual forces. And ultimately, only by creating an aesthetic experience that transcends the constraints of rationality and, as Jabotinsky maintained, reveals life's true virtues, could Hebrew culture fulfill its historical mission and (politically) liberate the Jewish people.

Jabotinsky wrote to the great master Boris Shatz: "Every true artist is a cavalier in his heart. Perhaps ultimately you and I are performing the same task, only from two different sides: You invoke in people their sense of beauty while I the sense of bravery, and these are two qualities that only a free man possesses, not a slave."[20] To the Revisionist leader, art and war were the highest manifestations of freedom, and they appealed to the same human instincts—what Benjamin saw as the essence of rightist aesthetics. War and art were the ultimate means to mobilize the Jewish nation and lead it on the path to political freedom.

Revisionism and Aesthetics

At the core of the Revisionist aesthetic stance was a criticism of the state of modern culture in general and of Hebrew culture in particular. In scores of articles on culture, art history, and aesthetics, Revisionist ideologues and activists lamented the decadent and limiting nature of modern art and called for the development of new artistic forms and expressions that would allow people to discover their true selves and serve the needs of the nation. The Revisionists claimed that a national revival movement needed artists and writers who would inspire the masses and motivate them to participate in the great battles that awaited them.

In a 1935 review of developments in modern Hebrew literature in *Ha-Yarden,* the writer M. Shamir called for an aesthetic expression that went beyond mere representation. Shamir argued that modern Hebrew literature followed developments in European culture in general, undergoing a radical transformation from classical patterns, which had dominated the end of the nineteenth century, to European-like modernism. Shamir identified modernism with a process of abstraction that attempts to provide an ultimate understanding of the cosmos. Modernism, he maintained, analyzes reality, breaks it down to its smallest particles, and then rearranges those images in a subjective fashion. But, he argued, the Jewish attempt to imitate European culture was dangerous; it led down the path of decadence and destruction, which has only one way out: "After entering European civilization, after experiencing all its marvelous achievements, our generation must arrive at the following conclusion: Fearful is man, for the entire world has vanished. From man, from the microcosms, all that is left is a pale clown in a public garden, and in this great emptiness rises the voice of the race, of the homeland, and the sensitive poet, whose blood is that of the blazing eastern heat, which freezes in the cold of the north."[21]

Shamir's was a Revisionist call to turn away from Western culture (the cold north). Instead, Shamir called for an authentic art, where words and symbols bring out what he regarded as the true human values—the race and the homeland. Only through these two primordial notions can a nation truly channel humans' spiritual forces and thus achieve the true calling of the aesthetic endeavor—to help people overcome reality, rather than understand and represent it.

Abba Achimeir felt a similar call away from rationalism and systematic thinking and toward art as a means to express truth and authenticity. Achimeir praised the philosophical work of the Jewish thinker Leo Shestov, who, according to Achimeir, had rejected the traditional language of philosophical reasoning and expressed his thought in a manner that subverts traditional philosophical representations.

Western philosophy, Achimeir argued, is enslaved by the system—a certain manner in which thinkers are expected to present and prove their logical conclusions. Western thought turns away from the real world and life's true experiences and toward a secluded territory of syllogisms and abstract formulas. But true thought, Achimeir maintained, finds its expression in a variety of literary media that escape the narrowness of Western metaphysics. Away from Germany (the modern home of Western metaphysics), in the United States (pragmatism) and Russia (literature), thinkers were able to find new means of self-expression that furthered Nietzsche's great revolt against abstract thought. And the only way to understand life's essentials, Achimeir argued, is by capturing the spirit of the great artists and poets who created rather than analyzed.[22]

Yevin, Achimeir's partner in the movement's maximalist camp, attempted to formulate a broad aesthetic theory in a series of articles about art and philosophy. In "An Attempt at an Aesthetic Outlook" Yevin claimed, "This, the aesthetic outlook, draws its essence from life—but it is filled with imagination and dreams. It comes to justify life, it gives into life—yet it rises and transcends it. It lacks the unity and completeness of ethical and utilitarian outlooks. It is as varied as a Persian rug; it collected the many colors of life, their glory and agony, their happiness and sorrow. . . . Yet it is the only free outlook, filled with light and promise. For it is the teaching of life in every sense of the word."[23]

For Yevin the aesthetic realm offers a unique escape in which conventional rules do not apply and where beauty, freed from any ethical consideration, reigns supreme. Yevin described his aesthetic approach as Copernican, in that it rejects any center, any one dominant factor that determines our judgment. In contrast to those fields of human interest with unifying factors that serve as gold standards, like morality in ethics or God in religion, aesthetics has no such ultimate criterion. In accepting an aesthetic outlook on life, humans free themselves from external limitations, or, as Yevin formulated it, "the aesthetic outlook knows no affinity. With great strength it demolishes all the shackles that confine things, and liberates them."[24]

Yevin associated aesthetics with absolute freedom and therefore advocated blurring the lines between art and life; he wanted to turn life itself into a work of art. He compared modernist culture, which he criticized, to the life of a prisoner in a jail cell Prisoners live a very monotonous life, confined to closed spaces and devoid of impressions from the outside world.[25] The prisoners' world is condensed into a very small place that they know so well that they do not need their senses to experience it; their cells are so familiar to them that they can tell the time of day by judging the shadows on the wall or pacing the room from side to side. Yet this expert knowledge, which far exceeds that of free men, does not mean that the prisoners understand life itself.

Modern culture, according to Yevin, finds itself in a situation similar to that of the prisoner. Modern humans too are surrounded by walls, spending their lives inside houses, trains, and restaurants. They filter life through the prisms of science, economics, and other analytical disciplines. Humans have learned to organize their lives in a way that is as harmonious as the sound of a finely tuned violin, but they have forgotten what life itself is all about.

Modern art, Yevin argued, falls into the same analytical trap. Impressionism, which for him was synonymous with modern art, analyzes reality and breaks it into particles, which it then reconstructs and claims is the true representation of reality. But this was not the purpose of art, according to Yevin. Art should not remove us from life's experiences; if anything, it should bring us closer to life.

Though he did not credit Spengler directly, Yevin's aesthetics echoed the older philosopher's criticism of impressionism and modern art. In *The Decline of the West* Spengler had argued: "Does it [impressionism] not signify the tendency—the deeply-necessary tendency—of a waking consciousness to feel pure endless space as the supreme and unqualified actuality, and all sense-images as secondary and conditioned actualities 'within it'? . . . Impressionism is the inverse of the Euclidean world feeling. It tries to get as far as possible from the language of plastic and as near as possible to that of music. The effect that is made upon us by things that receive and reflect light is made not because the things are there but as though they 'in themselves' are not there."[26]

According to Spengler, Western art had moved away from the world, from the natural order of things, and replaced it with transcendental categories that were supposed to reflect humans' unlimited (rational) mastery over the world. But, according to Spengler, this was not the sign of cultural greatness but of decadence. When a civilization loses its immediate experience with nature and the true life-giving forces of the world, it loses its own source of vitality and finds itself on the route to destruction.

For the Zionist revolution to avoid this decadent course, Yevin maintained, Hebrew art should break away from the false walls of modernity and act as a liberating force. Art has to be expressive and should express the true nature of human beings, not become a passive reaction to the world. While modernity and rationality have turned life into a (very efficient) jail, art can lead humanity to freedom by going back to life itself.

Art, according to Yevin, has a profound ethical role. Although art should detach itself from reality and from the sciences and disciplines that are bound by it, artists have to transcend reality and elevate themselves into an ideal world, a world where the true ethics of life rule. Art should address humans' destiny and their relations with the universe's fundamental powers and not be reduced to a mere representation of reality or a beautification of it.[27]

Modern artists, Yevin claimed, have fallen in love with their own creations. They are so mesmerized by the shallow beauty of their images, by their metaphors and brush strokes, that they forget the moral obligation of art, an obligation fulfilled in classics such as Job or *Don Quixote*. Modern artists neglect the true values of life and substitute empty ornaments in their stead. They fail to fulfill the utmost role of the artist, which is to help people discover their true potential and escape modernity's illusions of freedom and equality.

Contemporary Hebrew culture, Yevin wrote in the 1930s, followed the dangerous path of modern Western culture as a whole, neglecting national and ethical obligations and resorting to empty artistic images. After being confined to a ghetto for two thousand years, modern Jewish culture now was struck by the beauty of the "outside world" and had become intoxicated with modern aesthetics. However, unlike their Gentile counterparts, Jewish intellectuals could not afford a retreat into art for art's sake, for they were the beacons of an entire national movement in search of salvation. Hebrew literature and art therefore had to assume an ethical position and overcome their single-minded fascination with beauty.

But if Zionist artists should shun a solipsistic aestheticism, so too should they shun the realism espoused by such then-popular authors as Pasternak and Gorky. In 1933 Yevin wrote that Hebrew literature was in decline because the politics of the Zionist establishment, which placed universal values like Marxism before the particular needs of the nation, was eroding the national idea and the national appetite.[28]

Yevin regarded the novel in particular, and prose in general, as inferior forms of art, because they focus on reality and everyday life instead of the eternal and transcendent.[29] Hebrew culture, he claimed, should not follow in the footsteps of modern prose and describe the banal and trivial, nor should it criticize reality and try to mend it. Instead, it should become a medium for expressing the values that the Jewish nation must embrace in order to thrive—power and rage.[30]

Yevin's critique of banality also was one of the dominant themes of Jabotinsky's aesthetic view. Jabotinsky, though an established writer and translator, wrote relatively little about aesthetic theories and the relationship between arts and politics. However, in a select number of articles he did articulate a Revisionist stance with regard to the role of art.

In an appraisal of the work of Shaul Tchernichovsky, the great Hebrew revivalist poet, Jabotinsky observed: "In my youth, when I discovered the riches of the new Hebrew poetry, I found a major difference between this poetry and the poetry of other nations— with regard to its place in life. In the rest of the nations it no longer held a place in life, whereas in Hebrew culture it has a direct effect on life. This poetry has two major directions, anger and fervor. . . . Fervor is the positive element in nature, a natural and primordial force that can erupt at any time. . . . Tchernichovsky had the profound insight that identified this fervor that could be found even in the basest Jew."[31]

It seems clear that Tchernichovsky's belief in the power of Jewish "fervor" found a responsive chord in Jabotinsky, who repeatedly mentioned that Tchernichovsky was one of his favorite Hebrew poets. To Jabotinsky, Jewish fervor, which he found so masterfully depicted in Tchernichovsky, had to be behind the Jewish political transformation. He wanted all Jewish artists and writers to follow Tchernichovsky's example and express this "natural and primordial force" through their art.

Jabotinsky thus seemed to advocate what Benjamin critically described as art for the purpose of self-expression of the masses. Jabotinsky believed that art could mobilize people by invoking certain images and symbols. He wanted art to lead the Jewish masses beyond the moral and rational restrictions that modern culture had imposed on them.

Jabotinsky found in the development of modern forms of popular dancing a prime example of the process by which culture had attempted to suppress humans' true urges. Historically, Jabotinsky claimed, dancing had been a medium that allowed people to express both their sexual desires and religious zeal and therefore was part of both mating rituals and religious celebrations. Dancing also provided an opportunity to escape the ordinariness of everyday existence and to violate normal societal conventions and discover and express our hidden passions and desires. Primitive and popular forms of dance were spontaneous. They did not have predetermined patterns and moves, and they allowed individuals to express themselves freely.

Modern European culture, according to Jabotinsky, set out to control the act of dancing. In modern European forms of dancing, people are not allowed to jump off the ground or otherwise to depart from the strict patterns of modern dances. Even the waltz, which brings the man and woman close together, keeps them in a position where they cannot move either away from or closer to each other, thus subduing the sexual tension.

Modern European culture, then, had moved away from the initial drive that drew people to dancing in "young" cultures. Young cultures"—a highly expressive term that Jabotinsky used only in his writings about dance, perhaps because the act of dancing suggests youthful vigor—are those cultures whose imagination has not been weakened by the passage of time. People in these cultures still can imagine things beyond the widely accepted and the conventional, and they still possess an uninhibited sense of love and desire.

According to Jabotinsky, the age of a culture is not measured in years but by enthusiasm and vitality. He wanted the Jews to become a "young culture" again, and he sought out cultural models that they could emulate. One such model was dance forms that were popular in the United States at that time, like the polka, which, according to Jabotinsky, challenges modern dance patterns and provides a return to dancing's original qualities of passion and motion.[32] He did not want the Zionist revolution to follow the strict norms of modern European culture but to discover the "young" qualities in each nation and to cultivate them.

Jabotinsky wanted art and the aesthetic experience to take people on a journey beyond the limits of civilization; hence his fascination with American adventure stories about the western frontier, which he viewed as fantasies about people living unimaginable lives. However, this was a controlled and monitored journey, because there was no need to alter social and historical conditions to achieve these goals. To the Revisionist leader a true revolution was a purely symbolic act and did not involve a fundamental restructuring of social and class constructions.

As Mark Neocleous has argued, the revolution of the Right was intended to be primarily a cultural one—a national spiritual revolution rather than a transformation of the material conditions of exploitation or of the structures of social domination.[33] And a revolution that is predominantly cultural depends for its success on its leaders' finding the right signs, which would effectively trigger the collective consciousness of the nation. Following Sorel, this process might be described as the creation of a new human by releasing the subconscious from the limitations imposed on it by history through myth and collective symbols.[34]

In his analysis of American art and culture Jabotinsky described the unique revolutionary power of American cinema: "Revolutionary is not that which speaks directly about a revolt against the authorities but that which incites you to rebel against them. Movies that show us poverty, oppression, and so forth—this is not revolutionary; this is simply (almost always) a boring morality tale, and the viewing masses do not enjoy them. On the other hand, they are great fans of plays about luxury, palaces, private cars, and private gardens. And this is what Americans are so good at making. Throughout history, never have the poor been exposed so clearly to wealth, that which the masses lack and desire. . . . Jealousy is the primary revolutionary factor; it is the only one."[35]

Jabotinsky in effect reversed Benjamin's call for the politicization of art. Benjamin wanted art to expose the inherent contradictions and injustices of modern society. Jabotinsky celebrated these differences, seeing in them a means to mobilize the masses. He did not want art to tell people truths about their economic and social conditions, truths that might lead them to a Marxist revolution. He wanted the lower classes to be mesmerized by displays of wealth so that they would strive to achieve wealth for themselves.

Though images of poverty and its attendant pathos might be useful in fomenting a social revolution that would pit class against class and tear nations asunder, Jabotinsky hoped for what in some ways was the exact opposite—a national revolution in which both rich and poor (who would want to emulate the rich, not destroy them) would unite behind a common goal.

Jabotinsky's analysis of American cinema could not be more different from the Marxist cultural critique, which has been so influential among Western intellectuals of the modern era. True art, according to a neo–Marxist like Benjamin, should uncover the means by which modern popular culture serves the needs of certain economic and social elites by seducing the masses with illusions of prosperity.

Modern consumer culture, the (neo) Marxists contended, suppresses proletarian rage by creating the fallacy of a mobile society. Mainstream culture creates, to borrow Roland Barthes's terminology, myths and images that are freely available (as symbols) to the entire public but only when the symbols appear in advertising, movies, and the media. Real access to these cultural status symbols is in fact limited to the well-connected few. According to de Saussure's theory of representation, signifiers are arbitrary; they have no intrinsic link to the objects that they represent. However, Marxists countered that in modern capitalistic society, certain images and symbols become naturally and inextricably linked to their objects[36]: In the 1930s the media represented cars and luxury homes as tangible expressions of the American dream, objects that all Americans should aspire to possess. These symbols of wealth acquired new meanings as marks of success that transcended their original meanings as mere consumer goods.

Jabotinsky, however, was not interested in the origins of the myths of modern capitalism. In his analysis images and symbols are not linked to certain objects just to encourage consumption of those objects. Cultural symbols in and of themselves are entities with power to mobilize the masses and ignite revolutionary fervor. (Presumably, this would have been a surprise to U.S. capitalists, whose purpose in manufacturing these cultural symbols was hardly revolutionary in nature.) Jabotinsky called on artists to try to achieve what large U.S. companies had achieved—to create a series of images and symbols that would communicate with the masses on a subliminal irrational level and impel them to social action.

The Revisionists thought that the most influential recent trends in art—impressionism, cubism, constructivism, for example—were based on the artists' attempt to break reality into small particles, analyze it, and reconstruct it in an artistic (rational) manner. Revisionists advocated instead a sort of idealized realism, which uses life as its source of images but can provide a real alternative to life.

Modern art, the radical Right (and the Revisionists) maintained, offers a fragmented experience. It provides people with an alienated depiction of reality, an abstracted representation that is foreign to the human spirit.[37] As Russell Berman has argued, the Right valued the pure image, the popular aesthetic representation that unites people with easily recognizable depictions of real objects. (This was in direct contradiction to Benjamin's fascination with montages— both cinematic and those created on surfaces—that broke the expected sequence of images and rearranged them in a way that critiques and analyzes reality and reveals its limitations.[38])

The artistic medium that best embodies the Right's aesthetic ideals is film. As Alice Kaplan has suggested in her study of the French Right: "Crowds watching films learn from the screen to know themselves as a crowd: movie going becomes a group rite, or a place where strangers gather to dream together. The crowd comes to know itself as film. . . . In the film experience the spectators do not merely control a model that remains exterior to their untouched subjectivity; rather, their subjectivity is altered and enlarged by the film."[39]

Film, though a close approximation of reality, is also one of the most passive media, and viewers are no longer required to sort through and analyze the reality around them. According to Benjamin, whereas traditional art requires the spectator to focus on the aesthetic object, the viewers absorb the movie as entertainment, and it becomes one with their life.[40]

Unlike traditional artistic media, which maintain the boundaries between life and art, film blurs these boundaries and turns life into an aesthetic experience. The movie shows the spectator the true purpose of life through the acts of its realistic though idealized heroes and makes individuals feel as if they too are heroes. At a time when traditional artistic media (literature, painting) were deconstructing reality (cubism) or showing its lowly sides (socialist realism), movies of the 1930s provided a unifying, uplifting experience that united the masses around heroic virtues.

Paraphrasing Althusser, Kaplan said that ideology provides people with the illusion of recognizing themselves, each other, and reality itself.[41] As such, film is the ultimate ideological medium because both art and people become one entity; heroes and masses converge on the same representational plane.

In their study of the history of Hebrew movies, Nathan and Ya'acov Gross have argued that in the era before statehood, the socialist-dominated Zionist establishment regarded the art of filmmaking as contrary to the spirit of pioneering.[42] The Revisionists, on the other hand, regarded the cinema as a powerful political and propagandist tool, and they produced propaganda films that featured their leader. In 1934 the daily *Hazit ha-Am* praised Jabotinsky as a leader who not only provided a new ideological direction for his movement but introduced new technologies and representational media (film) to his followers as well.[43]

Jabotinsky, for his part, regarded film as one of the great achievements of the modern age. He claimed, "Every day the cinema brings in rays of light and happiness to the harsh and repressed lives of the masses, it soothes their tensed nerves, gives them hope for the future, and stimulates them to comprehend beauty that until the arrival of cinema they did not know."[44] And in one of his accounts of American culture and its important contributions to modern society, he wrote: "From all the influences that were so powerful on the European youth, this [cinema] is the strongest. The great American actors remind them that on the other side of the border there are offices and factories where there are—or were—life of war and great acts. For this savagery that dominates the lives of the European youth today, especially in the fascist lands, the American cinema occupies a prominent role."[45] The ultimate role of art, according to Jabotinsky, is to lead the nation and especially its youth on a course of heroism and self-sacrifice, and cinema is the medium best suited for this task.

In 1934 a review in the Revisionist daily *Ha-Yarden* called an American movie, whose title in Hebrew translates as *The Victory of Youth,* "a hooligan movie in spirit and form, hooliganism that provides the people with a sense of beauty and honesty. . . . The notion of hooliganism is simple—the youth must lead the nation. The youth must warn the people against corruption, and where the authorities and laws are weak they must seize control of the centers of power."[46] The Revisionists regarded movies as having the ability to give the masses a direct experience of the very characteristics that can lead a nation to independence and revitalization. Film is the ultimate experience of life as art—realistic in appearance but free from the practical limitations of ordinary life.

Jabotinsky's attempt to capture the essence of art received interesting expression in his analysis of artistic, mainly literary, representations of war. Jabotinsky had an ambiguous view of the experience of war. On the one hand, he maintained that for the population at large war is a difficult experience; people's ordinary lives, which are already demanding and challenging in their tenuousness during times of peace, become even more difficult in wartime. Yet he also viewed war as the ultimate arena in which individuals can discover their true power. He wrote, "War is bad, it is terrible, but people in war are more beautiful than in ordinary everyday life."[47]

When examining the literature that dealt with war, Jabotinsky arrived at similar conclusions. He argued (not unlike Yevin did in his criticism of modern novels) that the realistic depiction of war in fiction is usually pacifist in intention and fails to describe the heroic aspects of war. Realistic war fiction focuses on the effects of war on ordinary life and on war's material consequences.[48] However, other representations of the war experience escape the banal and explore the heroic qualities that only war can bring out in people.

Jabotinsky was impressed, for example, by a book on the Boer War that describes an Afrikaner commando unit.[49] The book, he claimed, achieved the unique richness of great American adventure novels. He commented that it was rare that a nonfiction book could accomplish this and that the book had done so by focusing on the feats of young soldiers. Jabotinsky wrote that the author of this "short masterpiece" was able to convey in two paragraphs what most better-known writers could not do in hundreds of pages for one simple reason: The author himself was a soldier and thereby underwent the unique aesthetic experience that in modern society only war can provide.[50]

Jabotinsky rejected the socialist, pacifist artists' focus on the plight of ordinary people and instead yearned for a literature that would describe war's gifts to soldiers—transformative personal experiences and a unique opportunity for expression of the self. Art should celebrate the extraordinary, not the mundane.

The contemplation of aesthetics was to the Revisionist leader and his followers a supremely political act. Jabotinsky's political writings advocated a disdain for the material world of money, possessions, and necessity and urged the Jews toward a transcendent life of heroic virtue. Similarly, he discounted art that focuses on the sufferings of ordinary people and called for art that expresses the possibility of transfiguration through battle. Showing that this was possible in the artistic realm could only strengthen his conviction that it was possible in the world of politics.

Jabotinsky and the Revisionists wanted to release politics and art as well as words and meanings from the grip of objectivity. The Revisionists wanted to model reality as an independent power play between signs and symbols, in which the role of the artist (politician) is to find and manipulate these symbols, regardless of any objective (material) consideration.

The Artist as a Revisionist Leader

The writer whose works most closely embodied the aesthetic ideals of Zionist revisionism was the poet Uri Zvi Greenberg. Greenberg's artistic career spanned many decades and underwent several important stylistic transformations. His poetics changed over the years from an urgent expressionism in the early 1920s to a more lyrical and contemplative mysticism.[51]

Greenberg came out of the radical modernist circles of Jewish poets in Poland that included Peretz Markish. Yet, while Markish was a supporter of the Bolshevik Revolution who moved to the Soviet Union, Greenberg emigrated to Mandatory Palestine in 1924. After a period of writing for socialist publications, he found in the Revisionist movement under Jabotinsky a more welcoming home for his ideological tendencies, and Greenberg soon became its main poetic voice. Though he did not officially join the Revisionist movement until 1928, his works from 1925 on, especially in the literary publication *Sadan,* which he edited, revealed his nationalistic leanings and a strong anti-Western cultural stance.

From his Yiddish poetry of the early 1920s to the Hebrew poetry of the later 1920s and 1930s, Greenberg developed a distinct poetic voice that accompanied the emergence of his aesthetic position as nationalistic poet-prophet. As the literary critic Reuven Shoham wrote in 1997, "The radical negation of western culture necessitated finding a positive alternative. He [Greenberg] found this alternative in an antithetical return to an archetypical worldview that draws on ancient myths. . . . This is a return out of a deep understanding of modernistic poetics that can be termed nationalistic poetics."[52]

In rejecting the West and its values, Greenberg made an artistic and ideological decision to return to historical and mythical formulas that transcend what he perceived as the limited power of the stylistic options open to Western poets. He deserted the modernist mission of reinventing representation in an attempt to describe and understand reality better, and he set out to reveal the ancient mythical structures that, he felt, were part of the Hebrew nation and its people.

In his Revisionist poetry Greenberg created a mythological cosmos, where he, the poet, stands as the prophetic herald of a transcendental vision. In the 1931 poem "Burnt Writing" he wrote:

Light me as a burning bush, my God, and the invisible fire
that consumes to ashes marvelous young branches
    and their blessed fruits . . .

In ardor you will inscribe in them in burning letters words of prophecy
And you will command my flesh: to be a vessel
    to their consuming rage
And to time: to cast blood on my hands and writing pen.[53]

The poet in "Burnt Writing" is at one with the prophetic words and their divine source. Greenberg was neither primarily an observer of the physical world nor a purveyor of aesthetically pleasing metaphors organized in artistic manner. Greenberg saw himself in his role of poet as part of a metaphysical reality, someone who communed with divine entities. He was the burning bush. The words that Green-berg wrote were not his own; in fact, they were not a human creation. They were the words inscribed on him, as his own flesh had become the book; he himself was the vessel of the sacred word.

In another poem, "Burden," Greenberg wrote that, as with many biblical prophets, his words were not soothing but harsh. Greenberg distinguished himself from artists who attempted either to beautify reality or to create imaginary realities. Greenberg's mission, like Jabo-tinsky's, was to be an unwilling seer:

> Artist I tell you: God cursed me.
> He did not place savoriness in my mouth . . .
>
> God placed an ember in my mouth—an ember of truth
> and I will place it on the tablet of your life.[54]

Greenberg rejected the traditional role of the poet as a creator and arranger of signs. Instead, he viewed himself as part of a metaphysi-cal reality where words were at one with all other things.[55] Greenberg made the leap into the realm of the Kantian thing-in-itself, which the subjective self could not experience. Greenberg placed himself in a cosmos where rational subjects could not be separated from the ob-jects of their perceptions by a set of rational categories. In Green-berg's poetic world, art, science, and other means of abstraction that attempt to provide a representation of reality are thus an illusion. Truth can be revealed only through an unmediated encounter with words that come from a divine source and are transmitted through the prophet-poet.

Like his fellow Revisionists, Greenberg accused modern Hebrew writers of neglecting their national role. He argued that there was no "godly tremble" in the modern Hebrew literature, no "transcenden-tal urgency." He claimed that Hebrew writers were trying to adopt a universal language, one that was devoid of a pulse and a heart. A na-tional literature, he argued, had to be egoistic and impulsive. A poet was not a factory worker who assembles all-purpose symbols and images into universal messages.[56] Literature had to become one with the nation and the homeland; the nation, the people, and their poetry are indivisible.

In *A Poet and a Legislator,* a laudatory critique of Greenberg's literary work, Yevin observed that Greenberg's poetic language went from the modern and the abstract to biblical and medieval Jewish elements. Greenberg rejected the universal language of abstraction, which relies on arbitrary symbols and sought to rediscover in his poetry the forceful Hebrew language that had kept the Jewish spirit alive.[57] The dormant power of the nation lay in the race and its collective memory, Yevin maintained, and the way to release this potential was by drawing on Jews' national consciousness, unleashing their violent nature, and using it for the good of the nation.[58]

Despite his reliance on traditional poetic expressions, Greenberg did not want to reverse the course of history and return to the Hebrews' biblical heyday (when the Hebrew kingdom manifested the great Hebrew might). As a poet who early in his career associated with futurist circles, Greenberg, like his fellow Revisionists, embraced technology. In *Against Ninety-Nine,* his aesthetic manifesto, he declared that "the Dynamics of all that is called 'man' and all that is called 'inanimate' is one that rules from inside and from outside over all of the universe."[59]

To Greenberg machines and power sources are as much a part of the world as humans are. And with regard to their poetic uses he claimed: "Steel and steam, electricity and concrete, and the poet can rise to the skies in an airplane, if he longed for the moon rather than earth."[60] Greenberg celebrated physical forces and energy, seeing in them a parallel to the artistic impulse: "Musical instruments are the machines that man uses for his creations—and there is a great violin, set along side the tracks, for thousand of miles: the telegraph wire: man's violin."[61] The new poet, Greenberg wrote, does not need a pen, he needs a hammer.[62]

Words in Greenberg's poetic world were great building blocks; they were the matter from which the universe is constructed. Therefore, the poet, who is uniquely skilled with words, carries the obligation to understand and use their eternal qualities. Literature is not a set of "lead imprints" that a writer left for later generations; it is the art of the eternal that is to be achieved in the present.[63]

Greenberg's worldview recognized no boundaries and differences. Machine and human, words and technology are one. No

temporal limitations exist, and the present is all encompassing.
Greenberg criticized the poets who sat on an imaginary Olympus,
with its external perspective on life. He rejected what he saw as an
artificial division between art and life, poetry and politics. "Here
what is needed is a magical power to assemble under the right vision
those who are cosmically scattered, scattered between body and
soul. This is a process of purification that is needed to give permanent spiritual validity, so there will exist no voids, and this is where
literature is needed."[64]

Greenberg, who rejected the poetry of empty aesthetic formulas
and sought to return to the world, to words that are one with the objective reality, wrote in "The Layout of My Homeland,"

> I am not the master of reduction and the champion
>   of diminishing devices
> Therefore I would not be able to channel into a little nutshell
> the desires of raging blood.
> And I learn the art of rhythm from the sea:
> I chose you the Mediterranean to be my teacher of poetry . . .
>
> Forgive me, for I was born by mistake not on your shores
> and the language of the Hebrews was not my mother's tongue,
>   but that of my blood.[65]

To Greenberg poetic words were one with nature; they were not
representations that reduced reality to a series of systematic symbols.
For Benjamin the perfect language, what he termed the "Language of
the Garden of Eden," was one that lucidly represents reality, an idyllic system that lies completely outside the world.[66] To Greenberg, on
the other hand, the ideal language is *part* of reality.

Not merely a rhetorical device, the word, to Greenberg, is a powerful entity in itself. In a 1932 poem he wrote:

> From Russia and Poland, Yemen and Germany,
>   from the Balkans and Caucasus we are,
> not gold diggers, but men who chisel rocks.
> As alchemists, here, we have transformed a dead pile,
>   and we called Tel Hai the mound of life . . .[67]

Material factors alone would not revive the Jewish homeland. Greenberg called for the use of alchemy—the occult "science" that draws on spirituality to transform and reshape material elements— as the means to transform the Jews from a Diaspora people to a nation of pioneers. To search for answers in the real world is to dig for gold that is not there. Visionaries know that it takes words, poetry, and ideas to change rocks into gold, "dead pile" into a "mound of life." The Jews would need to transcend the limits of objectivity to forge their destiny.

Aesthetic Politics

Jabotinsky once wrote that one achievement of Wagner's music was its ability to bring down the tyranny of harmonies and chords. Wagner, he said, created sounds that challenge the rational rules of music and liberate the human spirit from the grip of false restrictions.[68] The message of Jabotinsky and his followers was that language and art should serve as the forum where power can express itself fully without any artificial limitations, and the role of the leader—ideally, both an artist and politician—is to uncover that power.

The ultimate human experience, the Revisionists claimed, is that of an army unit, whose harmony and coordination are the highest form of art. However, as Adolph Garbovsky wrote in *Ha-Yarden*, "Destiny assigned the Revisionists a bleak position. They want to make history with a nation that has no grasp of history. They want to generate heroic acts with a nation that embraces the ideal of mercy."[69]

The Revisionists, in their place at the political and social margins of the Yishuv, were never in a position to shape the Jewish community in Palestine according to their national (and aesthetic) ideology. Only in Beitar, their youth movement, did they find a forum in which to try out their synthesis of art and politics.

The Italian educational system was one of the models that Beitar tried to emulate. In the Revisionist publication *Mishmar ha-Yarden*, Yitzhak Ben-Menachem described the principles of the physical education of the youth in Italy under the auspices of the Balilla, the national youth federation.[70] The Balilla placed special emphasis on water sports as well as skiing and motorcycle riding, all of which require not just skill but courage—the main trait that the youth responsible for the nation's future should possess, Ben-Menachem wrote. Members of the Balilla demonstrated what they had learned by engaging in marches and athletic competitions during national holidays. This emphasis on the development of the youths' bravery and on public manifestations of athleticism and discipline were at the core of Beitar's educational program.

In 1932 the Beitarist publication *Avukah* described the opening of the first Maccabi Games in Tel Aviv. These "Jewish Olympics," the writer claimed, were a clear sign that after nearly two thousand years, Jewish heroism and strength were again manifesting themselves on the historical scene.

The article alluded to Yoseph Klausner, the historian associated with Revisionism who asserted that the process of national redemption would include a transition from the power of the spirit to the spirit of power, and maintained that the games showed that a new phase was about to begin in the history of the Jewish nation: "The spirit of learning, that very spirit that confined the Jew to his private sphere, to an existence that suppressed his national character, now gives way—as the Maccabi Games show—to the spirit of power in Israel."[71] According to the Revisionist newspaper, the Maccabi Games also proved the importance of physical education in the process of national rejuvenation, because an education that promotes the nation's courage and strength would be instrumental in developing nationalist sentiment and pride.

Along with physical education, the creation of a sense of order and harmony was central to the Beitarist educational vision. Yitzhak Sciachi, a Revisionist activist in Italy, claimed that for Beitarist youth, style was discipline.[72] The members of Beitar, he maintained, had to embrace order and discipline as life's main principles, for they were the keys to true national freedom.

As we have seen, Jabotinsky likened Beitar to a smoothly operating machine. "The greatest achievement of a free mass of people is the ability to operate together as one with the absolute precision of a machine. . . . When we listen to an orchestra and choir, as over one hundred individuals follow the commands of one conductor, we are left with the impression of absolute unity. It is the result of a great effort that each individual has made. . . . We would like to turn the entire nation into such an orchestra; and the first step in achieving this goal is Beitar."[73]

Much like their Italian counterparts in the Balilla, members of Beitar were called upon to exhibit their knowledge in public marches. The Revisionist daily *Hazit ha-Am* described such a march in Tel Aviv in April 1933. Beitar members put on their brown uniforms and marched through the streets of the first Hebrew city.[74] As they marched—in perfect order, according to the Revisionist daily— members of the socialist youth movements, dressed in red, yelled at them, "Vladimir Hitler." In reaction, whenever they heard the name *Jabotinsky,* the Beitarists saluted with a gesture that looked exactly like the "Nazi Heil." When the marchers reached the Maccabi stadium in the center of the city, they carried out a series of drills and performed martial arts exercises that showed off their athletic abilities and sense of order.

Thus the Beitarists, acting in machinelike fashion, transcended their personal subjective limitations and became one as a group. The inclusion of individuals in the collective freed them from ethical or moral considerations. Individuals became part of an aesthetic experience, a perfect machine that operated without external interference. Individuals could express their authentic wish for power and control without fear of retribution, as their actions were affirmed by the mass of people around them. This was the futurist aesthetic vision of machine and war, of destruction and firepower, where art replaced the world as the sole criterion for right and wrong.

The marching of the young Beitarists was not only an exhibition of the young Revisionists' conditioning and dedication. It was also a realization of their leader's aesthetic vision of order and harmony, which he described in *Samson*. In the novel Jabotinsky described Samson's reaction to a religious ceremony that he attended in the Philistine city of Gaza: "One day, he was present at a festival at the Temple of Gaza. Outside in the square a multitude of young men and girls were gathered for the festive dances. . . . All were dressed alike in white garments. . . . The dancers had been arranged in two groups according to height, the young men on the right and the girls on the left. A beardless priest led the dances. . . . Suddenly with a rapid, almost inconspicuous movement, the priest raised his baton, and all the white figures in the square sank down on their left knee and threw their right arm toward the heaven—a single movement, a single, abrupt, murmurous harmony."[75]

In bringing Jabotinsky's novel to life, the young Beitarists erased the differences between fiction and reality, between art and politics. Shlomo Zemach, one of the philosophical voices of Labor Zionism, argued that "art is the apex of human activity. . . . The artistic act creates a complete world that does not come back to the natural world but stands alongside nature and reality. It is a reality of images; it is a restrained reality where man lives with himself and only with himself."[76] According to Zemach, art preserves a sense of discontinuity that separates the artistic experience from real life. The Beitarists, on the other hand, bridged the gap between the two spheres. They lived out their leader's aesthetic vision, fulfilling the Right's ideal of aestheticizing politics.

Ze'ev Jabotinsky. Courtesy Jabotinsky Institute.

Abba Achimeir, Uri Zvi Greenberg, and Yehoshua Heschel Yevin. Courtesy Jabotinsky Institute.

Jabotinsky in uniform. Courtesy Jabotinsky Institute.

Jabotinsky and a group of Beitarists. Courtesy Jabotinsky Institute.

Jabotinsky in Johannesburg with young supporters. Courtesy Jabotinsky Institute.

5

Land, Space, and Gender

Visions of the Future Hebrew State

Because the land was then the chief hero. We sang dozens of
songs about earth. But that was joined by the blood. Because
there is not one inch of our soil that was not expiated in
blood. Earth my earth merciful until my death. . . . I will
betroth you with blood.

Haim Gouri, The Odysseus Complex

Power is everywhere; it is omnipresent, assigned to Being. It
is everywhere in space.

Henri Lefebvre, The Survival of Capitalism

In *Oded the Wanderer* (1930), one of the first Hebrew films produced
in Palestine, a teacher, points at the barren landscape around him and
tells a group of students: "The Valley of Jezreel was desolate like these
mountains before your fathers' hands touched it. And what they have
begun, you must continue."[1] For the Zionist movement, creating a
modern Jewish society in an independent state involved organizing
and reshaping the Israeli landscape. The new Jews, the basis for the
future Jewish state, were called upon to alter both the physical and
cultural geography of their reclaimed land; to change the land of Israel from a barren, backward space into a productive modern environment; and to create a society of workers, where both men and
women would live off the products of their own land and labor.

According to James Diamond, Judaism, as a monotheistic religion,
was based on a fundamental suspicion of space and the spatial, which
Jews perceive as the domain of idols, monotheism's archenemy.

Jewish nationalism, on the other hand, was an attempt to re-encounter the spatial, to move away from history and memory, and to embrace the natural and the material.[2]

For David Ben Gurion and Labor Zionism this entailed the transformation of the old Jews into the New Hebrews who, by the fruits of their colonizing labor, transform the land's economy and culture and create a new spirit of work and creativity.[3] To the Zionist Revisionists, on the other hand, such an endeavor did not entail a process of liberation from the bonds of the Diaspora but rather the creation of new barriers. For them the return to the spatial had to include a return to humans' true nature, to their authentic urges, which could exist only in an open, uncivilized sphere.

The Revisionists believed that the great efforts at colonizing and working the land were misguided and that the only way to gain true independence was by developing Jewish national power. As Yevin argued, the strength of Zionism did not lie in its ability to build and settle but in its ability to develop Jewish strength, which should be the only moral objective of the movement.[4]

These differences between the two main Zionist factions were apparent in the different ways that the two camps understood the Tel Hai incident of 1920, when eight Zionist pioneers were killed defending a small Jewish settlement in the north of Israel. As Yael Zerubavel showed in her important study of Tel Hai as an Israeli myth of creation, Labor emphasized the pioneering aspects of settling and working the land, whereas the Revisionists emphasized the militaristic and heroic elements of the story.[5] An editorial in the Revisionist daily *Hazit ha-Am* summarized these differences. It proclaimed that in the spirit of Nietzschean heroism, the true life is but a prelude to a heroic death and that Yoseph Trumpeldor—the leader of the Tel Hai pioneers—exemplified this spirit in his valiant death. Therefore, although the socialists can claim the memory his life and his colonial experience, his heroic death was purely Revisionist.[6]

While much has been written on the importance of *kibbush ha-adama* (conquering of the land) and *kibbush ha-avoda* (conquering of labor) in Labor's Zionist ideology, the Revisionists' vision of the future Israeli landscape has been presented only in negative terms, as a rejection of Labor's colonial program. However, the Revisionists did develop a unique view of the spatial characteristics (both physical and spiritual) of the Land of Israel, which evolved from their overall ideological platform; it emphasized the importance of the development of a strong national ethos of power and heroism as the only way for the Jewish people to establish an independent modern state.

Furthermore, the role of women in the Hebrew state, as the Revisionists perceived it, was informed by their vision of the Israeli landscape, or, to paraphrase Doreen Massey, the production of "the geographical" influenced gender and gender relations in Zionist Revisionist thought.[7] The Revisionists saw the Hebrew state as an authentic masculine space that accommodated the needs and desires of the new Hebrew man, whereas women were restricted to the home, the feminine space.

Zionist Space/Revisionist Space

Shlomo Zemach wrote in 1950 about the importance of working the land as part of the Zionist ethos. He argued that in the centuries preceding the Zionist migration to Israel, fellahim (Arab farmers) worked the majority of the land. And while the fellahim inherited a rich agricultural tradition from biblical and Roman times, their cultural stagnation made them give in to the powers of nature.[8] Thus, according to Zemach, when the Zionist settlers came to the Land of Israel, they entered an uncivilized space that was shaped for centuries by the brute forces of nature, and they had a singular opportunity to mold the landscape and create a healthy and productive society through colonization. They had a chance to escape what the socialist Zionist ideologue Nachman Sirkin described as a vicious historical cycle: Jews were forced to aimlessly migrate from one territory to another for nearly two thousand years.[9] Thus in the twentieth century they had a unique opportunity to reestablish what A. D. Gordon, the moral voice of socialist Zionism, called the necessary link between humans and nature by way of working the land.[10]

The Zionist perception of Jewish history offered distinct periods of Jewish activism (before the destruction of the Second Temple and after the emergence of Zionism) and what the psychologist and critic

Benjamin Beit Hallahmi has described as "the long period of submission and passivity, which should be erased from the collective
memory, a black hole."[11] The Zionist consciousness perceived the Diaspora as a great natural force and that over coming it required a tremendous collective effort and energy. The wild Israeli terrain symbolized a similar natural force, but it also represented an opportunity
to tame nature, to absolve the Jewish people of the shadow of its passive past. As Ben Gurion claimed, the return to the land, the source
of vitality, creativity, and health, was the only way to rid the Jewish
people of the curse of the Diaspora.[12]

As Michel Foucault showed in his analysis of the relations
between space, knowledge, and power, modern society needed engineers and technicians to design space so that it could meet the needs
of modern economies and technologies.[13] The modern landscape
became an engineering project that reflected society's dominance,
over both individuals within the polity, and over nature, the opposite
of modern rationality. By colonizing Palestine and civilizing the native landscape, Zionism established its dominance over the land. The
control of the elements reflected the movement's ability to control
the forces of history and to create a revolutionary new society that
would become a "normal nation" with a clear geographical and historical mission.[14]

For the Revisionists, on the other hand, this very process meant
that the Land of Israel, like the Diaspora, would become a trap, a restrictive and alienating space that would prevent the Jewish nation
from achieving true freedom. As Hen Merhavia explained to the
members of Beitar, Zionism's greatest tragedy stemmed from its reduction to a materialistic movement by its leaders. Instead of becoming a revolutionary movement that restores the Hebrew national
spirit, Zionism was reduced to a utilitarian movement whose merits
are judged by its ability to develop the land agriculturally. Thus, according to Merhavia, Zionism had become nothing but a continua-
tion of the cultural heritage of Diaspora, which limited the Jewish
existence to a constant search for materialistic benefits.[15]

In his historical novel, *Samson,* Jabotinsky described a meeting
in the desert between the great warrior judge and a wise elder of
the Sons of Cain. The old man tells Samson that his people are the

descendants of Cain, the father of all tillers of the soil who killed his brother and whose sins still haunt his offspring. The elder explains to Samson, "Cain was evil because he asked to divide the land into estates and raped it so it will produce not that which God ordered, but that which was planted by man in his evil intent."[16] When Samson fails to see the relation between working the land and evil, the old man says, "It is a sin to rape the land. She is our mother. A son should never master his mother. It is not good. . . . She is the almighty queen, and there are no rulers but her—not presidents and not judges—all is sin."[17]

The ideological message of Samson's encounter with the Sons of Cain was unequivocal: Humans should not immerse themselves in futile attempts to overcome nature. Humans' true powers lay elsewhere, in developing their own physical and spiritual powers. Cain's sin was trying to outdo nature and produce more than the land could bear. This was the source of his hubris, and when God did not acknowledge Cain's efforts, he was overcome by his rage and killed his brother.

In the desert, following his encounter with the Sons of Cain, Jabotinsky's Samson freed himself from the constant struggle to tame nature and discovered his great strength as a warrior. In fact, Jabotinsky wrote, Samson's spiritual powers became so great that by merely standing by the side of the road, he made traveling merchants stop and give him their goods.[18]

Revisionist ideology called upon Jabotinsky's disciples to follow the same path, to become what Yoseph Klausner, the Revisionist historian and author, described as the ideal warrior, "the warrior of nature as part of nature, and the warrior of life as part of life itself."[19] Such a warrior could only exist outside the tight grip of a materialistic civilization, out in the open Israeli space.

For the Revisionists the process of colonization was a process of building artificial obstacles that limit humans' natural urges. Abba Achimeir called upon the Jews to go outside the walls of the old cities of Israel and to escape the limitations of an ideology—socialist Zionism—that forced them to become settlers confined to their homes and fields. These walls and artificial barriers, he argued, provided a false sense of security. Jewish power could not rely on matter; it had to depend on the spiritual strength of the people, which can flourish only outside the walls and comforts of a settlement.[20] The

Zionist movement, he claimed, must prepare its members for what another Revisionist activist, Z. E. Cohen, described as a vicious world of struggle and power in which only the strong who are willing to fight will survive.[21]

In developing their vision of the Jewish settlement in Palestine, the Revisionists felt that the Zionist movement could benefit from examining the experiences of other nations that migrated to uncivilized territories and developed a healthy national ethos. Jabotinsky, who, as we have seen, wrote extensively about American culture, admired American frontier narratives. He was fascinated by the experiences of people who went beyond the populated areas east of the Mississippi into the open spaces of the American West, which, as he put it, "had no plows or courthouses."[22]

Jabotinsky argued that the emerging Hebrew nation needed a young generation that, like the heroes of the American frontier, were ready for great adventure and turmoil. It needed, he wrote, "young people who can ride horses, climb trees, swim in the water and use a fist and a gun, people of great imagination and a strong will that aspire to participate in the war of life."[23] He wanted the New Hebrews to follow the conquerors of the American West, who, as Georges Sorel described them, were the twentieth century's only true warriors, a real master type, in the full Nietzschean sense.[24]

According to Jabotinsky, another people whose entire national identity was formed by such a pioneering spirit were the Boers of South Africa. Like the Zionists, they escaped an oppressive power and sought liberation in the vast empty spaces that lay beyond the control of the European powers in Africa.

The Boer nation, Jabotinsky argued, was born as a result of the trek across the wild South African terrain.[25] Racially, Afrikaners remained purely European, but what made white South Africans so different from citizens of other European nations was the environment in which they developed. Instead of the cold wet climate, overpopulation, and suffocating social order of their old homeland, the Boers found that Africa offered a perfect climate and, even more important, an uncivilized open space.

Jabotinsky claimed that the Boers became expert equestrians and expert marksmen.[26] They were able to live the true life of warriors, possible only in a land without any form of social, political, or moral order. In their historical isolation the Boers maintained some of their original European characteristics, but over the centuries they developed what Jabotinsky regarded as Mediterranean traits.[27] They became talented merchants and businesspeople; they excelled in academia, especially in law, and, unlike the people of northern Europe, the Boers were temperamental, witty, and tended to live a carefree life.[28] Presumably, in comparing the Boers to the people of the Mediterranean, Jabotinsky was making the claim that Zionism, in order to allow for the healthy psychological development of the Hebrew nation as a vibrant Mediterranean culture, had to maintain the natural untamed qualities of the Jewish homeland.

Ben Gurion, also aware of the experience of other nations, warned the people of the young Jewish Yishuv that if they did not learn from history, the entire Zionist colonial enterprise would be in danger. He looked at the historical fate of the great city-state of Carthage and argued that although Hannibal was a brilliant military leader, Carthage's lack of an agricultural infrastructure ultimately led to its defeat by the Roman village-state. Mediocre generals led the Romans, but they were tied to their land and were one with the soil.[29] To the socialist Zionist leader the lesson of this historical tale was clear: If the massive urbanization that the Yishuv was experiencing continued, the entire Zionist dream would be in jeopardy. He feared that Tel Aviv would become a modern Carthage, a thriving Hebrew commercial center that would not withstand the constant struggles with its enemies.[30]

In contrast, the Revisionist colonizing program championed the Carthaginian city-state model. It was composed of a strong, primarily urban, center where the entire population would be concentrated, while the rest of the land would remain an open space where a Hebrew army actively protected the true interests of the Yishuv.

These two opposing approaches to the colonization of Palestine were clearly articulated in the 1920 debate in the Yishuv's Va'ad

Zemani (temporary committee) regarding the settlement in Tel Hai. The proponents of the settlement, predominantly Laborites, argued that the Zionist movement had a duty to colonize every part of the Land of Israel. The opponents, including Jabotinsky, claimed that leaving settlers unprotected in a hostile environment between French-controlled Lebanon and British Palestine, and where Arab bands roamed free of the control of either colonial power, was simply irresponsible. In his speech before the committee Jabotinsky claimed, "I think that all those who are in the French zone [Tel Hai] must return to Israel. . . . People said: we will just go there and work without the need for military protection. . . . I am here to debunk the second illusion, that we can just work and not fight." Later in his speech he begged the settlers: "Return from there and build here what is already built!"[31]

Throughout the 1920s and 1930s Jabotinsky and the Revisionists did acknowledge that some agricultural settlements would be needed for the future state. However, they maintained that these should be limited to the few places in Palestine that have sufficient irrigation to support agriculture in the harsh Mediterranean climate. The Revisionists claimed that the agricultural settlements in Palestine should be geographically small and based on intensive agricultural methods that would make the settlements economically profitable.[32]

In 1929 Jabotinsky wrote, "Here in the Land of Israel, they [the British] see strong young men who work the land, dry marshlands, who are proud of their heroics as the builders of the land. . . . Yet they cannot protect their community and need the English to have mercy on them. . . . Therefore, the British scorn us."[33] In order to overcome the scorn of others and create a true independent state, Jabotinsky maintained, the Zionist movement should concentrate its efforts on the development of Jewish militarism, not on the settlement of the land.

Rediscovering the Spiritual Space

While pioneering involved discovering new open spaces, it was not only a physical endeavor for the Revisionists. It was also a process of spiritual liberation, by way of a cultural—primarily artistic—journey to new cultural spaces that lay outside what they perceived as the restrictive realm of modern civilization.

For Abba Achimeir the other side of modern civilization was found in the works of Dostoyevsky who, Achimeir claimed, used his training as an engineer to dismantle the strict scientific principles of modern Western civilization and reveal their inability to provide true spiritual comfort.[34] Dostoyevsky, Achimeir argued, unveiled modernity's attempts to mask these failures with hollow rational constructions that only accentuate humans' sense of cultural and social alienation.

For Yevin, Achimeir's fellow maximalist, the ability to escape the limitations of modern civilization lay in the realization that life should be viewed as an aesthetic experience. Yevin maintained that a culture can be considered authentic only when it realizes that life is not a neatly arranged and rational sequence of events. True art, he argued, transcends the conventional boundaries of reality and thus comes closer to the truth. The aesthetic experience liberates humans, transforming their world from an oppressive space into a autonomous sphere, free from false constraints.[35]

In Jabotinsky's view Edgar Allen Poe epitomized the search for the authentic and liberated spiritual space: "Who was the first who tried to capture the devil who seduces us away from rationality? Who was the first to lift the veil from the 'healthy' soul and gazed into that dark den of witches, hidden in every human's mind? . . . Edgar Poe. . . . In 1849 he died under a fence on the route between Baltimore and Richmond, a wandering drunk, a poet and a storyteller. He died under the fence, but he managed to drill in that fence a window into the darkness of the consciousness beyond."[36]

Jabotinsky, who translated Poe into Hebrew, sought to lead the new Jews into those very spaces where people could express their true spiritual powers. He sought to go outside civilized boundaries, to that decadent sphere that lies beyond good and evil, beyond the accepted norms that restricted our true desires.[37]

Uri Zvi Greenberg too looked westward to find cultural alternatives. The Revisionist writer detected in the poetic voices of black America an authentic cultural alternative to the hollowness of Western civilization. In a letter to Avraham Elmaliah, the editor of the cultural journal *Mizrah-Ma'arav* (East-West), Greenberg criticized what he considered the tendency of Jews to neglect their own racial and national heritage and blindly to follow certain aspects of European culture.[38]

Greenberg denounced the eagerness of Jews to accept such notions as pacifism, which he argued had nothing to do the with the teachings of the Hebrew prophets but with the decadent influence of German liberalism on Jewish intellectuals. He also condemned the tendency of those who were the victims of European violence to admire the culture of their oppressors without realizing that they were victims of that culture.

Instead, Greenberg pointed to the black poets in the United States who knew very well that the only true poetic expression was a song of rage that grew from one's own racial consciousness and not from an abstract and empty universal artistic formula. This sort of poetry, Greenberg argued, defied the classical European poetic rules. It did not describe the heavens and the stars, the setting of the sun, or sound of the waves, the empty metaphors that dominated European poetry and its Hebrew imitations; instead, the black poets dealt with humans' most basic needs and desires, as an organic part of their soul.

According to Greenberg, to find their true self humans have to go beyond the false cultural conventions that engulfed him and seek new artistic forms of expression that could only flourish away from the core of Western civilization. Greenberg wrote: "I despise (as a Hebrew poet who does not conform to the ideals of Western pacifism) Christianity and its classical version in Hebrew."[39] The truth lay in authenticity, and the search for truth involved seeking out that which could uncover one's spiritual essence.

By creating an outpost of European civilization in the ancient homeland, Greenberg warned, the Jews would not come closer to their true nature; they would only create an alienating cultural space that would represent the values and the history of the Jews' greatest oppressors. In order to truly return to its homeland, to what Greenberg regarded as the nation's true racial consciousness, the Hebrew nation had to rediscover its authentic voice. It had to follow the example of the black American poets who, in defiance of the dominant (white) Western culture, were able to find their authentic voice.

Jabotinsky found in another product of black American culture, jazz—which he considered the true expression of the American pioneering spirit—another example of a cultural journey beyond the fence of civilization:

> There was a time, a hundred years ago, that music theorists argued that there are "musical" sounds and "non-musical" sounds. . . . In short, a fence and inside the fence a limited number of sound combinations. The first to create a hole in that fence was Wagner, who entered dissonance into music, but only in a limited way. . . . And then came the American who listened to the sounds of the Black neighborhoods and simply brought down all the fences. He not only canceled the difference between a chord and a dissonance but also questioned the mere concept of musical sound. He proved that music includes the sound of noise, scratching, banging, commotion, squeaking, shouting, whispering, and more. The leash was loosened. And this is what we call Jazz. A new leap of pioneering.[40]

Jazz developed and created new spiritual spaces in the areas that modern culture had yet to penetrate and dominate, in the black neighborhoods of big American cities. The Land of Israel, which had stood for centuries on the other side of civilization's fence, offered similar opportunities. Israel should therefore be preserved as a culturally autonomous sphere—much like the African American communities and American frontier—where an authentic culture could be formed and developed.

Jabotinsky's view of music as a means to transcend the limitations of thought and civilization is rooted in the Nietzschean tradition. In *The Case of Wagner* Nietzsche claimed that music liberates the mind and gives the thought wings. He viewed it as a bolt of lightning that flashes through the gray sky of rational thought and its abstraction of the world.[41] To Nietzsche reason and truth were nothing but illusions that culture imposed on that primal force, the will to power, that was at the heart of humans' authentic actions. In its purest form, away from rationality and thought, music could unmask this illusion and bring us closer to that force, to the true philosophy of mankind. Wagner's irregular melodies questioned the foundations of a civilization that subjugated music to reason and helped to create a culture where music in its freest form reigned. Jabotinsky sought a similar quality in art and music. He wanted it to allow the Jewish people to transcend the false boundaries of civilization and explore new and authentic places, where the will reigned supreme.

The Revisionists were not the only Zionists to follow in Nietzsche's cultural and intellectual footsteps. Other Zionist thinkers and writers—most notably, Berdichevsky in the mid-1890s—found in Nietzsche's critique of the Judeo-Christian tradition a way to escape the heritage of the Diaspora and rejuvenate the Hebrew nation.[42] Berdichevsky saw in Nietzsche's teachings a call to abandon culture and return to nature and the land, the two most vital sources of the nation.[43] He wanted the Jews to return to their "natural" state, the epoch of courage and strength before the Jewish people were encumbered by the ethical and religious teachings of the Torah.

For the Revisionists, however, the (Nietzschean) criticism of modern culture did not entail a return to a savage state. It involved the destruction of the fundamental difference between culture and life, in which culture—and its two main characteristics, rationality and morality—was seen as superior to the authentic life according to the will to power. They wanted culture to become one with nature, to accommodate humans' true desires and needs and not to restrict and repress them. But as the champions of modern technology, the Revisionists did not want simply to return to nature, to a primitive human state.

Space and Technology

For A. D. Gordon, who perhaps more than any other individual represented the pioneering ideals of the early settlers in Palestine, the return to the homeland meant a return to the soil, to the basic elements that allow for the development of a healthy, vibrant society. It involved a move away from the insalubrious Diaspora and a return to nature and health. He argued that the nation is predicated upon some cosmic element that "may best be described as the blending of the natural landscape of the Homeland with the spirit of the people inhabiting it."[44]

In defining the goals of Zionism Gordon stated, "In the countries of the *Galut* we are compelled to lead an inanimate existence, lacking in national creativity. . . . We come to our Homeland in order to be planted in our natural soil from which we have been uprooted, to strike our roots deep into life-giving substances, and to stretch out our branches in the sustaining and creating air and sunlight of the Homeland."[45]

Gordon expressed the romantic side of the Jewish national revival, a sentiment that a return to the homeland meant a return to nature, to the goodness and simplicity of a lost past in which the Jewish nation had thrived. However, to the Revisionists—despite their vision of the Israeli landscape as an uncultivated space—the return to the old homeland did not entail a romantic return to a primitive state.

The Revisionists firmly believed that industrialism was the way of the future. They distinguished between a false, utopian approach to the study of society, which followed Rousseau's idealization of simple farm life, and a realistic social analysis that acknowledged that industry and technology were the way of the future.[46] They felt that the ideas expressed by the advanced and radical elements of contemporary European culture, of which they were great admirers, did not mean a return to barbarism. In fact, they believed with all their might that they represented a profound process by which false cosmopolitan ideals, which were contrary to humans' true nature, were being replaced by true national values.[47]

The Revisionists were admirers of modern technology and Italian futurism. Jabotinsky even suggested that F. T. Marinetti would have been a great jazz enthusiast, an admirer of the music of street noises, and, like the Italian prophet of technology, he wanted to fashion Beitar after a machine.[48] However, the Revisionist ideologues did not envision a modern technological space that organized every aspect of human life. To them the machine was not a goal in itself but a means to an end, a tool that freed people from physical labor and allowed them to concentrate on developing their true characteristics. As Jabotinsky put it, "True social salvation will not come out of class war: it will be the result of the mind, of ingenuity, of technological inventions . . . that would allow us someday to transform 'labor' into pleasure and wage-slavery into 'paid leisurely activities.'"[49]

Ezra Pound, writing in 1928 about the evolution of the modern urban space, envisioned future cities as a place where "the right-angle street plan has lost its use. The new city is built on stream line and follows the natural flow of the traffic."[50] Pound did not want technology to create modern gothic constructions that reflected humans' ability to overcome nature. Instead he wanted the future metropolises to become part of nature, an integral part of the natural order of things. Expressing this very sentiment, the Revisionists warned that if technology became the dominant force in society, people would turn into robots or golems.[51] And Achimeir claimed that if technology were to dominate, people would lose their true nature and would turn into slaves of the technological world.[52]

Technology, the Revisionists maintained, was part of the natural world. It was not an external force that humans developed in order to master nature and reshape the land; it was a natural power that had to be treated as any other natural element. In an observation that can be understood as a precursor of the Heideggerian distinction between premodern and modern technologies—a distinction between manufactured instruments that only channel natural forces to use them better and modern technologies that absorb natural forces, store them, and then use them in a way that challenges nature—they wanted technology to become part of the natural world, not to alter it.[53] As Uri Zvi Greenberg put it, steel, steam, electricity, and concrete have become part of the human body, some of the necessary components that provide for one's existence.[54]

Jabotinsky felt that the machine should be restricted to what he referred to as the sphere of necessity, which was secondary to what he called the realm of play. To Jabotinsky, as we have seen, necessity belonged to the world of matter, while play was part of the spiritual world. In "necessity" he included all the defensive acts that an organism performs in order to ensure its existence. Play, on the other hand, included acts of aggression that are the result of the urge to maximize one's potential or to expand one's habitat.[55]

For the Revisionists, then, machines and technology were not meant to dominate every aspect of our life but should exist independently in a culture that was not necessarily governed by rational or scientific principles. According to Jabotinsky, the Boers, the free, wandering warriors of the South African wilderness—who nonetheless enjoyed the material fruits of modern civilization—exemplified this duality. They were fortunate to have the native African population as

cheap labor that relieved the Boers from manual work.[56] The freedom from physical labor, he claimed, liberated the Boers from the
boundaries of the life of necessity and created among them a vibrant
royal instinct. But the native population was not part of the Boer
landscape. In the areas controlled by the Boers, the natives were restricted to the farm and the mine, to the secondary realm of necessity, to the fringes of the open South African landscape.

To Jabotinsky—who believed that by the year 2030 physical labor
would no longer be needed because machines (and robots) would
perform any type of work—technology in the Zionist state could
serve a function analogous to the Boers' African laborers: freeing the
New Hebrews from mundane physical activities to explore their true
nature.[57] In the ideal Revisionist space, then, technology would be
restricted to the workplace, to the factory, to the areas that provided
for society's necessities, while the majority of the land would remain
an open uncivilized space that nourishes the playful instincts of its
male inhabitants.

Space, Place, and Gender

In the futurist manifesto Marinetti wrote: "We want to glorify war . . .
militarism, patriotism, the destructive gesture of freedom fighters,
beautiful ideas one dies for and scorn for women. We want to destroy
museums, libraries, academies of every kind, and fight against mo-
ralism, feminism and any opportunistic or utilitarian cowardice."[58]

Marinetti made a division between the masculine realm of militarism and heroism and the feminine world that was rooted in tradition and sought practical solutions rather than decisive violent
acts. The masculine space was the battlefield, where the virile games
of life could be played. The feminine space, on the other hand, was
the home, the place that provided society's necessities.

These differences and spatial designations were shared by most
contemporary European radical right-wing movements and were
expressed—without the harsh misogynist rhetoric—by the Zionist
Revisionists as they meditated on the future of the Hebrew nation.[59]

For the Revisionists, as the elder of the Sons of Cain told Samson
in Jabotinsky's historical novel, humans were part of nature, not its
master. Humans, they claimed, should not try to reshape the natural

world in an attempt to create a new order that rested on some abstract rational speculation because any such attempt would inevitably lead to turmoil and destruction. The difference between the sexes, the natural hierarchy of men and women, was part of this sacred (natural) realm, which should not be subject to any rational or moral reconfiguration.

For Labor Zionism the Jewish national revival entailed the creation of a new society that would challenge traditional (Diaspora) social divisions, including gender. Since the second Aliya (the second major wave of Jewish immigration to Palestine—1904–14) and the rise to dominance of the Labor movement, Zionism fostered the image of *halutzim* (male pioneers) and *halutzot* (female pioneers) who together conquered the Palestinian wilderness. In the boldest social experiment of socialist Zionism, the kibbutz, women were portrayed as the equals of their male comrades, and literary and cinematic representations of that period depicted women soldiers fighting alongside men in the military organizations that fought for the nation's independence. Historically, this equality between the sexes was an ideological construct rather than an accurate depiction of the times. As the historian Eyal Kafkafi has shown, while the Yishuv presented an official image of an egalitarian society, since its early history it denied women real access to the economic and political centers of power.[60] Lesley Hazleton has similarly argued that the claim of gender equality in the prestatehood Jewish community in Palestine was nothing but a well-perpetrated myth. According to Hazleton, most of the *halutzot* did not work in the fields but in the kitchen or the laundry room, and on the battlefield predominantly men were sent out to combat while women served mainly as nurses.[61]

But regardless of its historical basis, the ideal of greater gender equality was a staple of Zionist ideology and drew substantial criticism from the Revisionists, who objected to the notion that Zionism could be based on a progressive social program that questioned traditional gender roles. The Revisionists called for a return to what they perceived as the "natural" social order, where men dominated the public sphere and the private sphere, the home, was solely the domain of women.

Like other right-wing ideological movements of the period, re-visionism claimed that the breakdown of the "natural" order was rooted in contemporary social and moral theories that stripped humanity of its true qualities and turned it into an abstract rational entity.[62]

Achimeir claimed that the moral foundations of socialism—the social platform of mainstream Zionism—rested on Kant's moral categories, which prevented both men and women from acting according to their true nature. These philosophical imperatives, he argued, treated humans as mere variables in a logical equation. They did not treat them as men and women, as individuals with unique characteristics and desires that were part of their individual nature and not some universal formula.[63] This rational and impersonal nature of socialism, he said, resulted in a large number of suicides among female members of socialist groups in the Yishuv. Socialism deprived women of their eternal feminine characteristics and turned them into members of a faceless social class, causing alienation and ultimately a propensity toward suicide.

Achimeir warned that Zionism should keep away from the Bolshevik model. In Soviet society, he argued, women had taken over every aspect of life and men became irrelevant.[64] Instead, he called on Zionism to create a society of (male) heroes who would rise above the crowd and lead the nation on the path of power and conviction.[65]

Y. H. Yevin's attack on David Vogel's 1929 novel, *Married Life,* further developed the antifeminism of the Revisionists.[66] The novel, Yevin claimed, was a prime example of the genre of romantic realism that had dominated the Modern Hebrew novel. It was a celebration of feebleness, of feminine values. The male protagonist in the book was weak both physically and mentally and was inferior to his wife: He was the opposite of the ideal Revisionist male. And good conquered evil in the story only when the woman sacrificed herself, when masculinity prevailed.

In his aesthetic criticism Yevin objected to the modern fascination with the banality of everyday life. He viewed the tendency of modern art to depict the life of simple people as a sign of the cultural decline of the twentieth century. Modern man had become a prisoner, surrounded by walls, spending his life inside houses, trains, and restaurants.[67] Yevin longed for a culture that celebrated heroes and admired great men who overcame the triviality of ordinary life. Art, he felt, should lead man out to the open, outside the close spaces of modernity that restricted man's true self.

To Yevin, the growing role of women in contemporary culture was another sign of the move away from masculine virtues, from the sphere of great acts, to the home, the feminine-dominated space that was governed by rational laws. Modern culture, he argued, broke reality into the smallest particles, into featureless entities that were then reconstructed in a manner that was purely rational, devoid of any true values.[68] In this way modern culture served the weak. It erased the fundamental differences among people that are at the heart of human experience and created a false consciousness of universal equality. By limiting man to the house, the office, and the train, modern society suppressed man's natural urges and turned the world into a feminine sphere.

The ideological role of revisionism, then, was to help the Hebrew man discover his true potential and escape the false illusions of freedom and equality that modern culture offered. Zionist society had to break the walls of modernity, which provided a false sense of security, and create a masculine society of heroes that could flourish only away from the home and the workplace, in the open wild spaces where true gender differences existed. Zionism had to perform the Nietzschean task of breaking away from the feminine realm of truth to a masculine world of heroic virtues.

If to the Revisionists the vast open spaces of the Hebrew land were to become a masculine sphere of play, the home and the family were to be the domain of the Hebrew women. However, they considered the domestic role of women in the Hebrew state to be revolutionary, because women would thereby serve the needs of the nation. Writing in *Madrich Beitar* (The Beitar Guide), the Revisionist activist Avraham Meikovich distinguished between the Diaspora family unit and its Zionist counterpart.[69] In the Diaspora the entire Jewish experience revolved around education. Men were responsible for educating the young male scholars, and women were responsible for educating the girls in the home. In Palestine, however, men were no longer restricted to Yeshiva learning; their world shifted out into the open. Thus women, who were now the sole masters of the domestic realm, were entrusted with the education of both boys and girls. The responsibility of women was to educate the entire future generation of the nation and ensure that both genders were prepared for their future roles.

Meikovich differentiated between what he considered the feminine ethos of the ghetto, in which both men and women were confined to a house that served as an educational institution (the home and the Yeshiva) and the Zionist ethos, which was virile in nature. Zionism's revolutionary quality, he believed, is revealed in its reinstatement of the natural differences between the genders, placing men in their natural habitat and turning the home into a feminine sphere.

In the "Principles of Beitar," the ideological platform of the Revisionist youth movement, Jabotinsky observed that "the woman is a unique creature with special functions, which are of great importance: she must be proud of her 'uniqueness' and receive the appropriate education she requires."[70] The greatest quality that women possessed, Jabotinsky argued, was their organizational skills. Since its earliest stages, human society featured a clear division between the males who went out to hunt and the females who transformed what the men brought from the outside into meals, clothes, and a comfortable home.

In fact, Jabotinsky warned that women should not be exposed to the dangers that lay outside the house. A woman should always be protected because, he argued, "her health and life, which are the basis for the nation's future, are much more important than the life and health of men."[71]

The field was the space where men could live the true life of a warrior and make the ultimate sacrifice in the name of the nation. Women, on the other hand, were restricted from entering that sphere, as they did not possess the natural qualities that would allow them to play on the field of battle. For a woman the ultimate mission was staying alive and maintaining the health of the next generation. The woman therefore had to sacrifice her individual wants and desires and could never achieve the greatness of the fighting man.

Although Jabotinsky celebrated women's unique organizational skill and their ability to operate within established social frameworks, he feared their sexuality. He believed that, kept unchecked, their wildness would lead society down a path of destruction. The Revisionist leader, who sought to fashion society in a manner most suitable for man to express his violent, irrational characteristics, believed that a woman's wildness, her sexuality, would threaten the very foundations of the social order. Jabotinsky, who wanted men to escape the constraints of modern culture and explore their authentic subconscious side, feared that if women were allowed this freedom, they would use their sexuality to dominate and feminize society.

In "Tristan da Runha," a treatise about the development of a utopian society on a deserted island in the South Atlantic—the members of that fictional society were criminals banished to this island—Jabotinsky discussed the role of gender relations in the development of a healthy society and the need to control women's raw sexuality. This is how Jabotinsky, who wrote this treatise from the point of view of a newspaper correspondent, characterized the effects of the arrival of the first group of women to the island: "Any description of the developments that followed on the island during the next years would be out of place in a daily paper. Enough to say that it was permanent chaos . . . brawls, fights, and even murders dangerously increased during that period."[72]

At that time on the island, Jabotinsky wrote, men's mortality rates were very high, whereas women, who did not work and did not have children, prospered as men battled over them. Order finally came to the fictional island when laws were passed that regulated relations between the sexes. As Jabotinsky put it, "A woman gradually became a sort of partner, interested in her husband's work and welfare. She began to mend his clothes, which would have been impossible in the preceding period. . . . The first births on the island occurred in the seventeenth year. . . . It is not necessary to say what a moral revolution it produced in the mentality of the women themselves."[73] Only when women found their true social roles as mothers and wives was order achieved and society able to flourish.

The most complete description of the ideal Revisionist woman appears in Jabotinsky's novel *The Five*—necessarily a fictionalized account, because, unlike Labor, the Revisionist movement did not conduct such social experiments as the kibbutz, where their social vision was put into practice.

In the novel, which depicted the disintegration of an assimilated Jewish family in turn-of-the-century Odessa, the central character was the family's oldest daughter, Marusya, who, with her great beauty and extraordinary charm, possessed the feminine ideals of the time. However, it was not her life (her many affairs and her marriage) that elevated her to the level of a feminine role model but her death in a domestic fire, which allowed her to manifest what Jabotinsky considered to be the highest feminine attributes. In her last moments, as she realized she could not save herself and was engulfed by flames, Marusya performed the most heroic act that a woman and a mother can perform, saving the life of her son, Mishka.

The story of Marusya's family, the Milgroms, is told by a narrator who was a friend of the family, who upon hearing about the deadly fire came to her house to learn what actually happened. From the accounts of a neighbor who witnessed the fire, and of a pharmacist's assistant who rushed to the family's aid, the narrator gleaned that the most curious fact about the fire was that the door of the kitchen where she died was locked from the inside and that someone later found the key in the street below the kitchen's open window. According to the neighbor, the fire broke out while Marusya was boiling milk for her young son; a draft came through the window, and Marusya's dress caught on fire. At that moment Mishka was in the hall just outside the kitchen. The pharmacist's assistant, who rushed up the stairs to the kitchen, completes the account from his perspective inside the house:

> She jumped at the door or crawls to it, and turns the key. In her place, I would have first rushed outside: but she locked herself in with a key, because out in the hall is Mishka. But wait, that's not all. Why was the key found in the street? It is clear. Not only you and I, but any person would have run out in a situation like this. And Mrs.

Kozodoy [Marusya], after all, is also human, she also wants to run, and moment by moment her desire to escape grows stronger. . . . And she realizes that she cannot hold herself, that she has to rush outside! And there is Mishka. . . . And here she says to herself: No! I must not! And to eliminate any temptation she threw the key to the street.[74]

In her last moments Marusya placed the well-being of her son before her own, thus embodying the ideals of womanly heroism: protecting her family. She was a true feminine hero, because she fought her battle for life and death inside the home while providing for her young son.

Before the accounts of the horrible fire and Marusya's heroics, the narrator of *The Five* provides a detailed description of the house, depicting the various rooms, staircases, and balconies. Jabotinsky thereby created a map of the heroine's habitat—her battlefield—which was contained within the walls of her home. Men fought in open spaces, while a woman's fight, in the Revisionist paradigm, was fought in the home for the health and well-being of her offspring.

In *The Five* the narrator's visit to Marusya's house is followed by his receipt, in a dream, of a letter from the dead heroine. In the letter Marusya describes her last moments and how she had to battle her natural instincts. She rejects the notion that she is a heroic woman and claims that she was only acting according to her true nature as a woman. She then tells the narrator what the true strength of a woman is: "If the day comes, my dear, and your entire world falls apart, and you are betrayed and left by all, and you have nothing to lean on—then find a woman and lean on her."[75] To the Revisionists this was a woman's ultimate role—to provide support for her man, to nourish and nurture him, making sure that the home was a healthy environment for their children to grow in, freeing the man to participate in the battles he would face in the open spaces.

The idea of turning the Israeli landscape into a healthy environment was at the heart of the Zionist ethos. Zionists described their efforts as a process by which they turned malaria-infested marshlands into productive settlements, and dry, lifeless deserts into blooming fields. The Revisionists regarded these Zionist ideals as feminine activities that should not define a national revival movement. Health and hygiene were the responsibility of women, whereas men could thrive only in wild and dangerous conditions.

Revisionist Zionists called upon the female members of Beitar to undergo "domestic training." They were supposed to take control of the domestic unit and maintain the nation's health.[76] What mainstream Zionism considered the foremost mission of the Zionist enterprise, the creation of a healthy and productive society of workers, the Revisionists regarded as strictly feminine.[77]

Zionism represented a revolt against the feminine image of the "ghetto Jew."[78] It was an attempt to create a new, virile Hebrew man who thrives outside the walls of the Yeshiva and the synagogue.[79] Zionism strove to overcome the historical perception of the Diaspora male Jew, whom the dominant European culture viewed as feminine in his weakness and passivity. As the literary critic Michael Gluzman styled it, Herzl's Zionist vision was informed by his desire to refute the anti-Semitic stereotype of the Jew as effeminate, an image that Jews have internalized. Herzl believed that the transition to Palestine would lead to a physical and spiritual transformation of the Hebrew man, who would rediscover his (normal) masculinity. [80]

The Revisionists, however, claimed that, under the domination of the socialists, Zionism itself embodied a feminine ethos—a weak way of life that could flourish only in feminine spaces. To them the settlement in the Yishuv formed a reincarnation of the shtetl in the homeland—a space that was feminine, not masculine, that restricted rather than liberated. Echoing Max Nordau's call to create a new strong Jew and to make masculinity the symbol of the new Zionist society, the Revisionists felt that the only way to fully liberate the Jewish nation after two millennia in bondage was by developing a virile national spirit in a masculine space of action and struggle.

The Wandering Jew and the Return to the Homeland

The writings of (post)modern European thinkers on the relationship between Jewish identity and spatiality offer a perspective on the debates about these issues among early Zionists.

In "Edmond Jabès and the Question of the Book," Jacques Derrida has said that "the situation of the Jew becomes exemplary of the situation of the poet, the man of speech and of writing."[81] Judaism, Derrida claims, is a movement away from the homeland and the Book, to the eternal wandering, to the endless game of exegesis.

Much like the Zionist ideologues of both the Right and the Left, Derrida reduces Judaism (in its exilic state) to the role of the poet and the rabbi, who are both the masters of writing and of the exchange of meaning. He equates Judaism with what Nordau called "coffeehouse Jews," who, from the perspective of the dominant western culture, lived an abnormal life detached from manual labor.[82] The Jews, Derrida claims, operate in the margins, in an endless search for signification that always falls into the middle area between the core and the periphery, in the commentary that accompanies the ancient (original) text.

Working from a postmodern perspective, Lyotard—in *Heidegger and "the jews,"*—distinguished between the Jews (with an upper case *J*), the historical Jewish people whom Europe tried to convert, expel, and exterminate, and the "jews" (in quotation marks and a lower case *j*), as the object that Western discourse could not command, a constant reminder of its limitations. According to Lyotard, "the jews," who are never at home wherever they are, evade the West's wish to master and control.[83] The dominant Western discourse that attempts to represent all facets of reality cannot master "the jews." Therefore throughout history Europe has tried to eliminate the Jews—the object that would not succumb to the Western paradigm. The West tried to destroy this group, which steadfastly maintained its Otherness and wandered on the periphery of European civilization.

Derrida and Lyotard have celebrated the marginality of Judaism within the framework of the dominant European culture, what Max Silverman has called the image of the Jew as a nomad: "The Jew, then, simply becomes the figure (or trope) employed to define a new universalism, the reified marker of all resistance to rootedness, fixity and closure—the nomad *par excellence*." [84]

This very image of social, political, and cultural marginality was at the heart of the Zionist revolt against the Diaspora. Both the postmodern and Zionist view of the Jewish experience in the Diaspora reduces it to one essential characteristic, that of the wandering Jew who is restricted to the margins of European civilization. (Though it serves different purposes—for the postmodern thinkers as a sign of Western metaphysics' shortcomings and for the Zionists as a proof of their historical necessity—both ignore the complexity and richness of Jewish history.[85]) The early Zionists sought to lead the Jews away from what they perceived as the fringes of European civilization, back to the mainstream of world history. As the post-Zionist critics Ariella Azoulay and Adi Ophir have put it: "We [modern Israel] are the last landing place for the wandering Jew, the one that Europe could not bear."[86]

Under Labor's leadership Zionism sought to return the Jews to the (original) land in order to create a productive society and to create the new Jew as a pioneer.[87] The Israeli space presented a unique opportunity to liberate the Jews by transforming them into a productive nation that does not rely on others for its subsistence. Yet to the Revisionists, Labor's colonizing scheme was the very opposite of a liberating process. To them the socialist Zionist space was an oppressive sphere that deprived humans of the ability to express their true identity and instead turned them into slaves. In a world that, as the Revisionist activist E. Z. Cohen claimed, "God created as a place where the strong eat and the weak are eaten," only people who were free from any false restrictions could live truly liberated lives.[88]

Michel Foucault described the modern landscape as a series of connected sites through which everything was monitored and controlled. He maintained that no colonizing or architectural project could be perceived as liberating: "I do not think that there is anything that is functionally—by its very nature—absolutely liberating. Liberty is practice. So there may, in fact, always be a certain number of projects whose aim is to modify some constraints, to loosen, or even to break them, but none of these projects can, simply by its nature, assure that people will have liberty automatically, that it will be established by the project itself. The liberty of men is never assured by the institutions and laws that are intended to guarantee them. . . . I think that it can never be inherent in the structure of things to guarantee the exercise of freedom."[89]

The Revisionists perceived Labor's spatial vision similarly, not as an enlightened project that would liberate the Jews from the bonds of the Diaspora but as a series of interconnected settlements that would suffocate the native landscape and control every aspect of one's life.

The Revisionists rejected the view that progress liberates or, as Yevin put it, "that there is 'progress' in the world, that the world is improving and advancing, even if slowly, toward the implementation of general justice."[90] They felt that Western culture and its many political and social faces (liberalism, socialism, rationalism) turned men into slaves. The Revisionists wanted to remain on the other side of the fence, outside the core of Western civilization. But unlike contemporary postmodern critics, the Revisionists' idea of Otherness did not entail hiding away in a textual universe of endless interpretations; it meant entering the (masculine) arena of struggle and war.

Writing in the Revisionist publication *Mishmar ha-Yarden,* the Beitarist activist Hen Merhavia claimed that in Jewish history the glorious periods were those of wars and conquests. The Haskalah (Enlightenment) represented everything that stood in opposition to the ethos of those magnificent epochs, and the Zionist movement, he warned, followed the dangerous footsteps of the Haskalah. The true Zionist spirit, he stated, had to embrace war and conquests and stay away from the cultural legacy of the Enlightenment, which suffocated the Jews in a modern spiritual ghetto.[91]

The Revisionists' was a creative world, where individuals created an environment that served their authentic needs, where jazz musicians challenged traditional standards and formed new worlds. Theirs was a society of warriors who controlled and shaped their lives instead of reacting to life's challenges passively. On the eve of the first Maccabi athletic games in Tel Aviv, the Revisionist publication *Avukah* declared that the games marked the rebirth of Hebrew power in Israel. After the spirit of learning (Haskalah) had taken over Israel and shut it in for centuries, the rule of power reappeared and set it free.[92]

In the Revisionist spatial scheme the only place where the new Hebrews could thrive and escape the limitations of false spirituality was out in the open spaces that offered absolute freedom. Ultimately, for the Revisionists, only a landscape that did not tie individuals and did not restrict every aspect of their lives could create a true Zionist alternative to the Diaspora and not form a new Diaspora, a new alienating space, in the homeland. The poet Ya'acov Cohen captured this very sentiment in his poem *Biryonim* (Zealots):

In blood and fire Judah fell
In blood and fire Judah will rise!

The earth's heart will beat with the stampede of knights on horses,
The entire space will be filled by the thundering sounds of cannons....
Battalions of horsemen, like forests of spears, will sweep the land—blazes,
All the voices of the land will unite in a call for a war of the strong.[93]

Labor Zionism too maintained that blood would have to be spilled to realize the goals of the movement. As Haim Gouri, one of the greatest poetic voices of Labor Zionism, has claimed, the land was not just the source of life and health but also called for sacrifices; the redemption of the land would require people to die for it.[94] But fighting was not perceived as a goal in itself; rather, it was a necessary evil on the road to independence. Labor Zionism emphasized that the Jews had to earn the land; they had to claim it by working, developing, and fighting for it. But the fighting was seen as a means to an end, an initial stage in an overall program that saw the redemption of the land as the only way to liberate the people.

Just before the creation of the State of Israel, Ben Gurion tried to explain the origins of the Zionist pioneering spirit: "In the soul of man, in the soul of every man there are unlimited sources of wants and desires, talents and willingness that can be revealed, operated and strengthened. The secret of pioneering is the secret of releasing man's most inner forces and guiding them to a higher cause."[95]

Ben Gurion claimed that the forces that are involved in the spirit of pioneering were both positive (building and working the land) and negative (fighting and death) and that both served the same ultimate goal, the creation of an independent society of workers. To the Revisionists, on the other hand, the land had no intrinsic value; it did not serve as the final cause and did not possess the mystical forces that could emancipate the nation. The fighting itself, the expression of physical power, for which the land served only as a stage, was the true objective of revisionism, for fighting was the ultimate expression of a true national consciousness.

6

Neither East nor West

Revisionism and the Mediterranean World

> The Orient is not only adjacent to Europe; it is also the place of
> Europe's greatest and richest and oldest colonies, the source
> of its civilizations and languages, its cultural contestant, and
> one of its deepest and most recurring image of the Other. In
> addition, the Orient has helped to define Europe (or the West)
> as its contrasting image, idea, personality, experience.
>
> Edward Said, *Orientalism*

In 1997 Ofir Ha-Ivry, the editor-in-chief of *Azure,* an Israeli right-
wing publication, wrote an article titled "The New Prince" about the
maverick Italian businessman and politician Silvio Berlusconi.[1] Italy,
according to Ha-Ivry, has held a unique position in the history of
Western political history. "Its vigorous social and cultural conservatism," he wrote, "has enabled this once-beleaguered nation to become an industrial power without paying the price in bloodshed or
suffering that often leads to leftist regimes." And under Berlusconi,
Ha-Ivry argued, Italian conservatism crystallized ideologically as a
healthy synthesis of the economic freedom of classical liberalism
and the social and cultural conservatism of Catholicism, a synthesis
that promises economic prosperity and political and social stability
that other nations (including Israel) should adopt as a political
model.

In finding in Italy a viable model for the Israeli Right, an alternative to what he saw as the pro-Arab and Western tendencies that have
plagued the Israeli intellectual and political establishment, Ha-Ivry

was echoing the viewpoint of his ideological forefathers in the Revisionist movement. The Revisionists in the 1930s were fascinated with Italy and, not foreseeing the terrible fate of many Italian Jews a decade later, viewed the Italian leadership of their time both as a potential ally and prototype.

One basic characteristic of Zionism was the desire to bring the Jewish people back into the general course of world history. This goal could be accomplished by looking both forward to the West and back to the East in the form of ancient Israeli history. Zionism wanted to bring the Jewish people back to a position where Jews live a normal life as citizens of a productive and independent nation on its own land. To mainstream Zionists this meant bringing together two seemingly opposing principles. Socialism, the most progressive and contemporary of movements, would provide the organizing principle for the new Jewish society, whose spiritual underpinnings would reach back across the millennia to the Jewish glory days, the pre-exilic Jewish kingdom when the Jews ruled their own land.

The Revisionists also wanted to follow this general path. As Jabotinsky claimed, "The Diaspora means that others create and control our history; Zionism means that the Israeli nation begins, as an independent nation, to make its own history."[2] But in contrast to the dominant Zionist view, the Revisionists wanted to explore an alternative historical narrative in which history's dominant powers suppressed virile and vital life forces. The Revisionists wanted to explore the Dionysian forces in human history that, in the end, the Apollonian narrative of progress and rationality always overshadows.

While drawing freely on ancient imagery and forebears, the Revisionists did not romanticize the ancient East as a paradise lost, nor did they long for a return to a simpler, more spiritual time. In fact, they argued that part of the mission of the Jewish national revival and the return to the ancient Hebrew homeland was to bring the West and its technological heritage to the East. They did not view the Jewish people of the twentieth century as part of the Orient but as part of the scientifically advanced European world. As the protagonist of Jabotinsky's short story *Edmee*, put it, "The East? It is entirely foreign to me. . . . I was born a Westerner in spite of the tell-tale shape of my nose."[3]

At the same time, however, the Revisionists regarded modern Europe as a decadent culture, a civilization that had lost its vitality and turned away from its core values. They did not want the emerging Hebrew nation to become a purely rational, mechanistic culture but a more authentic culture that embraces vitality, violence, and the natural will to power.

Italy, caught between the primitive East and the decadent West, offered the Revisionists a viable political and historical model of a glorious Mediterranean civilization that, like the ancient Israeli kingdom, had been crushed by foreign powers but was ready to reclaim its hegemony through the affirmation of manhood and national pride. To the Revisionists, Italy was an emerging regional power with which the Zionist movement should form an alliance in order to advance the movement's political goals. To the Revisionists modern Italy represented the ideal synthesis—a nation that drew on its past as a source of national inspiration and symbolism but created a society that was both fully modernized and predicated on the healthiest and strongest ideals.

Neither East nor West

In a 1927 article titled "The Arabesque Fashion," Jabotinsky, citing Max Nordau, claimed that "we are going to the Land of Israel in order to advance Europe's moral boundaries to the Euphrates."[4] In this article Jabotinsky challenged what he called the "Orientalist" tendencies that had gained popularity among Zionists who saw the East and its inhabitants as morally superior to the West, because the East had not been contaminated by Western civilization and had maintained its original virtuous characteristics. According to Jabotinsky, this tendency to romanticize the Orient rested on the false assumption that the East and the West were fundamentally different. The only difference between the two, he claimed, was that while Europe was technologically advanced, the East by and large was not.

In an article about Jewish culture in the Middle Ages, Jabotinsky criticized the use of the expression "the Arab revival," which historians used in discussing the cultural background of the golden age of Spanish Jewry. He argued that this revival indeed took place in lands controlled by Arabs but that this in itself was not enough to describe as Arabic the great cultural production in those lands in medieval times. Jabotinsky claimed that the great Moorish architecture of Spain was in fact designed by Greeks and that Arab science was mostly the creation of non-Arabs.[5]

The East, Jabotinsky claimed, was a primitive expression of Western culture—the historical equivalent of Europe of the Middle Ages.[6] The calmness, restraint, and peacefulness of the East were a reflection of the Orient's primitive nature, not the outcome of a profound approach to life. Jabotinsky maintained that no moral difference existed between the predominantly Christian West and the Muslim world. He wrote, "Islam, *like any other religion,* possesses the greatest moral attributes and serves as a very positive educational factor."[7] Both cultures stem from the same moral foundations and rest on similar philosophical and epistemological pillars, but they are situated in different evolutionary phases in the technological development of those principles.

In a series of articles in *Ha-Yarden* titled "The Arabesque Style," the Revisionist writer A. Assar redefined Jabotinsky's analysis of the differences between East and West in metaphysical terms.[8] According to Assar, the difference between Eastern and Western cultures lies in the relationship between matter and form. In Western culture the individual, the subject, stands outside the objective world of matter. The subject acts purposefully to give matter its form, its meaning. Eastern culture, on the other hand, is entirely material. There is no fundamental difference between subject and object, and the raw qualities of the objective reality determine everything. Eastern culture, he maintained, seeks to give aesthetic form to the objective matter without relying on some overall pattern; no transcendental design shapes and gives meaning to the objective world.

However, according to Assar, although the differences between the Eastern and Western cultural models are important, they are the opposite ends of a single evolutionary process, which is an epistemological process of separation in which the subject detaches himself from the objective material world.

Assar's (and Jabotinsky's) analyses of the evolution from Eastern to Western modes of thought followed the model set forth by the philosophers of the Enlightenment, who associated progress with technological advancements (the ability to master nature). Yet, while the latter and their followers viewed progress as a process that brings about greater knowledge and understanding of the world, and guarantees individuals greater freedom and control over their lives, to the Zionist Revisionists this was a narrative of the decay and, ultimately, the destruction of the human spirit.

Assar criticized both the Eastern mode of thought that is controlled by the concept of an alien objective reality, as well as the Western worldview, which limits individuals to a static set of rational rules. He called for an epistemological system in which objective reality (or our perception of it) does not initiate and control every human action, either as its physical source or as the object of intellectual contemplation. He envisioned a world that is governed by the pure will to power. Assar wanted to go beyond the scope of the cultures that had developed along the East-West geographical axis and that were founded on the basic object-subject opposition.

In the traditional historiographical approach to world history, ancient Israel is located at an important crossroads between the ancient cultures of the Near East and the classical Greek and Roman world. In this narrative of the transmission and development of intellectual and cultural modes from East to West, ancient Israel is credited with the creation of monotheism and with the development of the ethical and moral foundations of the major religions of the Near East and the West.[9]

Ben Gurion saw this moral and religious heritage as the greatest contribution of the Jewish people to the world: "The Books which were created and sanctified in Israel gave the Jewish people and the entire human race a moral and religious legacy that would never be matched; it is a legacy that holds an eternal, national, and universal vision that brings light to the darkest of human conditions and can guide the individual and society in the path of justice, peace, grace, and truth."[10]

The Zionist Revisionists, on the other hand, maintained that true national rejuvenation lay elsewhere, in the discovery of the authentic powers that allowed the ancient Hebrew nation to flourish as a dominant regional power. They did not want to reduce the legacy of ancient Israel to another (however important) phase in the long process of the rise of Western culture; instead they sought to accentuate Israel's uniqueness as a political entity that was part of a thriving Mediterranean world.

Israel as a Mediterranean Culture

Abba Achimeir, writing about the intellectual legacy of Jabotinsky, wrote: "He was a typical man of the Mediterranean. . . . He truly liked two cities: Odessa and Rome. . . . He loved them because they represented to him the Mediterranean. . . . The Mediterranean and the East, the countries by the azure sea and the countries close to the desert. Jabotinsky loved the Mediterranean countries and hated the East. In his hatred of the East he expressed the Mediterranean outlook of the Revisionist movement."[11]

To the Revisionists regional dominance could be defined in several ways. Abba Achimeir, for example, rejected what he characterized as the traditional Zionist view, according to which the beginning of the Jewish Diaspora after the destruction of the Second Temple marked the start of a long process of decline. He maintained that, on the contrary, the Diaspora in its early stages was a process of colonization, which is the mark of a strong nation that expands its natural borders, just as the Greeks and Romans expanded to new territories when their cultures were at their height.

Achimeir examined Jewish history through what he regarded as strictly secular factors: the realization of national goals. Thus the first two centuries of the common era were in fact the high mark in Israeli history and not, as modern Jewish and non-Jewish historians have suggested, a period of decline. At that period Judaism was a revolutionary force that dominated most of the Mediterranean east of the Greek mainland. What ended that great epoch were the internal conflicts in the homeland. The victory of Yavne over Jerusalem, of the religious and moralistic component of the Jewish community in Israel over the secular and nationalistic forces brought about the imminent decline of the Jewish empire.

Therefore, what many saw as the symbol of the greatest achievement of the ancient Israeli civilization—Jewish theology—was for

Achimeir and the Revisionists the sign of its decline. For Achimeir the historical transition from East to West (in the geographical limits of the eastern part of the Mediterranean) that ancient Israel experienced was the result of territorial growth and expansion, not a cultural process.[12]

To the Revisionists the greatness of ancient Israel was not predicated upon its intellectual or moral contributions, which were universal and extraterritorial by nature, but on its strength as a territorial power. Hen Merhavia, the Beitarist leader and editor of different Beitarist publications, argued that Zionism should see itself as a source of a revived civic spirit that would return the Hebrew nation to its past glory, not as a movement that rebuilds the spiritual center in Israel and brings the Jewish people back to their holy land.[13]

Dov Chomsky, writing for the *Beitar Guide,* similarly argued that Zionism must try to dissociate the Jewish nation from the term that came to symbolize it in the Diaspora—*Am ha-Sefer* (the people of the book). The reduction of the Jewish experience to that of messenger for the moral teachings of the biblical prophets, he claimed, was nothing but an attempt to justify the anomaly of the Jewish condition in the Diaspora in which a nation that had lost its territorial base had had to relinquish its historical self.

Judaism in the Diaspora had to reinvent itself as a spiritual (feminine, defensive) entity devoid of any nationalistic or territorial aspirations. Zionism, then, in order to overcome this deviant historical condition, must stop emphasizing the spiritual (and holy) nature of the Jewish people and instead cultivate its nationalistic and virile heritage.[14]

To Jabotinsky too the character that captured the essence of this (alternative) ancient Israeli spirit was that of Samson, the warrior-judge, whose relations with the Philistines—the people who came from the heart of the Mediterranean world—allowed him to realize his heroic nature.

Jabotinsky's Samson was destined from birth to live the life of a Nazarene and adhere to the strictest demands of the Jewish religion. But from a young age Samson was torn between his calling and his desire to experience life to the fullest. In his home, where he was known as Shimshon, he was a leader and a judge and lived according to the strict rules that govern the life of the Nazarene (no alcohol or other physical pleasures). But when he went outside his home, he was known as Taish, a man of earthly desires. As Jabotinsky described him, "Two Samsons, two kinds of life. . . . A stern judge without friendship or happiness; a clown that enjoys life."[15]

The Samson in Jabotinsky's novel was a complex character driven by discontent and by a constant search for an alternative way of life. As the critic Alice Stone Nakhimovsky has pointed out, one phrase that he repeated throughout the novel was "Here I am not myself."[16] He did not find happiness at home fulfilling his duties as a judge, nor did he find it in his endless wanderings, except among the Philistines: "Here, in the land of the Philistines, he was used from an early age to play the game of life without any questions or fears."[17]

In the religious tradition of the East, living as a Nazarene, Samson could not uncover the basic truths that would serve him as a leader. The moral and religious fundamentals of Jewish monotheism left him torn and alienated. Only his experience with pagans, who carried the ancient traditions of the Mediterranean world and were descended from the Minoan civilization, provided him with real peace, and only with them did he discover his true nature.

In describing the formation of the Hebrew nation, the Bible presents (for the contemporary reader) a general historiographical transition from East to West, from the great ancient civilizations of Mesopotamia and Egypt to the Holy Land. Abraham, the patriarch of the Hebrew nation, came from the East to the Promised Land. He was asked to leave his homeland and move westward to a new country as a sign of his commitment to his newly discovered god. Moses led the Jews from Egypt on their way to Israel, a journey in which they became a nation. And the conquest of Israel by Joshua, the establishment of Hebrew sovereignty over the land, also advanced from the eastern bank of the Jordan to the heart of Canaan.

In *Samson* Jabotinsky went against this geographical theme, claiming that the most critical movement in his analysis of the formative period in ancient Israeli history was from West to East, from the heart of the Mediterranean to its eastern shores. To Jabotinsky the opportunity to live independently and explore its true nature as a nation on its own land was what formed the Jewish nation, not the cultural and theological progression of monotheism from East to West. Jabotinsky depicted the Philistines, whom the Bible portrays as the Other of the Hebrew nation, as a source of the Hebrew nation's vitality. The values that the Philistines brought with them from the Mediterranean West were Samson's key to an authentic and healthy life. And the message of the novel was unmistakable: The Philistines' values are the heroic values that the Jewish nation must adopt.

Jabotinsky's search for the Mediterranean origins of the Hebrew nation was not restricted to the literary realm but was also historical and philological. Jabotinsky was a champion of the revival of the Hebrew language. However, this linguistic revival raised a unique practical question of how to transform a language that was dead for centuries into a living tongue. This question was particularly difficult in the case of Hebrew, which has no natural vowels, thus bringing into question the proper pronunciation.

To Jabotinsky, finding the correct Hebrew sounds was not merely a scientific endeavor but a national mission; these sounds would evoke in the nation's youth the true national characteristics that had all but disappeared in the Diaspora. And like Itamar Ben-Avi, Eliezer Ben Yehudah's son, Jabotinsky advocated at one point the adoption of the Latin alphabet, which would render the study of the spoken language easier and bring the speakers of Hebrew closer to the language's true sounds.

In a 1934 letter to Leone Carpi, the leader of the Revisionist movement in Italy, Jabotinsky asked about recent studies of Etruscan civilization, specifically to find out whether the ancient Etruscans and the ancient Hebrews had any linguistic or cultural similarities.[18] Presumably, Jabotinsky hoped that such similarities did exist, as he frequently tried to associate Hebrew culture with the Mediterranean world.

As part of his criticism of the Orientalist tendencies of some Zionists, Jabotinsky objected to the notion that modern Hebrew should sound like another Semitic language, Arabic. He felt that ancient Hebrew had little in common with a language that originated in the Arabian peninsula. In an essay titled "The Hebrew Accent," he claimed that the attempt to rediscover the original and pure Hebrew sound required an aesthetic principle. And, according to Jabotinsky, the European sound, particularly that of Italian and other languages that developed along the shores of the Mediterranean, is the pure sound that modern Hebrew must emulate.

Jabotinsky claimed that the Semitic sounds of Arabic were but a series of noises without distinction or character. Moreover, he argued that the ancient Hebrews, according to the Bible, had little contact with the Arabs and that Jerusalem, with its cool breezes and snowy winters, had little in common with the hot and tropical Arabian world.[19] Modern Hebrew, then, must rid itself of Arabic sounds and adopt the noble sounds of the Mediterranean languages that not only are more aesthetically pleasing but also are historically closer to the ancient Hebrew tongue.[20]

The notion of a return to the Mediterranean world of the ancient Hebrews was the topic of a 1932 letter from Jabotinsky to Yitzhak Sciachi, a leader of the Revisionist movement in Italy.[21] In the letter Jabotinsky stated that the Hebrew movement must undergo a radical change in its international orientation. Zionists can no longer rest their hopes on Great Britain and must seek other allies that will better serve the movement's goals. And this redirection, Jabotinsky claimed, could not be based solely on political concerns but had to be predicated upon cultural and spiritual considerations as well. The Zionist movement should adopt Mediterranean and Latin cultural models. It must, he wrote, "turn the masses into a Latin people (by means of a linguistic education). Beitarism must be an educational program that brings new contents to the nation."[22]

Jabotinsky and the Revisionists did not see the Jews as a people of the East and its cultural heritage (religion) but as a Mediterranean nation that returns to its glorious epoch as a regional political power.[23]

Between North and South

Though revisionism did not view the East as the original Hebrew home, Revisionists too objected to the notion that Western European culture should serve as the guiding light for the emerging Jewish state. When looking back at ancient Hebrew history in terms of cultural geography, revisionism focused on the East-West axis, and the Revisionists' preference was clearly for the Mediterranean West. However, in discussing the future of the Hebrew nation, the focus shifted to a north-south axis, to the tension between the Atlantic and Latin worlds, between northern Europe and Europe's Mediterranean countries.

In his 1932 letter to Sciachi, Jabotinsky had said that it was time for the movement to abandon its pro-Nordic tendencies. Two years later, in an article titled "On the Shores of the Mediterranean Sea," M. A. Perlmutter developed this theme further.[24] Perlmutter called for a revival of Mediterranean culture, for a return to the glory of Greece, Italy, and Israel. He claimed that only the creation of an alternative to the decadent Atlantic culture of the North would allow the nations of the Mediterranean world to resurrect their past glory.

An interesting application of the Revisionist sense of a historical tension between the Atlantic north and the Mediterranean south was an article in *Mishmar ha-Yarden* that drew an analogy between the fate of the Jewish people and that of the Irish.[25]

According to the article, Ireland became part of the Roman cultural world in the first century and was the only European country not affected by the Barbarian migration that swept Europe after the decline of the Roman Empire. During a time when Europe sank into ignorance, Ireland, much like the Jewish culture of the time, maintained its Mediterranean heritage and served as Europe's only cultural center. However, this golden age came to an end when Ireland was attacked from northern Europe, first by the Normans and later by the English, who brought Irish independence to an end and all but destroyed the authentic Irish character. The north, with its barbaric (Germanic) heritage, crushed the heroic Latin spirit.[26]

Abba Achimeir found examples of the north-south dichotomy somewhat closer to his own day. In 1927, in an analysis of the political situation in contemporary Spain, Achimeir drew a clear line between the south, which was led by Barcelona and the north, led by Madrid; Barcelona challenged the liberal and republican establishment in Madrid. Achimeir regarded Barcelona as a symbol of a true (anarchist) popular spirit that promised rejuvenation, whereas Madrid represented the decadence and stagnation of European civilization.[27]

In 1935 Achimeir applied this analysis to the United States. He predicted that in the 1936 campaign, Franklin D. Roosevelt, the representative of the northeast, the traditionalist European part of the country, would lose the election to Huey Long of Louisiana, who represented the emerging south, which challenged the authority of the old establishment.[28]

For the Revisionists the north represented the despised cultural heritage of rationalism, liberalism, socialism, and abstraction. It was a culture that had lost its vital connection to the fundamental principles that provide for an authentic life and replaced the true needs of the individual with empty universal rules.[29] Northern culture suppressed the real desires of its people and substituted for them false ideals that led only to alienation and resentment. In the name of universalism and humanism northern intellectuals wanted to eliminate the nation and the state, the two institutions and concepts that allow for authentic existence.

According to the Revisionists, few cultures showed signs of escaping the immanent decay that Western civilization was facing. Of these, the most notable was the reemerging Mediterranean power of Italy.

Italy

For a confluence of reasons the Revisionists of the 1920s and 1930s looked to Italy as a source of ideological, historical, and cultural inspiration. In "An Eastern Orientation in the Hebrew Policy," the Revisionist activist A. Faran claimed that Zionism was based on two basic tenets: Anglophilia mixed with pro-Arab pacifism that was rooted in German romanticism. However, the time had come to reject these two approaches and adopt a third option, Levantinism, which Faran saw as only appropriate for a culture that originated on and sought to return to the shores of the Mediterranean.[30]

Revisionism rejected both the Arab and Muslim East and the northern Europe and instead looked to the Mediterranean, which stood both as a historical reminder of the roots of the Jewish people and, in the case of modern Italy, as a living example of a glorious culture that was reclaiming its hegemony through the affirmation of power and national pride.

In the 1920s and 1930s the Revisionists looked at different national movements for inspiration. Achimeir, for example, wrote in 1930 that the Zionist movement must follow Sinn Fein's fundamental principle that a national movement cannot rely on the kindness of other nations but only on its own power and resources.[31]

The Revisionists also identified with Polish nationalism and its long struggle against Poland's oppressors. As the historian Laurence Weinbaum suggested, Jabotinsky and the Revisionists saw in Poland a suppressed nation that nevertheless continued to struggle to reclaim its independence.[32] Jabotinsky even suggested in a 1935 speech before Beitar members in Krakow that soil from Trumpeldor's grave in Palestine be brought to Jozef Pilsudski's grave as a symbol of the two national movements' close relations.[33] But it was Italy that served as the ultimate national model for the Zionist Revisionist movement.

From Jabotinsky's days as a student in Rome at the end of the nineteenth century, when he developed an admiration for Garibaldi and the Italian fight for national independence, the Revisionists expressed interest in modern Italy as a role model for the Zionist movement. Yet, until the beginning of the 1930s, the movement, like the rest of the Zionist establishment, still regarded Britain as the Jews' most reliable ally.

By 1932, however, Jabotinsky was writing, "Just as we all treated Czarist legislation with contempt, so must we treat British rule in our country now. . . . The time has passed when we saw it as our duty— even when it was unpleasant or inconvenient—to give our moral sanction to British rule. No longer!"[34]

If Britain could no longer be trusted to advance the Zionist cause, the movement had to seek other alternatives, and to the Revisionists the most natural alternative was Italy, the growing power that challenged Britain for dominance in the region.[35]

The Revisionists felt that Italy and Israel shared a common historical heritage and common national aspirations and that Italian fascism and Zionist revisionism provided the purest expression of those aspirations. In 1935 Hen Merhavia wrote:

> I cannot emphasize enough the fact that I see my movement, Beitar, as a movement of the highest moral level. Therefore I have to say

that I also see in fascism, as long as it is not aggressive, a moral movement of a nation that wants to control its destiny, rule over its country, and be free on its own land. This morality necessarily leads to a
corporative form of government, to absolute unity of the nation,
and to a virtuous culture that brings progress in all realms of life, science, and human activity. Like our movement, the Italians want to
establish a nucleus of an exemplary life of morality and purity. Like
us, the Italian fascists look back to their historical heritage. We seek
to return to the kingdom of the House of David; they want to return
to the glory of the Roman Empire.[36]

The history of relations between the Zionist Revisionists and fascist Italy dates to 1922, when Jabotinsky, still a member of the Zionist
Executive, was sent by the World Zionist Organization to help win
international support for the British Mandate and the creation of a
Jewish national home in Palestine. Jabotinsky was scheduled to meet
Mussolini during that visit, but the meeting, for reasons that remain
unclear, did not take place. Jabotinsky, however, did send Mussolini a
letter in which he tried to win the Italian's support for the Zionist
cause.[37]

Jabotinsky started the letter rather strangely, declaring that he was
aware of Mussolini's opposition to Zionism and that therefore Jabotinsky assumed that they were enemies. Jabotinsky then turned to his
main point, using a mostly linguistic and cultural argument to try to
convince Mussolini to abandon his pan-Arabic policy. Jabotinsky
claimed that only a strong Jewish presence along the Mediterranean
could ensure the hegemony of the Italian language in the region.

Jabotinsky argued that because Hebrew culture was not fully
developed, Jews everywhere relied on a second (European) language.
If Italy were to ally with the Jews, he continued, the new Jewish state
would adopt Italian language and culture and establish their dominance throughout the region. The Arabs, Jabotinsky wrote, did not
possess the cultural or intellectual tradition of the Jews, so only the
Jews could truly help advance Italian objectives in the area.

Moreover, Jabotinsky claimed in the letter that the Arabs and Italians would soon find themselves fighting each other in what would
essentially be a cultural war for control of the Middle East. (He
pointed out the problems that the French were experiencing in

North Africa.) In such a war the Jewish state, separated physically from the Arab world by the deserts of the East, would serve as a buffer zone between Europe, Asia, and Africa.

Jabotinsky concluded his letter to Mussolini by comparing the vitality of the Jewish nation to that of the Italian fascists, and he expressed his interest in Mussolini's personality and his movement. Yet for the next decade Jabotinsky continued to view an alliance with Britain as the Zionist movement's only international option, changing his mind only in the early 1930s.

By then other Revisionists already had expressed their interest in Italy as a potential model and partner. Most noteworthy, perhaps, were Achimeir's columns "From the Diary of a Fascist," published in *Doar ha-Yom* in 1928, but other Revisionists, particularly Beitar activists, professed their support of Italy's fascist regime in those years. For example, Ze'ev Shem-Tov, one of the heads of Beitar in Warsaw, wrote that the movement had to concentrate on one political ideology: fascism. He argued that for the good of the Jewish nation, Beitar should adopt the fascist model and blindly follow its one leader, Jabotinsky, with absolute devotion.[38]

In the second half of the 1920s revisionism also established itself as a growing force among Italian Zionists. The movement's first Italian branch, the Raggruppamento d'Italia, was founded in 1925. And although the Milan branch had only four members in 1927, by 1928 the number had grown fivefold. In the next two years branches were opened at different Italian universities, primarily by Jewish students from eastern Europe. In the elections for the 15th Zionist Congress the Revisionists received 75 percent of the votes in Milan, and in 1929 they received more than a quarter of the votes in the entire country.[39]

In 1930 the first issues of *L'Idea Sionistica*, edited by Leone Carpi, came out. The publication had a distinctly anti-British stance and championed cooperation between the Italian government and the Zionist movement.

The first Revisionist Conference in Italy convened in Milan in February 1932. The anti-British, pro-Italian slant of the fifty delegates was clear from the conference's political resolution: "The Conference puts on record that Great Britain is conducting an openly anti-Zionist policy in Palestine. . . . The Conference insists that World Jewry should put in a concrete political form the traditional sympathy with Italy, and express its hopes that, as a Mediterranean power, Italy will show interest in the establishment of the Jewish home in Palestine."[40]

Before the elections to the 16th Zionist Congress, Sciachi wrote to his fellow Italian Revisionists that they should not be ashamed to be called the fascists of the Zionist movement. Moreover, he claimed, they should be honored to be compared to a national movement that had been so successful in rejuvenating and leading forward a great nation like Italy.[41]

Carpi, addressing the first New Zionist Organization Conference in Vienna in 1935, made a similar argument, claiming that the Revisionists and fascists had much in common. He argued that the two movements had a similar national and social platform and that they both represented the truest national values.[42]

If the Revisionists' interest in Italy in the late 1920s was restricted to activists in Italy and a few activists elsewhere, by the early 1930s this interest had grown dramatically, particularly because of the growing disappointment with British policy in Palestine. That the fascination with Italy had spread to Palestine is clear from trends in the Revisionist dailies *Hazit ha-Am* and *Ha-Yarden* and the Beitarist publications. Stories about Italy, as well as articles from Italian papers that covered political, economic, cultural, and artistic matters, at times overshadowed the coverage of local affairs and Zionist politics. The Revisionist dailies wrote favorably about Italian colonialism (especially during the war in Ethiopia); they published several speeches by Mussolini; and they printed several articles that distinguished between Hitler's Nazism and Mussolini's fascism. In fact, articulating the differences between Hitler's brand of fascism and the Italian model was a dominant theme in the Revisionist publications. A. Revere, for example, wrote in the Italian Revisionist publication *L'Idea Sionistica* about the great gulf between Italian fascism and Hitler's anti-Semitism and praised Mussolini for his attacks on Hitler.[43] Abba Achimeir, using the Revisionist distinction between northern (Atlantic) and Latin cultures, suggested that Hitler's anti-Semitism—which diverted his movement from its pure Italian (fascist) origins—derived from Anglo-Saxon sources. Achimeir argued that the slavery of blacks in the United States was the direct outcome of this racist Anglo-Saxon heritage.[44]

As the opening paragraph of Jabotinsky's letter to Mussolini indicated, in the 1920s the Italian leader was not a supporter of the Zionist cause and viewed the Arabs as Italy's natural allies in the Middle East. By the early 1930s, however, Italy's Middle East policy had changed and had become more favorable toward the Zionist movement.[45]

In 1933 the Italian foreign ministry (Mussolini was then also the foreign minister) began circulating internal memoranda stipulating that ending the British Mandate in Palestine and creating a strong Jewish state were in Italy's best interests.[46] The favorable political climate made it much easier for Zionist groups to operate in Italy, especially Revisionists whose local leaders had close ties to Italian officials.

But did the Italian government treat the Revisionists differently from other Zionists? This question is hard to answer, and to judge by Mussolini's own actions, the answer would have to be no. Despite his relentless efforts, Jabotinsky was unable to arrange a meeting with the Italian leader, whereas Chaim Weitzmann met with Mussolini four times between 1923 and 1934.[47] It is important to remember, however, that Mussolini was not well versed in the different Zionist ideological currents and that, as official head of state, he probably found it appropriate to meet only with the head of the Zionist movement. In fact, we have information that suggests that Italian authorities did view the Revisionists as likely ideological partners.

In March 1932 the Italian newspaper *Il Piccolo della Sera* offered coverage of the first conference of Italian Zionist Revisionists. The Italian paper's coverage included a short outline of the Revisionist ideological platform as well as a short biography of Jabotinsky as a political leader, writer, Italian scholar, and translator of Dante's *The Divine Comedy* into Hebrew. The article summarized Jabotinsky's speech, underlining his insistence that liberating Palestine from the British would require an exercise of power. At the end of the article the paper's correspondent wrote, "Italy, which has its colonial interests to protect, cannot fail to appreciate the importance of the statements made by the leader of the Revisionist movement."[48]

The editors of *Il Piccolo della Sera* headlined the article "The First Conference of Italian Zionists-Revisionists—Uselessness of Cooperating with the World Organization." The Revisionists, in the editors' view, had much in common, both culturally and politically, with the Italian regime and its aspirations in the region. The Revisionists thus presented an alternative to the World Zionist Organization and were perceived as potential partners for the Italian government and people in the Middle East. A report to the Revisionist Executive Board interpreted this article, and, presumably, others like it, as an indication that the Italian press, and by implication the government, saw Jabotinsky and his movement as likely allies that opened up new possibilities for Italy in the region.

Raffaele Guariglia, who was head of Middle Eastern desk at the Italian Foreign Ministry, expressed similar views in a memorandum that he sent his superiors in November 1935. Guariglia wrote that Jabotinsky exhibited superior intellectual qualities and a strong character and was free of that brand of Jewish mysticism that beleaguered the Jewish people as a whole in the modern era. To Guariglia, Jabotinsky symbolized a new type of Jewish leader. Guariglia associated Judaism and its leaders with mysticism, spirituality, and idealism, qualities that were in direct contrast to what he saw as the true virtues of the modern era—power and vitality. Jabotinsky and his movement, however, represented the "new Jew," who turned away from traditional Jewish values and embraced the values championed by the Italian regime.[49]

In his 1932 letter to Sciachi, which finally gave an official seal of approval to the growing Revisionist interest in Italy, Jabotinsky brought up two other matters that he asked Sciachi to explore—the possibility of arranging a meeting between Jabotinsky and Mussolini, and the establishment of a military school for Beitar in Italy, which, he claimed, would be the most appropriate location for such a school.[50] Jabotinsky never met the Italian leader, and though his hopes for a comprehensive military school remained unfulfilled, the Revisionist movement was able to establish the Beitar Naval Academy in the Italian port city Civitavecchia.

The academy, which opened in 1934, represented both the Revisionists' commitment to the development of Jewish militarism and their hopes for a return to the Hebrew maritime spirit that had all but vanished in the Diaspora.

The titular "captain" of the school was the Italian marine scientist Nicola Fusco, but the man who ran the school and was the driving force behind it was the Beitarist leader Yirmiyahu Halperin. Through Jabotinsky's connections the Revisionists were able to procure a training boat from a wealthy Belgian supporter of the movement; the boat was named after the donor's wife, Sara. And cadets from all over Europe, and Palestine as well as South Africa, attended the school, which produced some future commanders of the Israeli navy.

The Revisionist leadership was well aware of the potential implications of opening a school in fascist Italy, as this would provide the Revisionists' opponents with propagandist material. Revisionist leaders wanted the cadets to keep away from any involvement in local politics. In November 1934 Jabotinsky conveyed a message to the cadets in Civitavecchia: "Do not forget even for a moment that you are visitors in this school and especially in this country. Be courteous. . . . Do not take part in any political dispute regarding Italian matters; do not opine about any Italian political issue. Do not criticize the existing Italian regime, the same regime that gave you the opportunity to attend this school."[51]

Nonetheless, the Beitar cadets were very involved in local politics. In his *History of Hebrew Seamanship* Halperin wrote that the cadets, despite opposition from their superiors, expressed public support for Mussolini's regime. During the Italian campaign in Ethiopia the Beitarist cadets marched alongside Italian soldiers in a demonstration in support of the war, and it was brought to Halperin's attention that they collected metal scraps and sent them to the Italian weapons industry.[52] The young Beitarist students felt at home in the Italian facility and identified with the local political culture; in Italy they felt as if they were living a true Beitarist life in an atmosphere of heroism, militarism, and nationalistic pride.

One event in Civitavecchia, perhaps more than any other, captures the Italian authorities' perception of the Revisionist cadets as true brothers in arms. On May 28, 1935, the Italian newspaper *Popolo di Roma* reported on the tragic drowning of a Revisionist naval cadet. After describing the accident, the paper detailed the ceremonies in

honor of the dead cadet, ceremonies that revealed the nature of relations between the Revisionists and Italian authorities: "In honor of
the missing cadet an emotional ceremony took place. On board the
ship *Domenico,* whose flag was flown at half mast, all of his comrades stood on board and they were accompanied by Mr. Halperin,
the head of the school; Mr. Fusco, the administrative secretary of the
local branch of the Fascist Party; a representative of the mayor; the
port's supervisor . . . and all of the cadets of the Lazio naval academy. . . . In the place where the accident occurred, the dead cadet's
comrades prayed according to their own [Jewish] tradition, performed a military ceremony, and tossed a bouquet of flowers to the
sea. All who were present then performed the *Saluto Romano* with
their heads uncovered."[53]

These expressions of solidarity between the Revisionist academy
and the Italian military were not merely the result of the emotions
of the moment, as indicated by an article about the Civitavecchia cadets in the official publication of the Italian professional maritime
schools, *Bollettino del Consorzio Scuole Profesionali per la Maestranza
Maritima.* The publication stated, "In agreement of all the relevant
authorities it has been confirmed that the views and the political and
social inclinations of the Revisionists are known and that they are
absolutely in accordance with the fascist doctrine. Therefore, as our
students they will bring the Italian and fascist culture to Palestine."[54]

The article went on to state that the Revisionist cadets were the
true pioneers of a civic blossoming in Palestine and that after they
developed their country, they would maintain close relations with
Italy, which would benefit both sides.

Interestingly, the Italian communists expressed this view of the
Zionist Revisionists in Civitavecchia as an integral part of the Italian
fascist system. In January 1938 the naval academy's training boat,
Sara 1, sailed around the Mediterranean. When the cadets arrived in
Tunisia, a series of clashes between the cadets and local Arab groups
broke out.

According to the Revisionists, the Arabs were responsible to the
violence.[55] The communist publication *L'Italiano di Tunisi* offered a
different version, claiming that Mussolini's regime supported a small
group of fascist Zionists that traveled around the world under

Fusco's leadership and spread the message of the new Zionism, which was fascist.[56]

The Civitavecchia academy occupied a special place in the Revisionists' iconography. In August 1937, as the Beitar Naval Academy's training boat, *Sara 1,* was about to arrive in Palestine, the Revisionist paper *Ha-Yarden* observed: "There is no wonder that maritime activities are considered the hardest and most masculine of any human activity. The people of Israel, who thousands of years ago were a people of the sea, were forced away from the sea during their years away from home; they were forced away from this great sphere of heroism. Only recently have we experienced a maritime awakening which will manifest itself with the arrival of the first Hebrew boat at the homeland's shores."[57]

Sara 1's voyage from Italy to Palestine was more than just a training sail from Italy to Palestine. To the Zionist Revisionists this was a journey across temporal and spatial boundaries. From a historical perspective it symbolized a return to the ancient origins of the Hebrew nation as a Mediterranean society that thrived as a maritime civilization.

But the voyage of the *Sara 1* also represented the Revisionist commitment to a future of heroism, action, and fighting that would revive the nation's glorious past as a regional power. Geographically, *Sara 1*'s voyage signified the Revisionists' desire to bring Italy and Israel closer together, to create a Mediterranean alliance that would drive the Atlantic powers away and restore Latin dominance over mare nostrum.

Epilogue
Revisionism Today

Zionism was an uneasy coalition of diverse dreams, and by
definition it would have been impossible for all those dreams
to have been fulfilled. . . . Israel is a fiery collection of arguments, and I like it this way, although it is no garden of roses.
. . . Israel is a living open street seminar about Jewish heritage, about the meaning of Judaism, about morality. . . . A
whole nation has been immersed for the past thirty years in a
debate which is superficially political or military but which is
essentially ethical, historical, even theological about the kind
of identity they want.

Amos Oz, "A Monologue: Behind the Sound and Fury"

From the mid-1970s to the early 1990s any discussion about the legacy of the Revisionist thought of the interwar period in modern-day
Israel would have focused on the Israeli Right's lead in the struggle
for "Greater Israel." The Likud—the modern political incarnation of
the Revisionist movement—has been regarded in general Israeli and
Zionist discourse as the movement that fights for the right of the
Jewish people to the Land of Israel.

Under the leadership of Menachem Begin, who succeeded Jabotinsky as leader of the Revisionist camp, the movement continued
the tradition of the Irgun, which saw itself as the vanguard in the
nation's fight for independence. And Likud's principal policy, when
it was in power from 1977 to 1992, was the establishment of Jewish
settlements in the territories occupied by Israel in the 1967 war and
the assurance of Israel's rule over these territories.[1]

The "Greater Israel" policy, which was the main political characteristic of Herut and later the Likud, was not, however, the sole reason for the Likud's political success since 1977. A chief factor in the
rise to power of the Israeli Right that year was the shift in political
orientation among the Eastern Jews—Jews who came from Arab and
Muslim countries—in Israel, who until 1973 had supported in large
numbers the Labor Party but after the Yom Kippur War embraced
Begin and the Likud as an antiestablishment alternative. The Likud,
as Yonathan Shapiro showed, allowed this population to shift its
struggle for status in Israeli society to the political realm. In return,
the Eastern Jews embraced the myths, symbols, and slogans of the
Zionist Right, whose leaders were also marginalized by the old Zionist leadership and, like the Eastern Jews, were pushed by Labor to the
fringes of Israeli society.[2]

In what some critics have described as the emergence of a post-
Zionist Israel, Begin's and Likud's rise to power marked the end of
the Labor Zionist ethos and the rise to prominence of new social and
cultural forces in Israel, and it ushered in a new cultural and social
chapter in Israeli history. Under the Likud a more pluralistic and
heterogeneous Israel has emerged; alongside the Ashkenazi Sabra, the
Moroccan singer and the national-religious yeshiva student dressed
in an army uniform came to symbolize the new and more complex
image of the prototypical Israeli. And by the 1990s Israeli society was
in a period of change and found itself in the midst of a heated debate
about its identity; various groups have resurrected some of the old
arguments made by Jabotinsky and his contemporaries as they attacked the core of Labor's Zionist ideology. By the end of the twentieth century (Labor) Zionism's critics from the Right not only offered
militaristic alternatives (as Begin and his generation of Likud leaders
did for half a century) to the policies of the old Israeli establishment,
they began to question the fundamental values of mainstream Zionism and its underlying historical and moral principles.

The most comprehensive ideological program that emerged from
the recent intellectual, cultural, and political assault on Labor's Zionist vision is, arguably, post-Zionism. Although on such issues as
Arab-Israeli relations the post-Zionists are on what is perceived to be

the extreme leftist flank of Israeli politics, an examination of post-Zionism reveals the shortcomings of the most widely used criteria for distinguishing between the Israeli Left and Israeli Right in recent years—attitudes toward Greater Israel and therefore toward territorial compromise. The post-Zionists demonstrate that in recent political discourse definitions of Left and Right are more multilayered than they have been since the days of the Yishuv. The post-Zionists (much like Jabotinsky and his supporters in the 1930s) offer a systematic criticism of the philosophical and ideological tenets of mainstream Zionism as part of a greater attack on the principles of modern Western culture. After examining the interpretation of Jabotinsky's ideological platform and its reduction into one political credo—territorial maximalism—by Begin and his followers, I would like to argue that comparing Jabotinsky's revisionism and post-Zionism would help deepen our understanding of the true ideological legacy of Jabotinsky and his early ideological supporters.

Israeli Revisionism from Begin to Netanyahu

While Menachem Begin was propelled to power largely by the support of Eastern Jews and traditional Jews who looked for a cultural alternative to Labor's secular and modern ideology, he (and his successor, Yitzhak Shamir) were mostly concerned the issue of Greater Israel. Begin, who had been a member of the Polish branch of Beitar, had led the attack against Jabotinsky for his inability or unwillingness to put his theories into practice. Begin objected to the cultural and intellectual character of the movement under Jabotinsky's leadership and wanted to turn it into a military organization. Under Begin's leadership the old guard of Revisionist intellectuals was removed from the movement's centers of power and was replaced with veterans of the Irgun.[3]

In 1945, on the fifth anniversary of Jabotinsky's death, Begin declared, "We are witnessing the victory parade of Jabotinsky's ideas. . . . This victory encompasses every aspect of our life."[4] But as a political leader, despite presenting himself as Jabotinsky's ideological heir, Begin all but ignored social and cultural issues, the trademark of Jabotinsky's brand of Zionist revisionism.

In the 1977 elections the Likud's manifesto declared that the right of the Jewish people to their land is eternal. The territories captured in the 1967 war, the manifesto declared, should therefore never be surrendered, and Jews will be sovereign between the sea and the Jordan River.[5] In his political manifesto from 1928, "What the Zionist Revisionists Want," Jabotinsky similarly declared that Zionism's first goal was the establishment of a Jewish majority on both sides of the Jordan. However, in the same paragraph he wrote, "This is not the ultimate goal of the Zionist movement, which is based on higher ideals such as addressing the hardship of Jews around the world and creating a New Hebrew culture."[6]

Ilan Peleg, in a study of Begin's foreign policy, has argued that Jabotinsky was to Begin what Marx was to Lenin: a revered intellectual whose ideas had to be changed to fit new realities.[7] Jabotinsky was, first and foremost, an intellectual, and his notions of power had to do with the creation of the new Jew and the revitalization of the Jewish national spirit; Begin, on the other hand, was a leader of a paramilitary organization and later a political party—and his notion of power had to do with practical questions of foreign policy and the use of military force.

Peleg has characterized Begin's ideology as neorevisionism.[8] Although Jabotinsky's worldview (and that of his Revisionist contemporaries) encompassed a host of issues (economics, aesthetics, gender, philosophy, and more) and drew on a variety of intellectual and ideological currents, Begin's ideology focused almost exclusively on two themes: military force and the utter rejection of the non-Jewish world.

Since his days as the leader of the Irgun, Begin used Jabotinsky's notion of the iron wall and believed that the development of military force should be the central policy of the Jewish state.[9] Jabotinsky spoke in the 1930s about the need to teach Hebrew youth how to shoot; Begin, in 1945, argued, "Now it is not enough to learn how to shoot; it is not enough to know how to shoot. In the name of historical justice, in the name of life's instinct, in the name of truth—we *must* shoot."[10]

In the early years of the state, Begin and other leaders of the Israeli Right argued that Israel should have continued to fight its war of liberation until it gained control of the entire area that had been under British mandatory rule, including Transjordan. In a 1949 speech before the Knesset, Begin claimed, "In our dealings with the Arab countries and other countries, we are faced with one critical issue—the eastern bank of the Jordan. . . . The eastern bank of the Jordan was and will always be an integral part of the Hebrew homeland."[11]

Israel (Scheib) Eldad was an intellectual and activist who in many ways was to Begin what Abba Achimeir was to Jabotinsky: a fiery orator and writer who drew on dramatic historical and philosophical images to deliver impassioned ideological arguments.[12] In 1961 he claimed that when Israel avoided crossing into Jordan to obey the cease-fire that was imposed on the Jewish nation, Israeli leaders (from the Labor movement) were not only stupid and cowardly but they showed that their essential character is one of obedience.[13] Two years later Eldad claimed that the truncated and partitioned Jewish state was not only physically small but that the entire national psyche was distorted because parts of the land had been taken from the Jewish people. "The partition was not isolated, it was a total partition, and not only are the national borders a mere caricature, all our thoughts and actions and our lives are distorted by these ridiculous borders . . . and this is not only a matter of little land or a small country, but a distortion of all forms, a lack of wholeness from within and from without."[14]

To Jabotinsky the land had no intrinsic value; it only had a practical role—to provide vast open expanses that would allow individuals to explore their true selves. In Eldad and Begin's worldview, however, the land was the most critical element of the nation's collective identity; it was the heart pumping life into the entire national body.

After 1967, when Israel occupied the West Bank, Gaza Strip, Golan Heights, and Sinai peninsula, Begin's and the Zionist Right's vision of territorial maximalism gained great popularity among different elements of Israeli society. The younger members of the national religious movement became the leading force in the settlement of the occupied territories, and certain elements of the Labor movement (especially those from Ahdut ha-Avodah) became leading activists in the Greater Israel movement. Yet, ultimately, as Ehud Sprinzak claimed in his study of the Israeli radical Right, veteran Revisionists, who have always been hostile to the 1948 partition of Palestine, were the most ecstatic leaders of the Greater Israel movement.[15] And it was the Likud and Begin who were the political leaders of the Greater Israel bloc and were able to lead it to victory at the polls.

Another important aspect of Begin's (and the Israeli Right's) political vision was his attitude toward the non-Jewish world. The critic Nurith Gertz has argued that Israeli culture had two dominant narratives with regard to the non-Jewish world: One saw Israel as part of the modern civilized world, whereas the other, championed by Begin and his supporters, viewed Israel as separated from the rest of the world and presented Israeli and Jewish history as the tale of a chosen people who are constantly experiencing catastrophic events of destruction and redemption.[16]

While Jabotinsky and his contemporaries saw themselves as European intellectuals, as soldiers in the cultural battle against the decay and disintegration of Western civilization, Begin's worldview was rooted in a deep suspicion of the non-Jewish world. Jabotinsky believed in cooperation with other countries (first Britain and later Italy) in order to achieve the political goals of the Zionist movement; Begin, on the other hand, came from a post-Holocaust perspective—he spent the first three years of World War II in Europe—and sought to rely solely on Jewish power to advance the Zionist cause. (In 1952 Begin was the most vociferous critic of Ben Gurion's reparations agreement with Germany. In a speech that year Begin declared, "A Jewish government that negotiates with Germany can no longer be a Jewish government. . . . Every German is a Nazi. Every German is a murderer."[17]) For Jabotinsky, Zionism was a Jewish response to the perceived general crisis that Western culture had been experiencing since the late nineteenth century. To Begin the creation of the state of Israel was a distinctively Jewish phenomenon, dialectically tied to the constant attempts by the Gentiles to destroy the Jewish people.[18]

For Begin the Holocaust was the greatest atrocity committed against the Jews; but it was not necessarily the last. To Begin the Jews were in a constant battle against Amalek, the tribe that attacked the Israelites from the rear on their way to the Promised Land during the exodus from Egypt and who came to symbolize the archetypical enemy of the Jewish people in each generation. After the Holocaust the Arabs were the modern-day Amelekites—the heirs of the Nazis, who were out to destroy the Jewish people. And in his depiction of the Arab threat Begin repeatedly drew on images from the Holocaust.

In a 1970 speech Begin reacted to various proposals that called for Israeli withdrawal from the territories captured in the 1967 war: "Would any country in the world accept such a solution; who can ask us to accept such a so-called peace with permanent bloodshed, with the killing of our children? How many Moishelach and Saralach must be killed after one and a half million Jewish children were massacred in our time? That would be the consequence of a repartition of the land of Israel."[19] In Begin's view the Arabs sought to complete what the Nazis had started, while the rest of the world aided the Arabs by demanding that Israel give up parts of the historic Jewish homeland. And for him, maintaining Jewish sovereignty over all of Greater Israel was the only way to ensure the survival of the Jewish people and prevent another Holocaust.[20]

This was the essence of his Zionist Revisionist outlook. What was in Jabotinsky's day a complex ideology that addressed a variety of issues and themes was reduced under Begin's leadership to a one-dimensional ideological platform: territorial maximalism, stirred by an existential fear of the non-Jewish world.

With the rise of a new generation of Likud leaders in the 1990s, however, some elements of the Revisionist movement have attempted to revert to its founding principles. Benjamin Netanyahu, the leader who brought the Likud back to power in 1996 (for a three-year term), realized that the party had to reinvent itself in order to meet the social and cultural demands of most of its supporters.

Netanyahu portrayed himself and his movement as leading the people's struggle for liberation from the cultural and ideological hold of the old leftist elites. He called for the creation of new academic institutions and media outlets that would allow for the development of an alternative Hebrew culture independent of established institutions.[21] His rise to power symbolized the decline of certain aspects of Begin's revisionism, which had focused almost exclusively on the issue of the Land of Israel and marked an attempt to reconstitute the Zionist Right as a cultural and social force.[22]

Netanyahu's supporters created a new academic research center, the Shalem Center, and a publication, *Azure*, to spearhead the intellectual and cultural battle against the Left. In *Azure*'s first issue the editors stated that the direction in which Israel's intellectual and political elite was leading the nation was predicated on a worldview that opposed everything that accepted the fundamental link between the Jewish state and the Jewish people.[23] Netanyahu and his supporters wanted to challenge Labor's intellectual and cultural heritage and revive Jabotinsky's monist ideal—to create a national culture for the Jewish nation that did not have to make any compromises, including territorial ones, in the name of universal values.

According to Yoram Hazony, perhaps the most outspoken of the intellectuals associated with Netanyahu, the idea behind the creation of the State of Israel was to form a Jewish state that is intrinsically Jewish, a state that directs all its powers to addressing the needs of the Jewish people.[24] Hazony has criticized what he sees as the Zionist establishment's attempts to turn Israel from a Jewish state into the state of the Jews, an idea that is based on the universalist heritage of the Enlightenment and the French Revolution. Hazony instead called for a revision in Zionism and a return to Herzl's Zionist principles, as did Jabotinsky more than six decades earlier.

In 1934 an editorial in *Hazit ha-Am* declared that "after the complete bankruptcy of socialism all over the world, and after the recent growth of the anti-Jewish hell in the Diaspora, only one ideal shines brightly in our skies . . . the royal idea of Israel in Zion as the only means of salvation for the poor Jewish masses. Now after this bankruptcy maybe the deceived Jewish youth would finally realize that it was tricked into worshipping an idol, the false ideal of 'humanism.' Zion is the only salvation."[25] For Netanyahu, Hazony, and the new leadership of the Zionist Right, the Israeli political scene had reverted to a cultural war between the agents of humanism and universalism on the one hand (the Left), and the representatives of the Jewish nation and its unique characteristics on the other hand (the

Right), that left the political scene much as it appeared to the Revisionists in the 1930s.

Although Netanyahu and his supporters have attempted to revive some elements of the revisionism of the prestatehood period, when the political debate focused primarily on the social and cultural identity of the future state, he and his party were primarily a political entity, not cultural crusaders. Other groups, however, that are more culturally oriented have filled the breach, spearheading a cultural battle against Labor and its heritage, a battle that reflects the recent fundamental changes in Israeli society.

The two main groups that have led the charge against the Zionist leftist establishment in the 1990s have been Shas, the ultra-orthodox, Sephardic movement, as well as a more loosely defined group of post-Zionist intellectuals, primarily academics and writers, who have offered a postmodern critique of old-school Zionism. Culturally, Shas represents the traditional ultra-orthodox sentiment that had always opposed Zionism as a secular movement that would inevitably lead the Jewish people to cultural and moral decay. Yet the movement combines its ultra-orthodox ideology with a popular, antielitist sentiment that has turned it into a powerful ethnic party that is supported by many nonreligious Sephardim (who in 1977 helped the Likud dethrone Labor).[26] The post-Zionists, on the other hand, represent (much as Jabotinsky and his supporters did in the 1930s) a secular (Western) opposition to Zionism, based on recent literary and philosophical trends.

Post-Zionism as a Revision of Zionism

Post-Zionism, which entered into the Israeli consciousness in the 1990s, draws on some basic features of postmodern thought. In using the term *post-Zionism,* I refer to a group of Israeli intellectuals (historians, sociologists, cultural critics, artists) who posit a paradigm shift in the perception of Israeli culture and history. Laurence Silberstein in *The Postzionist Debates* has described this group as the radical post-Zionist critics that as opposed to other critics of Zionism who relied on historical and social scientific methodology have turned to discursive and representational methodologies.[27] The post-Zionists' proclaimed aim is to challenge Zionism's accepted means of representation and undermine its self-perception as the only and necessary expression of Jewish history and culture. The post-Zionists, drawing on such recent critical theories as poststructuralism, gender studies, and postcolonialism, bring into question the discursive practices by which the Zionist and Israeli historical narratives and sociological representations were formulated.[28]

Following Jean-François Lyotard's assertion that "narrative is authority itself. It authorizes an unbreakable *we*, outside of which there can only be *they*," the post-Zionists argue that Zionist ideology represents the narrative of the interests of the old Israeli establishment vis-à-vis the Others, who were dispossessed of their land and rights or who were marginalized socially, culturally, and politically.[29] Ilan Pappe, perhaps the most outspoken of the post-Zionist ideologues, has encouraged his colleagues to employ linguistic and literary methodologies that allow, in what he considers an age of aggressive nationalism, for the dismantling of the authoritarian Israeli discourse and the means by which it dominates.[30]

In the post-Zionist scheme power does not reside within the political and social realm but rather in the systems of representation and the struggle to dominate them or, in the Foucauldian formulation, in the relations between the constitution of knowledge and the exercise of power.[31] And according to the post-Zionist critics, Israeli historiography played a critical role in the process of establishing Zionist dominance.[32] As Adi Ophir and Ariella Azoulay, two of the leading voices of the group, have maintained, it created a clear hierarchical relationship between the "White Jew" and his "Oriental Other."[33]

Zionism, the post-Zionists argue, represented Oriental Jews as a primitive community that had to adapt to the demands of a modern European society and renounce its cultural heritage. It depicted the survivors of the Holocaust as an example of the passivity of the Diaspora. It exploited their sufferings as justification for actions taken by Israel against the native Arab population, which in turn was portrayed as an enemy that attacked the peaceful Jewish Yishuv without provocation.[34] Postmodernists regard any attempt to represent reality as an economizing of language. Since it is impossible to represent reality in its entirety (it would require an infinite number of signs), we can only choose a limited number of signifiers and use them to tell one story that ostensibly represents reality in its whole. In the case of Zionist historiography, the post-Zionists have maintained, this economization has afforded the narrator, the Zionist historian, a dominant position that forces a specific understanding of history, while excluding those elements that do not fit within this limited perspective. The post-Zionists' ideological goal is to expose the methods by which this hegemonic historical narrative has dominated and to allow for the silenced elements in the dominant Israeli discourse to enter into the historical discussion.

In the immediate aftermath of the assassination of prime minister Yitzhak Rabin in 1995, his former chief of staff Shimon Sheves declared that, "The country was taken away from us."[35] He was paraphrasing a similar statement made by Yitzhak Ben Aharon, the former head of the *Histadrut,* after Labor's stunning defeat in the 1977 elections. These statements reflect a growing feeling among the old political elite that the state that they were responsible for building has undergone an irreversible transformation. As Ariella Azoulay in her postmodern jargon put it, the 1977 elections were a turning point in the cultural struggle for representation of the past. While under Labor, the Israeli past was represented exclusively by secular, male elite, after 1977 the Israeli cultural discourse opened up and allowed for Eastern Jews, the Revisionists, religious Jews and women to become part of Israeli to become part of the Israeli cultural landscape.[36]

It is important, in the context of the historiographical debate, to distinguish between the group that the historian Benny Morris termed the *New Historians* and the post-Zionists. The former is a group of historians that includes Morris, Avi Shlaim, and others, who use modern and positivistic methodological tools but challenge the traditional interpretation of historical documents by Israeli historians. They do not, however, question the theoretical and intellectual tenets of Zionist historiography. Instead, they strive to provide what they consider a true description of critical events in the formation of the State of Israel, especially the 1948 war and the flight of the Palestinian refugees. According to the post-Zionist scholar Ilan

Pappe, these historians, despite their important contributions to the study of the early years of the state, were unable to undermine the foundations of the Zionist consensus and ideology. Only scholars who are conscious of their methodology and constantly examine the relations between knowledge and politics can truly be considered post-Zionist, he has maintained. Post-Zionists argue that scholars who claim to be objective and operate from the assumption that there is only one linguistic regime are in fact part of the hegemonic narrative, which disguises its political obligations by claiming to be true and factual.[37]

In the traditional divisions of Israeli politics, in the framework of the Arab-Israeli conflict, the post-Zionists occupy the extreme left flank.[38] However, as the post-Zionists have traced the implications of their theories in a rapidly changing Israeli society, they have, much as other postmodernists have globally, found themselves proposing solutions to societal problems that could best be termed conservative or even reactionary. Adhering to the post-modern claim that any political entity is necessarily oppressive, the only moral option left for the Jews in Israel, they argue, is to nullify the modern Jewish state and its ideological foundations, and return to representations of traditional Judaism.

The post-Zionists regard the Zionist phase in Jewish history as an attempt to become part of the dominant Western culture, to participate in the discourse that seeks to master everything that does not fit within a rigid set of values. Instead, what they call for is a return to the ahistorical "Jews," those who represent the Other (in the case of the Jewish community in Israel, the Other would be the elements that formed Begin's new coalition) in the very discourse that they criticize.

From Amnon Raz Krakotzkin's call to define the Jewish existence in Israel as a diaspora, a cultural ghetto;[39] to Rabbi Michael Lerner's vision of a post-Zionist Israel that embodies Jewish renewal that could, as he put it, truly become a light unto the nations;[40] to Ophir and Azoulay's claim that the Zionist decision to grant primacy to Modern Hebrew over the languages of the immigrants caused the loss of Jewish cultural memory and dramatically narrowed its scope;[41]

to Danny Efraty's argument that, although Zionism preferred the nation of Israel to Judaism, post-Zionism would free Judaism from the grip of Israeli nationalism and allow it an autonomous existence and a renewed legitimacy[42]—various post-Zionist thinkers have sought to undermine the legitimacy of Israel as a modern Jewish state and instead offer a postmodern alternative that relies on traditional images and cultural conventions that rely on pre-Zionist images of Judaism.

The architectural critic Charles Jencks declared that modern architecture died when the infamous Pruitt-Igoe scheme was given the coup de grace in 1972. According to Jencks, this urban housing project epitomized the modern ambition to create an enlightened architectural space—a rational and healthy environment that was supposed to instill these virtues in its inhabitants. However, its failure (and ultimate destruction), according to Jencks, meant the end of the modern period in architecture and the birth of a new era—a postmodern era in which architects would no longer reinvent spaces but would eclectically rely on traditional forms and styles.[43]

Similarly, the post-Zionists see Zionism as an attempt to create a new national space that would imbue its inhabitants with the values of modernity that rationalize and legitimize the use of power—a space that, they claim, needs to be deconstructed and replaced with the array of cultural entities that comprise the Palestinian landscape, one of which is a Jewish cultural space in Palestine.

Postmodernism declared the death of the modern subject as the central point of the intelligible universe. Instead of an epistemological regime that has a clear center, it offers a deconstruction of texts, a process by which the one who manufactures the critique and exposes the text's power mechanism becomes himself part of the text. Thus the human subject loses its autonomous position and becomes but another symbol in an endless series of signs and images. Zionism, as a modernist movement, sought to create the new Hebrew subject as the centerpiece of its historical revolution. The post-Zionists, like the early Revisionists, seek to destroy this subject and abolish the differences—homeland/exile, Hebrew/Jew—that, they claim, constitute it.[44]

Hegel, from his dialectical viewpoint, scornfully equated Judaism with nihilism, with the desert, with eternal wanderings that lead to no objective goal. Judaism, he claimed, concealed God and offered no real opportunity to understand him as an objective presence. Judaism left only a trace of the divine, a name without a referent, and covered the endless wanderings in search of the transcendental with laws.[45] Lyotard, on the other hand, from a postmodern perspective, celebrated the wandering Jew as the one that managed to escape the Paulinian/Western desire to unify the divine and the world, to secularize culture. As we have seen, this is what Max Silverman described as the postmodern fascination with the Jew as the nomad par excellence.[46]

"The jews," as a sign of resistance to power, can exist only within a foreign dominant discourse that attempts to master and eventually annihilate them. Zionism attempted to alter the history of domination and elimination and transform the Jew from the passive Other, the constant object of persecutions, into an active historical subject, to overcome what it saw as the long period of submission and passivity that marked the Jewish experience in the Diaspora. For the Zionist ideologues, after the Jews lost their political independence and were forced out of their ancient homeland, they ceased to be a normal nation that controlled its historical destiny. And what the Zionists called for was the return of the Jewish people to the normal course of world history. Post-Zionism, on the other hand, has called on the Jews in Israel to leave this historical process, which is ultimately what the Revisionists called for more than sixty years earlier. To save the "jews," that which eludes the oppression of modern civilization, Israel, must be eliminated as a Zionist entity to make way for the desert, the only place where, to paraphrase Hegel, the "jew" can exist as the negator of dialectics.

At the core of the revision of mainstream Zionism by Jabotinsky (and his contemporary Revisionist ideologues) was an attempt to eliminate the movement's universal character, and, at the end, this is what the post-Zionists call for. The Revisionist ideologues believed that they were living at the end of an era. Like Nietzsche, Spengler, and Pound, they believed that Western civilization was about to make a radical leap from the age of rationalism and universalism to a new epoch of vitality and power. As the literary scholar Leon Surette has argued, Derrida, from a postmodern perspective, similarly felt that the era of logocentrism and rationality had come to an end and a new era free from the tyranny of rationality and its monopoly over truth had arrived.[47] The post-Zionists too believe that they are the heralds of a new era that would free the Jews in Palestine from the grip of Zionist ideology, or, as Laurence Silberstein put it, "To its proponents, Post Zionism is an outcome of a genuine need, the need to overcome a crisis of understanding, produced by the inability of the old categories to account for the world."[48]

For the post-Zionists the attempt to expose the means by which Zionism asserts its power leads to a call for a new form of power that is irrational and arbitrary but just as powerful, though unpredictable and thus more dangerous, as the one that they seek to replace. Zionism, they argue, is a structure that harnesses power for the service of a certain group (by tying it to a specific representation of reality), while they, on the other hand, seek to unleash this power and democratize it (make it accessible for everyone).

The Silver Platter in Memory of Hilmi Shusha, a pamphlet anthology that commemorates the murder of a Palestinian youth by a West Bank settler, is one of the more complete political and ideological manifestations of post-Zionism. One of its editors, Haim Lusky, described the anthology as an opportunity for the post-Zionists and post-Israelis to mourn publicly the death and suffering of the Other in a country and society, which like any other product of the Enlightenment, is in a state of turmoil and disintegration.[49]

In "Hilmi Shusha: A Eulogy Without Words," Adam Tennenbaum made the following argument in the pamphlet with regard to the debate between Zionists and post-Zionists: "This is not a struggle about peace. This is a struggle between different perceptions of violence, violence that nullifies the other and violence that accepts the other. . . . Thought itself, when it negates everything that has to be negated, becomes a supreme kind of violence. This violence is not dialectic because it leaves behind no memory; it is wasteful."[50]

Starting from the postmodern view of politics as an oppressive power, Tennenbaum issues a metaphorical battle cry, calling for a pure violence that is possible only at the level of representation. Tennenbaum regards the postmodern view of reality as a web of power relations that are recognizable only through linguistic practices, the only way to guarantee freedom from the restrictions imposed on us by modern culture and its political manifestations. He calls for the aesthetization of reality—a state in which one is not limited by necessity and can rise to a higher form of violence, which transcends the limits of history and politics—what he considers to be the postmodern/Zionist condition of liberated violence.[51]

While a leftist revolution, and Zionism in its early stages certainly wanted to be one, sought to alter real historical and social conditions, the postmodern revisionists of Zionism want to rearrange the sphere of symbolic practices to create a cultural environment that would free individuals from the constraints imposed on them by modern culture.

The literary critic Paul Morrison, following Walter Benjamin's assertion that the Right sees its salvation in giving the masses not their right but a chance to express themselves, has claimed that "poststructuralism, in turn, sees its subversive power in deconstructing expression. That is, the poststructuralist fetishization of the determining power of the signifier risks perpetuating the mystification it seeks to expose."[52] Ultimately, today's post-Zionist/postmodern critics of the Enlightenment project, who maintain that participating in a dialectic game under hegemonic discursive practices only reaffirms their authority, are engaged in a form of a symbolic/conservative revolution.

As the historian Daniel Gutwein put it, "[Post-Zionism] attacks the clear modernist and the social-democratic nature of Zionism and presents it as an oppressive force, the emancipation from which can be achieved only by the dissolution of its collectivist structure and by the privatization of Israeli identity."[53] To Gutwein, the multiculturalism of the post-Zionists is a neoliberal ideology that grew out of the interaction of such forces as globalization, privatization, and postmodernism; post-Zionist multiculturalism disguises the abuse and oppression that are an integral part of free-market competition while representing itself as a democratizing and liberating factor.[54]

The postmodernists see the politics of identity, which are determined by the totality of discursive practices, as the only path to political redemption. This form of political revisionism does not seek readily achievable goals, it does not pick and choose its battles—it is concerned with a grand campaign, one that attacks the core of the national identity, or, as Lyotard styled it, "Let us wage war on totality," a totality that becomes an aesthetic condition and replaces reality as the final arbiter in political and moral judgments. Rather than fight for rights, the postmodernists are concerned with ensuring access to representation and expression.

The theorist and critic Slavoj Žižek, writing about postmodern politics, has argued that proper politics are practiced when demands are not simply part of the negotiations of interests but function as the metaphoric condensation of the global restructuring of the entire social space. Žižek has drawn a clear distinction between this kind of politics and the postmodern politics of identity, whose goal is exactly the opposite—the assertion of one's particular identity within the existing social structure.[55] Žižek calls it incessant diversification—where the multiculturalist and the ethnic fundamentalist meet against the background of capitalist globalization. And that is precisely the nature of the post-Zionist political critique. It seeks to alter the way reality is represented while keeping the power structure intact.

The post-Zionist critique can exist only in a nonreferential, nonteleological play of language, in a semiotic desert that has no rational or transcendental center—a desert that becomes a republic of signs, where each and every member of the collective enjoys full access to symbolic capital, while firmly maintaining the existing material differences and power relations. The post-Zionists want to lead the Jews in Israel beyond the boundaries of modernity and rationality and go to what Jabotinsky described as the sphere that lies beyond reach of Western civilization and its ideological legacy.[56]

The writer and critic Gadi Taub has argued that post-Zionism was inspired by two postmodern intellectual traditions: the French poststructuralist assault on truth and universal values that brought such Nietzschean notions as will and power back to the mainstream of the academic and intellectual discourse; and American pragmatism, which in recent years under the guise of postmodernism has revived in American intellectual circles the Jeffersonian suspicion of all forms of centralized authority and collectivism and to liberate the individual by dismantling all centers of power.[57] According to Taub, "This all becomes very clear when we go back to the Zionist ideology that the post-Zionists rebelled against, an ideology that placed at its core a state-led economy, a wide social system and a tradition that emphasizes equality. The post-Zionists threw the social-democratic baby with the waters of the 'colonial' bathtub. They replaced the 'hegemonic oppression' of Zionism with a 'plurality of narratives' that undermines the Israeli collective memory."[58]

Zionism tried to bring together the particular needs of the Jewish people and the universal values in the tradition of the Enlightenment. Mainstream Zionism sought to create a state that would provide a particular group with a political framework (which they have been denied of for centuries) that would promote such ideals as equality and collective responsibility. The post-Zionists in the name of the postmodern attack on grand narratives and all forms of collectivism have sought to challenge Zionism's claims to be a liberating force and present it as an oppressive movement.

Removed from any true practical and political considerations, they are the modern-day champions of the cultural and intellectual attack on the heritage of the Enlightenment in the name of true Jewish salvation. As such they are the cultural and intellectual heirs of Jabotinsky's Revisionist vision, which sought to free the Zionist movement from the perceived tyranny of the Laborites and allow the Jewish people to discover their authentic (liberated) nature.

For nearly half a century Revisionist ideology was reduced to a rather limited version of Jabotinsky's view of Jewish-Arab relations in Palestine; revisionism became exclusively identified with the concept of the iron wall. The ideology of Jabotinsky, Achimeir, Greenberg, Yevin, and their fellow Revisionists addressed a multitude of subject matters that sought to refashion every aspect of modern Jewish life and create new forms of Jewish identity. For them new Jews were not going to be strictly defined by the parameters of their power relations with an external enemy. They envisioned new forms of power that sprang from the individual's own authentic urges and from the very contradictions that defined modern culture and the tensions that it created between the particular and the universal.

Revisionism was, first and foremost, an attack on modernity; it was an attempt to revise the course of Jewish history and release it from the hands of the champions of such ideals as progress, rationality, and universal rights. At the end of the twentieth century the post-Zionist debates rekindled some themes that the first generation of Revisionists explored: They brought the conflict between the adherents of the Enlightenment and their critics back to the center of the Israeli public discussion. The post-Zionists have redrawn the lines of the political debate in Israel between Left and Right, returning the Left's critics to the role that they occupied in the interwar period as the opponents of the Enlightenment project and its core values.

Notes

All translations into English, unless otherwise stated, are mine.

Introduction

1. *Ha-Yarden,* December 3, 1935.

2. Martin Buber, "Ha-Halutz ve-Olamo" (The pioneer and his world), quoted in Shimoni, *The Zionist Ideology,* 234.

3. Ben Gurion, "Avodah Ivrit" (Hebrew labor), in Becker, *Mishnato shel David Ben Gurion* (The teachings of David Ben Gurion), 245.

4. Benjamin Lubotzky, "He'ara al ha-Musar ve-ha-Hagana" (A remark on morality and defense), *Madrich Beitar* 3 (1933): n.p.

5. Y. Cohen, "Biryonim" (Hoodlums), in *Kitvei Ya'acov Cohen, Shirim* (The writings of Ya'acov Cohen, Poems), 293 – 94.

6. Leone Carpi, the head of the Revisionist Party in Italy who hosted the group in Italy, wrote to the movement's executive in Paris that the young Beitarists caused great damage to the hotel in which they stayed in Milan, and he asked that the movement's executive pay for the damages. See Carpi to Executive of Union of Zionist Revisionists, Zionist Central Archives, S25-2088.

Interestingly, in 1946 Brando played the part of David—a young Holocaust survivor on a journey to Palestine to join the underground militia—in the Broadway production of *A Flag Is Born,* a play written by Ben Hecht and produced by the American League for a Free Palestine, an organization created by Hillel Kook, the most prominent Revisionist activist in the United States in the 1940s. See Rafael Medoff, *Militant Zionism in America: The Rise and Impact of the Jabotinsky Movement in the United States, 1926–1948* (Tuscaloosa, Ala., 2002) 154 – 55.

7. See an internal memorandum of the Italian branch of Beitar regarding the establishment of a Beitar training school in Italy (Jabotinsky Institute [hereafter, JI] G14/2).

8. See Blum, *The Other Side of Modernism,* 145.

9. Abba Achimeir, "Fisiocratiut ve-Marksismus" (Physiocracy and Marxism), JI P5 14/2.

10. Jabotinsky, "Al ha-Ah—ha-Aleph Bet ha-Hadash" (On the fireplace—The new aleph bet), in *Ba-Derech la-Medinah* (On the way to the state), 89.

11. Jabotinsky, "Ra'ayon Beitar" (The idea of Beitar), in *Ba-Derech la-Medinah* (On the way to the state), 318.

12. Aronoff, "Myths, Symbols, and Rituals of the Emerging State," 175–92, esp. 177.

13. The Revisionists were not represented in most Israeli cultural and academic publications or on the staffs of major newspapers. The collected works of the major Revisionist ideologues were published by their families and ad hoc committees. The Jabotinsky Institute sponsored and published studies of the movement, as did other organizations affiliated with the movement, such as the Tel Hai fund and Misdar (Order) Jabotinsky, and the Revisionist journal *Ha-Umah.* The two major biographies of Jabotinsky, Joseph B. Schechtman's *Rebel and a Statesman* (n.d.) and Shmuel Katz's *Lone Wolf* (1996), were both written by close associates of Jabotinsky's.

14. The historian Benny Morris first used the term *New Historians* in his 1988 article "The New Historiography," 19–23; 99–102. The New Historians are Israeli historians, living in and outside Israel, who in the late 1980s began to question some of the most widely held beliefs about Israel's War of Independence. Benny Morris, Avi Shlaim and others have questioned the basic Zionist narrative that presents Israel as a peaceful victim of Arab aggression, and they lay much of the blame for the Palestinian refugee problem on the Israeli leadership.

15. See Segev, *1949: The First Israelis,* and *The Seventh Million;* Zarthal, *From Catastrophe to Power.* For a comprehensive sociological discussion of the differences between the "old" and "new" historians see Ram, "Zikaron ve-Zehut" (Memory and identity), 9–32.

16. Morris, *1948 and After,* 5.

17. See Weingrod, "How Israeli Culture Was Constructed," 228–39, esp. 228.

18. See Shavit, "Le'umiyut, Historiographia ve-Revisia Historit" (Nationalism, historiography, and historical revision), in Ginosar and Bareli *Tzionut* (Zionism), 264–76.

19. See Shapiro, *The Road to Power;* Shindler, *The Land Beyond Promise;*

Peleg, *Begin's Foreign Policy*; Sprinzak, *The Ascendance of Israel's Radical Right*; Rowland, *The Rhetoric of Menachem Begin*.

20. Shavit, *Jabotinsky and the Revisionist Movement*, 15.

21. Ibid., 23.

22. Sternhell, *Ha-Mahshava ha-Fashistit le-Gevanei'a* (The fascist thought and its variations), 9.

23. In using the term *radical Right*, I am alluding to what Ze'ev Sternhell described as the cultural and intellectual rebellion against the heritage of the Enlightenment that swept Europe at the end of the nineteenth century and the beginning of the twentieth century and preceded the rise of organized fascist parties, or what David Carroll termed *cultural fascism*. See Sternhell, *Yesodot ha-Fashism* (The birth of fascist ideology), 1, and Carroll, *French Literary Fascism*, esp. 6–7.

24. Foucault, "Power and Strategies," 139.

25. "Brith ha-Biryonim" (The brotherhood of hoodlums), JI K/14. See also Eldad, "Jabotinsky Distorted," 27–39, for an example of the Revisionists' reaction to the allegations that Jabotinsky was a fascist or influenced by fascist thought.

1. Between Left and Right

1. Jabotinsky, "Sipur Yami" (The story of my times), in *Autobiographia*, 27.

2. Ibid. As the historian Michael Stanslawski, in his study of Jabotinsky's early career, has shown—despite Jabotinsky's efforts in his later autobiographical writings, and the efforts of his followers, to portray him as committed to the Zionist cause from early in his public career—Jabotinsky became thoroughly involved in Zionist politics only in his midtwenties.

3. Stanislawski, *Zionism and the Fin de Siecle*, 130–32.

4. Jabotinsky, "Mored Or" (Rebel), in *Umah ve-Hevrah* (Nation and society), 99–110, esp. 102.

5. The historian Jehudah Reinharz has argued that Jabotinsky faced strong opposition to his militaristic ideas from both the official and unofficial Zionist leadership. He wrote that in a meeting in Copenhagen in June 1915, Zionist leaders rejected Jabotinsky's ideas and claimed that they would be impossible to realize and would put people in great danger. See Reinharz, *Chaim Weitzmann*, 80–82.

6. Jabotinsky to Allenby, in *Michtavim* (Letters), 32.

7. Jabotinsky to Churchill, May 7, 1921, PRO 733/17A.

8. For Jabotinsky's criticism of British policies in the early years of the British mandate in Palestine, see Jabotinsky, "Yehudei Hasut" (Jews of patronage), in *Umah ve-Hevrah* (Nation and society), 183–94.

9. At its height Ha-Tzohar won slightly more than 20 percent of the votes to the 17th Zionist Congress in 1931. In the next Zionist Congress (1933) Ha-Tzohar nearly doubled the number of votes it received. However, in the 18th congress the number of delegates decreased dramatically and the Revisionists had only a sixth of the overall number of delegates.

10. The most complete discussion of the split that led to the formation of Ha-Tzah is Even's *Ha-Pilug ba-Tzionut* (The schism in Zionism).

11. See Dov Alfon, "Ha-Gada ha-Ma'aravit, ha-Gada ha-Smalit" (The West Bank, the left bank), *Haaretz,* May 9, 2000.

12. According to Yonathan Shapiro, the Revisionists were driven by the totality of the principle of national pride, which prevented them from such practical activities as finding material resources to achieve their goals. See Shapiro, *The Road to Power,* 48.

13. Jabotinsky, "Shir ha-Giben" (Song of the humpback), in *Shirim* (Poems), 297–99.

14. See Stein-Ashkenazy, *Beitar be-Eretz-Israel* (Beitar in Eretz Israel), 141.

15. See Shapiro, *The Road to Power,* 56.

16. Around 1936 Jabotinsky embarked on a series of meetings with Polish officials to organize the evacuation of Polish Jewry (and Jews from other Eastern European countries) to Palestine. Jabotinsky felt that the only way to solve the problem of raging anti-Semitism in Poland was Jewish emigration—which for him also meant the establishment of a Jewish majority in Palestine. However, the program never materialized. See Weinbaum, "Jabotinsky and the Poles," in Polonsky, *Polin,* 5:156–72.

17. See Kister, *Etzel* (The Irgun), 78.

18. Begin, "Jabotinsky Set Us upon the Path of Freedom," v–vi.

19. Jabotinsky, "Ken Lishbor" (Yes, to bust), in *Ba-Sa'ar* (In the storm), 45–53.

20. The pamphlet was edited by a Mapai activist, Yoseph Bankover, and circulated by Ahdut Press. It was published at the height of the campaign for the 18th Zionist Congress and was intended to rally Jewish workers against the Revisionists, who were presented in the pamphlet as the enemies of Hebrew labor. See *Hazit ha-Bisquit,* Lavon Institute Archive.

21. Ben Gurion, *Tnuat ha-Poalim ve ha-Revisionismus* (The labor movement and revisionism), 57.

22. For example, Abba Achimeir's lawyer, Zvi Eliyahu Cohen, stated on behalf of his client that "if the Hitlerists renounced their anti-Semitism, then we would support them. Without the Hitlerists, Germany would have been lost. Yes, Hitler saved Germany" (*Doar ha-Yom,* March 5, 1932). Dr. Wolfgang Von Weisel, a leading Revisionist activist, claimed that the

Revisionists saw themselves as Hitler's partners and not the Marxists' (*Hazit ha-Am,* September 13, 1932), and an editorial in *Hazit ha-Am* declared that beneath the anti-Semitic cover of Nazism was an important principle of anti-Marxism that the Revisionists accepted wholeheartedly (*Hazit ha-Am,* March 30, 1933).

23. See *Hazit ha-Am,* June 9, 1933. See also Yohanan Fugravinsky, "Brith Stalin-Ben Gurion-Hitler" (The covenant of Stalin, Ben Gurion, and Hitler), *Hazit ha-Am,* June 16, 1933. In this article, which was published on the day of Arlozoroff's assassination, the writer described Arlozoroff as a petty merchant willing to deal with Hitler and who for money and wealth would be willing to deal away the most sacred Jewish assets and values.

24. One of the first acts of Menachem Begin as prime minister of Israel was to form an official inquiry committee that would investigate the Arlozoroff case. It reached no final conclusions regarding the identity of the killer or killers.

25. Minutes, Mapai Central Committee meeting, Labor Movement Archive (hereafter, LMA), 2-23-1934-7.

26. Ibid.

27. Eventually, the agreement was brought to a vote of all Histadrut members in 1935. Nearly 57 percent voted to reject the agreement.

28. Minutes, Mapai Central Committee meeting, LMA, 2-25-1934-8.

29. Ibid.

30. Ibid.

31. The debate about the agreements continued in 1935, and the rhetoric persisted as Labor activists continued to argue vehemently that dealing with the Revisionists meant dealing with and giving in to fascism (Minutes, Mapai Central Committee meeting, LMA, 2-22-1935-18). This view of the Revisionists as a radical right-wing movement was not limited to the political scene in Palestine. The leaders of American Jewry described the Revisionists in similar language. For example, in 1935 Rabbi Stephen Wise described the Revisionists as a movement governed by such concepts as militarism and social exploitation, and he argued that they were a Hebrew or Yiddish type of fascism. See David S. Wyman and Rafael Medoff, *A Race against Death: Peter Bergson, America, and the Holocaust* (New York, 2002), 19.

32. According to Ya'acov Shavit, because the Revisionists had no access to the centers of political and social power of prestatehood Palestine, even if they had certain fascist characteristics, they did not have the means to test them (Shavit, *Jabotinsky and the Revisionist Movement,* 372).

33. Ibid., 350.

34. Segev, *Yemey ha-Kalaniyot* (Two Palestines), 173. See also Jad

Ne'eman, "Mi Yiten 100 Lai la-Kolno'a" (Who would give 100 Israeli pounds for the cinema?), *Haaretz,* December 9, 1999. It is important to note, however, that not all those who are considered new historians share Segev's view of Zionist revisionism. Benny Morris, for example, wrote that he did not want to label his historiographical approach as Revisionist history because it "conjures up the faces of Ze'ev Jabotinsky and Menachem Begin, respectively, the founder/prophet and latter-day leader of the Revisionist Movement in Zionism. The Revisionists, unpragmatic, right-wing deviants from the mainstream of the Zionist experience, claimed all of Palestine and the east bank of the Jordan River for the Jews. Until 1977, their place was on the fringe of Zionist and Israeli history, though since then their vision, albeit in diluted from, has dominated the political arena in Jerusalem. To call the new history 'revisionism' is to cause unnecessary confusion and, to some, anguish" (Morris, *1948 and After,* 6).

35. Tom Segev, "Eich Omrim Transfer be-Ivrit" (How to say transfer in Hebrew), *Haaretz,* February 12, 1999.

36. See Heller, "Ha-Monism shel ha-Matarh o ha-Monism shel ha-Emtza'im?" (The monism of the goal and the monism of means?), 315 – 69. See also Stein-Ashkenazy, *Beitar be-Eretz Israel* (Beitar in Eretz Israel), 40, and Shavit, *Ha-Mitologiot shel ha-Yamin* (The mythologies of the right), 226.

37. Abba Achimeir's speech before the Conference of the Union of Zionists-Revisionists in Eretz Israel, April 29, 1932, JI G/2.

38. Ornstein, *Be-Kvalim* (In bondage), 54.

39. See Even, *Ha-Pilug ba-Tzionut* (The schism in Zionism), 116 –17.

40. In 1933 a group headed by Me'ir Grossman, a member of Ha-Tzohar's executive committee, called for the removal of the maximalists from the Revisionist movement. When its efforts failed, Grossman's group left the Revisionist movement and created a new party, the Hebrew State Party. Grossman's party, however, did not pose a real threat to Jabotinsky and the Revisionists. In the elections to the 18th Zionist Congress that year Jabotinsky's Revisionists received more than 95,000 votes, while Grossman's party received only slightly fewer than 12,000 votes. See Even, *Ha-Pilug ba-Tzionut* (The schism in Zionism), 158 – 59.

41. Abba Achimeir, "Keta'im mi-Yoman Soher" (Excerpts from a diary of a warden), *Ha-Yarden,* November 29, 1935.

42. Y. H. Yevin, "Hush ha-Bniya" (The sense of building), *Kuntras* 193 (1924): n.p.

43. Uri Zvi Greenberg, "El Ever Moskva" (Toward Moscow) *Kuntras* 157 (1924): n.p.

44. See Fischer, *History and Prophecy,* 159.

45. Abba Gaissinowitsch, "Bemerkungen zu Spenglers Auffassung Russlands" (Remarks on Spengler's concept of Russia), 29 – 40, Achimeir Archive.

46. In an article from 1927 Achimeir argued that only in Austria and Russia can one find true Marxism, because Marxism is a religion, and these two countries have a strong tradition of popular religion that accepts the religious beliefs of the political and social elites and does not question the characteristics of the dominant religion but just practices it faithfully. Abba Achimeir, "Yad Israel ve-Kol Ya'acov" (The hand of Israel and the voice of Jacob), *Haaretz*, November 24, 1927.

47. Gaissinowitsch, "Bemerkungen zu Spenglers Auffassung Russlands" (Remarks on Spengler's Concept of Russia), 57, Achimeir Archive.

48. Abba Achimeir, "Van der Valde o ha-Sotzialismus ha-Ma'aravi" (Van der Valde or Western socialism), *Haaretz*, September 13, 1928. Uri Zvi Greenberg also viewed communist Russia as a spiritual dictatorship that united and mobilized the masses. See *Kuntras* 11 (1925): n.p.

49. Sternhel, *Ha-Mahshava ha-Fashistit li-Gvaneiha* (The fascist thought and its variations), 27–28.

50. Y. H. Yevin, "Le-Tashtesh lo Narshe" (We will not allow to blur), *Doar ha-Yom*, September 26, 1929.

51. Abba Achimeir, "Zru'im ve-Pezurim" (Planted and scattered), *Hazit ha-Am*, August 16, 1932.

52. Jabotinsky, "Eglat ha-'Klei-Zemer'" (The musicians' wagon), in Ba-Derech la-Medinah (On the way to the state), 271.

53. Jabotinsky to Y. H. Yevin, August 9, 1932, JI 2/22/2/A1.

54. Jabotinsky, "Anu ha-Amerika'im" (We the Americans), *Ha-Tzafon*, June 4, 1926.

55. Jabotinsky, "Italia," *Ha-Yarden*, August 21, 1936.

56. See Jabotinsky, "Ilu Ha'iti Tzair bi-Shnat 1932" (If I were young in 1932), published in *Ha-Umah* 46 (March 1976): 181– 83. See also Haramaty, *Ha-Hinuch ha-Ivry be-Mishnat Jabotinsky* (The Hebrew education in Jabotinsky's teachings), 1– 4.

57. Abba Achimeir, "Leshe'elat ha-Rega, mi-Yomano shel Fashistan " (Issues of the present, From a diary of a fascist), *Doar ha-Yom*, October 10, 1928.

58. Y. H. Yevin, "Opozitzia o Tenuat Shihrur" (Opposition or a liberation movement), *Hazit ha-Am*, August 26, 1932.

59. Abba Achimeir, "A Speech in Fifth World Revisionist Conference in Vienna," *Hazit ha-Am*, September 13, 1932.

60. *Hazit ha-Am*, September 20, 1932.

61. The Statement of the President of the World Union of Zionist Revisionist, March 22, 1933. JI C/2.

62. Jabotinsky to Michael Samulovich, October 8, 1933, in *Michtavim* (Letters), 300–3.

63. Jabotinsky, "Manhig" (Leader), in *Zichronot Ben-Dori* (A contemporary's recollections), 216.

64. Jabotinsky, "Eineni Ma'amin" (I do not believe), in *Felitonim* (Feuilleton), 84. Raphaella Bilski Ben-Hur, in her study of Jabotinsky's social and political thought, has attempted to present Jabotinsky as a liberal and democratic ideologue. In discussing his commitment to the values of democracy, she used the same quote. However, she omitted the last sentence of that paragraph: "That prejudices would disappear by the grace of democracy—this, I believe, no sensible person would argue," where Jabotinsky clearly distinguished between democracy as an ideal and as a practical political doctrine. See Bilski Ben-Hur, *Kol Yahid Hu Melech* (Each individual a king), 43–44.

65. Jabotinsky, "Demokratia" (Democracy), *Ha-Yarden*, October 25, 1934.

66. Jabotinsky to the Beitar Cadets in Civitavecchia, November 20, 1934, JI A1/2/24/3.

67. Abba Achimeir, "Ha-Yehudim be-Germania" (The Jews in Germany), JI P5/2/10.

68. Jabotinsky to the Hebrew Youth in Poland, February 27, 1927, JI A1/17/2.

69. Aharon Zvi Propes wrote that when Jabotinsky visited the first Beitar branch in Latvia in 1925, the first thing he did was give the young members a lesson in military drills. See "Beitar: ha-Avar ve-ha-Atid" (Beitar the past and the future), *Ha-Umah* 40 (September 1974): 206.

70. Jabotinsky, "Shir Beitar" (The song of Beitar), in *Shirim* (Poems), 205.

71. Jabotinsky, "Sipur Yamay" (The story of my times), in *Autobiographia*, 29.

72. Ibid.

73. Ze'ev Jabotinsky, "Muvan ha-Avanturism" (The meaning of adventurism), *Hazit ha-Am*, August 5, 1932.

74. Jabotinsky to the Hebrew Youth in Poland, February 27, 1927, JI A1/17/2.

75. Jabotinsky, "Ra'ayon Beitar" (The idea of Beitar), 319–20.

76. Ibid., 323.

77. Ze'ev Jabotinsky, "Otto Max Nordau" (That Max Nordau), *Hazit ha-Am*, February 16, 1933.

78. Ze'ev Jabotinsky, "Hurdemu be-Kloroform" (Anaesthetized with chloroform), *Ha-Mashkif*, June 16, 1939, quoted in Shimoni, *The Zionist Ideology*, 314.

79. See Jabotinsky, "Sipur Yami" (The story of my times), in *Autobiographia*, 30.

80. Stanislawski, *Zionism and the Fin de Siecle*, 132–33.

81. Jabotinsky, "Hartza'a al ha-Historia ha-Israelit" (A lecture on Israeli history), in *Umah ve-Hevrah* (Nation and society), 161.

82. Y. H. Yevin, "Le-Hach'sharat ha-Dor" (For the preparation of the generation), *Doar ha-Yom*, July 2, 1930.

83. Ya'acov Cohen, "Jabotinsky," *Mishmar ha-Yarden* 5 (March 1935): n.p.

2. Monism

1. Gasman, *Haeckel's Monism and the Birth of Fascist Ideology*, 9–10. While Gasman makes a strong case for the importance of scientific monism in the development of fascist ideology, it is hard to ignore the large number of studies that point to the multitude of intellectual, social, and ideological factors that influenced and guided the ideologues of the European radical Right. See Trevor-Roper, "The Phenomenon of Fascism," 21; Neocleous, *Fascism*, ix; Sternhell, *Neither Right nor Left*, 3.

2. Gasman argues that this primitivism was at the core of the radical Right's rebellion against the humanistic and moral values of Western culture (*Haeckel's Monism*, 24). See also Ernst Nolte's analysis of the anti-transcendental nature of fascism in *Three Faces of Fascism*, 537–43.

3. Gasman, *Haeckel's Monism*, 30–31.

4. E. Cohen, "Israel as a Post-Zionist Society," 204.

5. Quoted in Arnoff, "Myths, Symbols, and Rituals," 178.

6. Ze'ev Jabotinsky, "Se'ara Mesaya'at" (A supporting storm), in *Ba-Sa'ar* (In the storm), 227. See Heller, "Ha-Monism shel ha-Matarh o ha-Monism shel ha-Emtzaim?" (Monism of goal or monism of means), 326, and "Ze'ev Jabotinsky and the Revisionist Revolt," 51–67.

7. Ze'ev Jabotinsky, "Tzion ve Komonism" (Zion and communism), in *Ba-Derech la-Medinah* (On the way to the state), 64.

8. Jabotinsky, "Al Tasimu Aleichem Sha'atnez" (Do not wear clothes of mixed fabrics), in *Ba-Derech la-Medinah* (On the way to the state), 74.

9. On the transformation of Judaism see Abba Achimeir, "Baruch mi-Magnaza ve ha-Na'ar Hana Ben Elyakum" (Baruch of Mainz and the young Hana Ben Elyakum), JI P5/2/8, and "Lo Ligro'a ki im le-Hosif" (Not to decrease but increase), *Doar Ha-Yom*, October 24, 1929.

10. "Ha-Tehiah shel Shlomo Neuman" (The revival of Shlomo Neuman), *Hazit ha-Am*, November 11, 1932.

11. Dov Chomsky, "Am ha-Sefer" (The People of the Book), *Madrich Beitar*, September 1933.

12. See Isaac Gurfinkel, "Shloshet ha-Hitzim" (The three arrows), *Ha-Yarden,* October 25, 1934.

13. A. Achimeir, "Ha-Mahapecha ha-Israelit ha-Gedolah" (The great Israeli revolution), in *Ha-Tziunut ha-Mahapchanit,* 242.

14. Spengler, *The Decline of the West,* 2:209.

15. Ibid., 207.

16. Ibid., 219.

17. Ibid., 323.

18. Abba Gaissinowitsch, "Bemerkungen zu Spenglers Auffassung Russlands" (Remarks on Spengler's Concept of Russia), 10.

19. Ibid., 11.

20. According to Achimeir, Greece and Rome underwent the same historical process of decline as a result of territorial losses. Achimeir argued that Europe, whose dominant forces migrated to North America in the modern age, is experiencing the same historical fate as the power shifts from the old continent to the New World. For Achimeir's analysis of the emerging American culture, see "Ha-Olam be-Tarpah" (The world in 1927–28), *Haaretz,* September 26, 1927.

21. Achimeir argued that during the Diaspora Jews preferred the book of Chronicles, which is more Jewish in nature and represents the clergy, to the Book of Kings, which is more political and secular in its historiographical outlook. This, according to Achimeir, typifies the Jewish Diaspora, which turned away from the political and the national and toward the Jewish and international. See Abba Achimeir, "Baruch of Mainz and the young Hana Ben Elyakum."

22. Abba Achimeir, "Raskolnikov ba-Keleh ha-Merkazi" (Raskolnikov in the central jail), *Ha-Yarden* 459 (1935), special edition.

23. Abba Achimeir, "Anti Mah o Madu'a Ein Anu Sotzialistim," (Against what, or why we are not socialists), JI P5/2/8.

24. See Abba Achimeir, *Brith Habiryonim* (The brotherhood of zealots), published by the Jabotinsky Institute, 5.

25. See Fischer, *History and Prophecy,* 230.

26. Abba Achimeir, "Michtav el ha-No'ar" (A letter to the youth), *Avukah,* September 1934.

27. Abba Achimeir, "Gniza" (Concealing), JI P5/2/9.

28. Y. H. Yevin, "Shki'at ha-Humanismus" (The decline of humanism), *Ha-Yarden,* January 18, 1935.

29. Y. H. Yevin, "Al ha-Emet ha-Peshutah Shelanu" (On our simple truth), *Hazit ha-Am,* June 17, 1932.

30. Y. H. Yevin, "Mah Zot 'Tziunut Ruhanit" (What is spiritual Zionism?), in Yevin, *Ketavim,* 358.

31. Ibid., 359.

32. Ibid., 359.

33. Jabotinsky, "Boris Shatz," in *Ha-Revisionism ha-Tziony Likrat Mifne* (Zionist revisionism approaching a turning point), 52 (emphasis added).

34. Gasman, *Haeckel's Monism*, 270. On the revisionist approach of the Italian syndicalists and their perception of violence as a revolutionary force, see Sternhell, *Ha-Mahshave ha-Fashistit* (The fascist thought and its variations), 28–29.

35. Ferri, *Socialism and Modern Science*, 95 (emphasis added).

36. Jabotinsky, "Geza" (Race), in *Umah ve Hevrah* (Nation and society), 126.

37. Ibid., 128.

38. Gasman, *Haeckel's Monism*, 26.

39. Jabotinsky, "Hilufei Mahma'ot" (Exchanges of compliments), in *Umah ve Hevrah* (Nation and society), 154.

40. Jabotinsky, "Tzion ve Komonism" (Zion and communism), in *Ba-Derech la-Medinah* (On the way to the state), 61.

41. Ze'ev Jabotinsky, "Tikkun ve-Hashlamat ha-Safa ha-Ivrit" (Mending and completing the Hebrew language), *Ha-Olam*, February 20, 1925.

42. The Beitarist leader Binyamin Lubotzky likened the linguistic condition of the Jews in the Diaspora to Europe in the Middle Ages. Medieval Europe did not have national institutions; it had one central authority—the papacy—and one cosmopolitan language of learning and writing, Latin. Similarly, Jews in the Diaspora were denied the national experience and were forced into a false cosmopolitan existence. See Greenberg, "Tikkun ha-Olam o Hatzalt ha-Umah" (Mending the world or saving the nation), in *Madrich Beitar* 2 (1932): n.p.

43. Uri Zvi Greenberg, "Al Heiter History ve-Shtika Metzuvah" (On historical permission and commanded silence), *Sedan* 3 (1925): n.p.

44. Quoted in Shalom Schwartz, *Jabotinsky Lohem ha-Umah* (Jabotinsky: The nation's warrior), 292.

45. Jabotinsky, "Al ha-Ah—ha-Aleph Bet ha-Hadash" (On the fireplace—The new aleph bet), in *Ba-Derech la-Medinah* (On the way to the state), 88–89.

46. See Shlomo Haramaty, *Ha-Hinuch ha-Ivry be-Mishnato shel Jabotinsky* (The Hebrew education in Jabotinsky's teachings), 59.

47. Jabotinsky, "Le-She'elat ha-Mivtah" (On the question of accent), *Ha-Olam*, February 20, 1925.

48. Jabotinsky, "Al ha-Ah" (On the fireplace), in *Ba-Derech la-Medinah* (On the way to the state), 89–90.

49. As Gasman has shown, Haeckel's monism was not atheistic. He developed a "monistic cosmonogy," which saw the universe as a single spirit that is one with the idea of God. Similarly, the Revisionist attack on the transcendental character of Diaspora Judaism was not atheistic but centered on the philosophical and ideological (Marxist) beliefs that Jews in the Diaspora developed (*Haeckel's Monism*, 60– 64).

50. Y. H. Yevin, "Le-Mi Anu Bonim" (To whom are we building?), *Doar ha-Yom*, July 8, 1930.

51. For Greenberg the Arabs are members of the nation of Edom, which in Greenberg's poetry is the cradle of Christianity, the civilization that throughout history persecuted the Jews. See Uri Zvi Greenberg, *Ezor Magen ve-Neum Ben ha-Dam* (Defense sphere and the speech of the mortal one), 30.

52. Quoted in Morris, *Righteous Victims*, 36.

53. Jabotinsky, "Al Kir ha-Barzel" (On the iron wall), in *Ba-Derech la-Medinah* (On the way to the state), 253.

54. Jabotinsky, "Geza" (Race), in *Umah ve Hevrah* (Nation and society), 128.

55. Jabotinsky, "Ba-Congerss ha-Tzioni 1931" (In the Zionist Congress, 1931), in *Neumim* (Speeches), 121.

56. Jabotinsky, "Rov" (Majority), in *Ba-Derech la-Medinah* (On the way to the state), 197.

57. Jabotinsky, "Ba-Congerss ha-Tzioni 1931" (In the Zionist Congress 1931), in *Neumim* (Speeches), 121.

58. Jabotinsky, "Shulhan Agol im ha-Aravim" (A roundtable with the Arabs), in *Ba-Derech la-Medinah* (On the way to the state), 245.

59. Jabotinsky, "Hartza'ah al ha-Historia ha-Israelit" (A lecture on Israeli history), in *Umah ve-Havrah* (Nation and society), 162.

60. See Lustick, *Arabs in the Jewish State*, 37.

61. In 1937, in light of the Great Arab Revolt, a commission headed by Lord Peel came up with a British partition plan that called for the establishment of two states—one Arab, one Jewish—in Palestine. On the debate about the partition plan see Shapira, *Land and Power*, 271.

62. According to the historian Kenneth W. Stein, by the early 1930s some Zionist leaders had seriously considered the transfer of Palestinian Arabs to Transjordan. See Stein, "One Hundred Years of Social Change," 72. According to Benny Morris, "Ben Gurion clearly wanted as few Arabs as possible to remain in the Jewish State. He hoped to see them flee. . . . But no expulsion policy was ever enunciated and Ben Gurion always refrained from issuing clear or written expulsion orders." See Morris, "Origins of the Palestinian Refugee Problem," 51.

63. In 1928 Jabotinsky published an essay titled "What Do the Revisionist Zionists Demand?" in which he listed a series of reforms that had to take place to achieve the goals of Zionism. With regard to the eastern bank of the Jordan River he claimed: "The first and foremost reform must involve the eastern bank of the Jordan, which is included in the British Mandate, but was taken out of the influence sphere of the Zionist movement. Tearing the eastern bank of the Jordan apart from the land of Israel is a grave historical wrong. . . . Historically, the eastern bank of the Jordan has always been part of the land of Israel; Jews settled there even before the conquest of western Israel." See Jabotinsky, "Ma Rotzim ha-Tzionim ha-Revisionistim" (What do the Revisionist Zionists demand?), in *Ba-Derech la-Medinah* (On the way to the state), 285.

64. Daniel Gasman, *Haeckel's Monism*, 15.

3. A Mobilized Society

1. Y. Kellerman, "Ha-Mishtar ha-Korporativi be-Italia" (The corporative regime in Italy), *Metzuda*, January 1938.

2. See Neocleous, *Fascism*, xi.

3. Pound, *Selected Prose, 1909–1965*, 298.

4. Goux, *Symbolic Economies*, 92.

5. Ibid., 93

6. Ibid., 99.

7. Spengler, *The Decline of the West*, 499–500.

8. Ibid., 481–82.

9. Ibid., 346.

10. See Marsh, *Money and Modernity*, 99.

11. Pound, "Gaudier-Breeska: A Memoir," quoted in Morrison, *The Poetics of Fascism*, 58.

12. Ze'ev Sternhell similarly argues that the radical Right always intended to use the technological advantages of capitalism and never challenged the notion of private property, yet at the same time it rejected the values of liberalism. See *Ha-Mahshava ha-Fashistit* (The fascist thought and its variations), 20. He argues that as the followers of Sorrel moved from socialism to the Right, they remained faithful to the idea that any progress is dependent on market economy: They accepted the reality of capitalist economy and did not challenge its primacy in the West (41–42).

13. See Thompson, *State Control in Fascist Italy*, vi.

14. Benjamin, "The Work of Art in the Age of Mechanical Reproduction," in *Illuminations*, 241.

15. Sternhell, *Ha-Mahshava ha-Fashistit* (The fascist thought and its variations), 24.

16. Neocleous, *Fascism,* 21.

17. According to Sternhell, what united society in the right-wing model was not the material condition of its members but common myths of common origin and national pride that mobilized the nation as a whole (Sternhell, *Yesodot ha-Fashism* [The birth of fascist ideology], 50).

18. Spengler, *The Decline of the West,* 507.

19. "Anu ve-Hem" (Us and them), *Beitar,* special supplement to *Hazit ha-Am,* April 1934.

20. Y. Yanai, "Ma Tzarich Lada'at ha-No'ar ha-Le'umi" (What the national youth has to know), *Avukah,* September 1935.

21. Abba Achimeir, "Michtav el ha-Noar" (A letter to the youth), *Avukah,* September 1935.

22. A. Asaar, "Het'ot ha-Homranut" (The sins of materialism), *Ha-Yarden,* April 12, 1935. The staff of the Jabotinsky Institute and I looked for Assar's first name for weeks but never found it, and similar searches for the full names of other key players also proved fruitless.

23. See Jabotinsky, "Tzion ve Comonism" (Zion and communism), in *Ba-Derech la-Medina* (On the way to the state), 64–65.

24. Aharon Spivak, "Anti–Marxismus" (Anti–Marxism), in Y. H. Yevin, ed., *Hazit ha-No'ar* (The youth front), June 1934 booklet.

25. Binyamin Lubotzky, "Tikkun Olam o Hatzalat ha-Uma" (Mending the world or saving the nation), *Madrich Beitar* 2 (1932): n.p.

26. Abba Achimeir, "Hirhurim shel Boor al Mas ha-Chnasa," (Thoughts of a layman on the income tax), JI P5/2/10, and "Ha-Golem me-Maharal" (The golem of Maharal), JI P5/2/9.

27. Abba Achimeir, "Ha-Mashber ha-Olami ve Sibotaiv" (The world crisis and its causes) *Beitar,* January 1933.

28. Jabotinsky, "Ra'ayon Beitar" (The idea of Beitar), in *Ba-Derech la-Medina* (On the way to the state), 320–21.

29. Heller, "Ze'ev Jabotinsky and the Revisionist Revolt against Materialism," 65.

30. Similarly, Shavit has claimed that Revisionist socioeconomic theory contained contradictory elements, making it look like an adjunct to Revisionists' national and political theory. See Shavit, *Jabotinsky and the Revisionist Movement,* 309.

31. Jabotinsky, "Ma'amad" (Class), in *Umah ve-Hevrah* (Nation and society), 247.

32. See Jabotinsky, "Mavoh le-Torat ha-Meshek (b)" (An introduction to the theory of the market), in *Umah ve-Hevrah* (Nation and society), 219–20.

33. Jabotinsky, "Ha-Muza shel ha-Ofna" (The muse of fashion), in *Felitonim* (Feuilletons), 216.

34. According to Sternhell, this notion of capitalism and private property as the only means to lead society in a revolution was at the heart of the Sorelian transition from antimaterialistic Marxism to the radical Right. See *Yesodot ha-Fascisim* (The birth of fascist ideology), 41–42.

35. Halevi, "Pan-Basilia," in Wirnik, Rubin, and Ramba, *Manhig ha-Dor* (The leader of the generation), 34.

36. Jabotinsky, "Ra'ayon Beitar" (The idea of Beitar), in *Ba-Derech la-Medina* (On the way to the state), 320.

37. In discussing the role of the state in the market, Jabotinsky likened the market to a playground: "What is this similar to? To a garden in which children play every day. In the garden there are five deep and dangerous holes in the ground that pose great peril to the children. And here come those social menders and suggest to strictly monitor the movement of the children—walk left, walk right, run at a certain pace and other such regulations. And I say that all these regulations are unnecessary: I suggest that we simply cover the five holes and let the children run freely." For Jabotinsky the socialists were engaged in futile attempts to rearrange society's infrastructure, whereas the more efficient way to social and economic remedy is found in the superstructure that can mask and hide all social illnesses. See Jabotinsky, "Ma'amad" (Class), in *Umah ve-Havrah* (Nation and society), 242.

38. Jabotinsky, "Al ha-Nep ha-Tziony" (On the Zionist *Nep*, in *Ba-Derech la-Medinah* (On the way to the state), 135.

39. Jabotinsky, "Mi-Zimrat ha-Aretz" (From the fruits of the land), in *Ba-Derech la-Medinah* (On the way to the state), 150.

40. Jabotinsky suggested that the question of "economic propaganda" exceeds in importance such questions as credit and interest. See "Mi-Zimrat ha-Aretz" (From the fruits of the land), in *Ba-Derech la-Medinah* (On the way to the state).

41. The Revisionist Workers Union: A memorandum to the party's branches in Palestine, JI B4/13.

42. Poleskin-Ya'ari, *Ze'ev Jabotinsky: Hayav ve-Pe'ulato* (Ze'ev Jabotinsky: His life and his acts), 46.

43. A manifesto of the National Committee of the National Workers Front, 1929, JI D1/A/4.

44. Jabotinsky, "Al ha-Nep ha-Tziony" (On the Zionist *Nep*), 136. In addition to mandatory national arbitration, Jabotinsky, drawing on the Italian model, suggested establishing a "parliament of trades," which would

represent the interests of both workers and employers in every economic field and ensure that they both work harmoniously.

45. Ben Gurion, *Mi-Ma'amad le-Am* (From class to nation), 225.

46. *Davar,* December 27, 1932, quoted in Shapira and Carpi, *Avodah Ivrit ve Baaya Aravit* (Hebrew Labor and an Arab problem), 146.

47. Jabotinsky, "Ma'amad" (Class), in *Umah ve-Havrah* (Nation and society), 242.

48. Jabotinsky, "Ha-Geulah ha-Sotzialit" (The social redemption), in *Reshimot* (Notes), 299.

49. Jabotinsky, " Ra'ayon ha-Yovel" (The idea of the jubilee), in *Umah ve-Hevrah* (Nation and society), 174.

50. Jabotinsky, "Prakim ba-Philosophia ha-Sotzialit shel ha-Tanach" (Chapters in the social philosophy of the Bible), in *Umah ve-Hevrah* (Nation and society), 186.

51. Ibid., 187.

52. See Jabotinsky, "Materialism Psycho-History (Psychohistorical materialism), in *Umah ve-Hevrah* (Nation and society), 205 – 6.

53. Jabotinsky, "Mavoh le-Torat ha-Meshek (a)" (An introduction to the theory of the market), in *Umah ve-Hevrah* (Nation and society), 197.

54. Schiller, *On the Aesthetic Education of Man,* 25 – 26.

55. Ibid., 80.

56. See Sychreva, *Schiller to Derrida,* 34.

57. Jabotinsky, "Mavoh le-Torat ha-Meshek (b)" (An introduction to the theory of the market), in *Umah ve-Hevrah* (Nation and society), 209.

58. Ibid., 216.

59. Zemach, *Al ha-Yafeh* (On the beautiful), 276 – 77.

60. See Jabotinsky to Ben Gurion, March 30, 1935, in *Michtavim* (Letters), 43. Jabotinsky wrote that the socialist Zionists were overtaken by the beauty of Marxist logic and failed to see its shortcomings.

61. Jabotinsky, "Mavoh le-Torat ha-Meshek (b)" (An introduction to the theory of the market), in *Umah ve-Hevrah* (Nation and society), 205.

62. Jabotinsky, *Shimshon* (Samson the Nazarite), 162.

63. Ibid., 86.

64. Jabotinsky, "Hirhurim al Calcala" (Thoughts about the economy), *Ha-Yarden,* February 3, 1935.

65. Yevin "Anchnu ha-Meshuga'im ve ha-Tza'akanim" (We the crazy and the loud), *Hazit ha-Am,* September 26, 1933.

66. Greenberg, "Ha-Col Macolet" (Everything in a store), in *Kelev Bait* House dog), 36.

67. Greenberg, "Banka'im Yehudim" (Jewish bankers), in *Kelev Bait* (House dog), 15.

68. Pound, *Selected Prose,* 351, 300.

69. In the early years of the State of Israel, the Labor-led government initiated an "austerity program" that included price controls, food rations, and the control of all foreign currency. Uri Zvi Greenberg, who was a member of Israel's first Knesset, was a staunch supporter of the program. As Tom Segev has pointed out, Greenberg wanted it to be the country's permanent constitution. See Segev, *1949,* 298.

70. Yevin, "Lemi Anu Bonim" (For whom are we building), *Do'ar ha-Yom,* July 8, 1930.

71. M. A. Perlmutter, "Al Saf ha-Tekufah—Sof ha-Milhama Beyn ha-Avodah ve ha-Technika" (On the Verge of an Era—The End of the War between Labor and Technology), *Ha-Yarden,* December 2, 1934.

72. Shapira, *Herev ha-Yonah* (The sword of the dove), 268.

73. Ben Gurion, *Mi-Ma'amad le-Am* (From class to nation), 279.

74. *Avukah,* September, 1935, p. 13.

75. See Halevi, "Pan-Basilia" in Wirnik, Rubin, and Ramba, *Manhig ha-Dor* (The leader of the generation), 32.

76. See Avineri's discussion of Borochov's synthesis of Marxism and Zionism in *The Making of Modern Zionism,* 145–50.

77. Ibid., 155.

78. Jabotinsky, "Al ha-Tekes" (On the ceremony), *Hazit ha-Am,* July 5, 1932.

4. The State of Pleasure

1. Aharon Propes, "Hag ha-Zimra" (The festival of singing), *Ba-Tnu'a* 6 (1935), supplement to *Ha-Yarden.*

2. "Be-Shevi ha-Tzura ha-Elohit—Reshamim Revisionistim be-Italia shel ha-Tzayar Re'uven" (In the grip of divine form—Revisionist impressions in Italy of the painter Rubin), *Ha-Tzafon,* June 10, 1927. Rubin (1893–1974), born in Romania and trained in Romania and Paris, was by the 1920s the leading artist in the Yishuv. His one-man show in 1932 launched the Tel Aviv Art Museum. He created an indigenous style of art that combined Western artistic techniques with Eastern motifs.

3. M. Shamir, "Tarbut Mamlachtit" (A national culture), *Ha-Yarden,* September 30, 1935.

4. Jean-François Lyotard, "Judiciousness in Dispute, or Kant after Marx," in *The Lyotard Reader,* 324–59. Kant solved the conflict by arguing that the existence of harmony in the representational sphere, as shown by our ability to understand and talk about art in a rational manner, testifies to the rationality that organizes the aesthetic reality. The critic Juliet Sychreva has written that "this harmony of the faculties in relating a representation

to a subject gives us a pleasure which we apprehend in the object represented, which we call beautiful. However, because this harmony is in our faculties, it is common to all humanity" (Sychreva, *Schiller to Derrida*, 21).

5. Ibid., 345.

6. Eagleton, "Ideology and Its Vicissitudes in Western Marxism," 195.

7. According to Alice Y. Kaplan, fascism sought to create the ideal male (machine) that would maximize the human potential, a process that includes negating femininity and its qualities. See Kaplan, *Reproductions of Banality*, 81.

8. Sorel, "Introduction to Reflections on Violence," in Sternhell, *Ha-Mahshava ha-Fashistit le-Gvaneiha* (The fascist thought and its variations), 75.

9. I draw here on Ciniza Blum's argument that the cultural crisis of modernity was a linguistic and metaphysical one that involved the collapse of transcendental values and old systems of belief, which rely on the anthropocentric notion of a rational control of reality. See Blum, *The Other Side of Modernism*, 3–4.

10. Maurice Barres, *Les Déracinés*, quoted in Carroll, *French Literary Fascism*, 40.

11. Benjamin, "The Work of Art in the Age of Mechanical Reproduction," 241.

12. Ibid.

13. Ibid., 242.

14. Ibid.

15. The letter is quoted in Lyotard, "The Story of Ruth," in *The Lyotard Reader*, 258.

16. Bullock and Jennings, *Walter Benjamin*, 283.

17. Ibid., 224.

18. Y. Triush, "Jabotinsky al Omanut" (Jabotinsky on art), in Wirnik, Rubin, and Ramba, *Manhig ha-Dor* (The leader of the generation), 138.

19. Ibid., 139.

20. Jabotinsky to Boris Shatz, in *Michtavim* (Letters), 305.

21. M. Shamir, "Bein ha-Cosmos ve-ha-Moledet" (Between the cosmos and the homeland), *Ha-Yarden*, December 6, 1935.

22. Abba Achimeir, "Ha-Philosoph Sholel ha-Philosophia" (The philosopher who negates philosophy), JI P5 2/18.

23. Yevin, "Nisayon shel Hashkafa Estetit" (An attempt at an aesthetic outlook), in *Ketavim* (Writings), 245–46.

24. Ibid., 238.

25. Yevin, "Tarbut Asirim" (A culture of prisoners), in *Ketavim* (Writings), 248.

26. Spengler, *The Decline of the West,* 285–86.

27. Yevin, "Musar ve-Omanut" (Ethics and art), in *Ketavim* (Writings), 257.

28. Y. H. Yevin, "Yom Katnot ba-Sifrut ha-Ivrit" (Small days in the Hebrew literature), *Beitar,* January 1933, p. 24.

29. Y. H. Yevin, "Pirpurei Mahapecha" (Convulsions of revolution), *Doar ha-Yom,* July 4, 1930.

30. Y. H. Yevin, "Ezor Magen" (Defense sphere), *Doar ha-Yom,* November 1, 1929.

31. Jabotinsky, "Meshorer ha-Ga'ash" (The poet of fervor), in *Al Omanut ve-Sifrut* (On literature and art), 381.

32. Jabotinsky, "Anu ha-Amerikaim" (We the Americans), *Ha-Tzafon,* June 4, 1926.

33. Neocleous, *Fascism,* 53.

34. See Sternhell, *Yesodot ha-Fashism* (The birth of fascist ideology), 89–109.

35. Jabotinsky, "Al America" (On America), in *Al Sifrut ve-Omanut* (On literature and art), 190–91.

36. See Moriarty, *Roland Barthes,* 24–25.

37. In her analysis of the realist qualities of fascist aesthetics in Italy, Ruth Ben-Ghiat has argued that "fascists claimed that while the materialistic mentality of leftist authors limited them to the mere production or documentation of reality, the New Italian novelists were free to transfigure reality and produce works that would chronicle the present and yet bear the imprint of an individual creative and ethical sensibility" (Ruth Ben-Ghiat, "Fascism, Writing, and Memory," 632).

38. See Berman, "The Wandering Z," xix.

39. Ibid., 155.

40. Benjamin, "The Work of Art in the Age of Mechanical Reproduction," 239.

41. Kaplan, *Reproductions of Banality,* 8.

42. Gross and Gross, *Ha-Seret ha-Ivry* (The Hebrew movie), 28.

43. *Hazit ha-Am,* February 12, 1934.

44. Triush, "Jabotinsky al Omanut" (Jabotinsky on art), in Wirnik, Rubin, and Ramba, *Manhig ha-Dor* (The leader of the generation), 143.

45. Jabotinsky, "Anu ha-Amerikaim" (We the Americans). Characteristically, Jabotinsky seems to be using savagery to describe a positive trait.

46. *Ha-Yarden,* November 19, 1934. Unlike reviews in newspapers today,

this review did not include any information about the director or actors. Moreover, despite repeated forays into movie websites, I have been unable to determine the English title of this film, much less any information about it.

47. Jabotinsky, "Ke-she-ha-Olam Haya Tza'ir" (When the world was young), in *Al Sifrut ve Omanut* (On literature and art), 335.

48. Jabotinsky, "Ma Kor'im ve Ma Hoshvim" (What we read and what we think), in *Al Sifrut ve Omanut* (On literature and art), 314.

49. Jabotinsky, "Ke-she-ha-Olam Haya Tzair," (When the world was young), in *Al Sifrut ve Omanut* (On literature and art), 329–35.

50. Ibid., 332.

51. See Barzel, "Uri Zvi Greenberg," 11–39.

52. Shoham, *Sneh Basar ve-Dam* (A living burning bush), 96–97.

53. Uri Zvi Greenberg, "be-Chtav ha-Michveh" (Burning writing), *Moznaim* 25 (1931): 1.

54. Greenberg, "Massa" (Journey), in *Kelev Bait* (House Dog), 65.

55. On the political meaning of Greenberg's poetic stance, see Hever, *Be-Shevi ha-Utopia* (Captives of utopia), esp. 78–79.

56. U. Z. Greenberg, "Al Heter Histori ve-Demama Metzuvah" (On a historical permission and commanded silence), *Sadan* 3 (1925): 6.

57. Yevin, *Meshorer Mehokek* (Poet legislator), 82, 33–34.

58. Ibid., 60.

59. Greenberg, *Klapei Tish'im ve-Tish'ah* (Against ninety-nine), 36.

60. Ibid., 45.

61. Ibid., 44.

62. Ibid., 40.

63. Ibid., 29.

64. Uri Zvi Greenberg, "Ha-Tnuah ve ha-Sifrut" (The movement and the literature), *Sadan* 5 (1927): 14.

65. Greenberg, "ke-Matkonet Moladeti" (In the layout of my homeland), in *Kelev Ba'it* (House Dog), 30.

66. See Gur-Ze'ev, *Ascolat Frankfurt ve-ha-Historia shel ha-Pesimism* (The Frankfurt School and the history of pessimism), 86.

67. Uri Zvi Greenberg, "Tel Hai," *Beitar,* March 19, 1932.

68. Jabotinsky, "Al Amerika" (On America), in *Al Sifrut ve-Omanut* (On literature and art), 189.

69. Adolph Garbovsky, "Ha-Tzionut ve ha-Revisionism" (Zionism and revisionism), *Ha-Yarden,* December 12, 1934.

70. Yitzhak Ben-Menachem, "Ha-Hinuch ha-Leumi be-Italia ve-ha-Balilla" (National education in Italy and the Balilla), *Mishmar ha-Yarden* 5 (March 1935): n.p.

71. "Ha-Macabia ha-Rishona Niftecha" (The first Maccabia opened), *Avukah*, March 29, 1932.

72. Yitzhak Sciachi, "Hashkafatenu al ha-Medinah" (Our view regarding the state), *Mishmar ha-Yarden* 6 (1935): n.p.

73. Jabotinsky, "Ra'ayon Beitar" (The idea of Beitar), in *Ba-Derech la-Medinah* (On the way to the state), 319–20.

74. *Hazit ha-Am*, April 23, 1933.

75. Ze'ev Jabotinsky, *Samson the Nazirite* (London, 1930), 179–80. See Avineri, *The Making of Modern Zionism*, 174.

76. Zemach, *Al ha-Yafeh* (On the beautiful), 368–69.

5. Land, Space, and Gender

1. Quoted in Shohat, *Israeli Cinema*, 33.

2. Diamond, *Homeland or Holy Land?* 122–23.

3. See Ben Gurion, *Mi-Ma'amad le-Am* (From class to nation), 266. For a discussion of Ben Gurion's perception of land see Tzahor, "Ben Gurion's Mythopoetics," in Wistrich and Ohanna, *The Shaping of Israeli Identity*, 61–84.

4. Y. H. Yevin, "Le-Tashtesh Lo Narshe," (We will not allow to blur), *Doar ha-Yom*, September 26, 1929.

5. Zerubavel, "New Beginning, Old Past: The Collective Memory of Pioneering in Israeli Culture," in Silberstein, *New Perspectives on Israeli History*, 193–215.

6. *Hazit ha-A*, March 3, 1933.

7. Massey, *Space, Place, and Gender*, 177.

8. Zemach, *Avodah ve-Adama* (Labor and land), 75–76.

9. Nachman Sirkin, "Kriah la-Noar ha-Yehudy" (A call to Hebrew youth), 17, in Slutsky, *Tenuat ha-Avodah ha-Erets Yisraelit* (The Israeli Labor movement), 17.

10. See Gordon, "Labor," in *A. D. Gordon*, 52–53.

11. Beit-Hallahmi, *Original Sins*, 122. See also Silberstein, *The Postzionism Debates*, 22.

12. Ben Gurion, "Matan Aretz" (Giving a land), in Becker, *Mishnato shel David Ben Gurion* (The teachings of David Ben Gurion), 126.

13. Foucault, "Space, Knowledge and Power," in *The Foucault Reader*, 243–44.

14. Derek J. Penslar, in his study of the early Zionist settlement in Palestine as a technocratic enterprise, argued that Labor settlement played a critical role in the political and socioeconomic development of the Yishuv. He wrote, "Scientific discourse—spare, practical and universal—was music to

the ears of Zionist ideologues hostile to rabbinic declamation and the shrill cry of the hawker. The technician, alongside the farmer and the warrior, became a Zionist ideal type, the embodiment of the relentlessly pragmatic spirit that Zionists toiled to instill into what would become the Jewish state" (Penslar, *Zionism and Technocracy,* 154).

15. Hen Merhavia, "Al Ekronei Beitar" (On the principles of Beitar), *Mishmar ha-Yarden* 5 (March 1935): n.p.

16. Jabotinsky, *Shimshon,* 169.

17. Ibid.

18. Ibid., 172.

19. Yoseph Klausner, "Tefisat Olamo shel Shaul Tchernichovsky" (Saul Tchernichovsky's worldview), *Beitar,* January 1933.

20. Abba Achimeir, "Hafsiku Linto'a Kotzim" (Stop planting thorns), *Doar ha-Yom,* October 21, 1929.

21. Z. E. Cohen, "Al Od She'ela Ahat" (About one more question), *Hazit ha-Am,* August 16, 1932.

22. Jabotinsky, "Al America," in *Al Sifrut ve-Omanut* (On literature and art), 186.

23. Jabotinsky, "Sankevich," in *Al Sifrut ve-Omanut* (On literature and art), 164.

24. Sorel wrote: "I believe that if the professor of philology had not been continually cropping up in Nietzsche he would have perceived that the master type still exists under our own eyes, and that it is this type which, at the present time, has created the extraordinary greatness of the United States. He would have been struck by the singular analogies which exist between the Yankee, ready for any kind of enterprise, and the ancient Greek sailor, sometimes pirate, sometimes a colonist or merchant; above all, he would have established a parallel between the ancient heroes and the man who sets out on the conquest of the Far West" (Georges Sorel, *Reflections on Violence,* 272).

25. Jabotinsky, "Ha-Bourim" (The Boers), in *Reshimot* (Notes), 217.

26. Ibid., 220.

27. Ibid., 221.

28. Ibid., 222.

29. David Ben Gurion, "Gormey ha-Tzionut ve-Tafkideiha be-Sha'ah Zo" (The causes of Zionism and its function in this hour), in *Mishmarot* (Watches), 332–33.

30. Ibid.

31. Jabotinsky, "Al Haganant ha-Galil ha-Elyon" (On the defense of the Upper Galilee), in *Ne'umim 1905–1925* (Speeches), 148.

32. See "Ekronot ha-Revisionism" (The principles of revisionism), in Shavit, *Merov la-Medinah* (From majority to a state), 327.

33. Ze'ev Jabotinsky, "She'elat ha-Bitahon" (The question of security), *Doar ha-Yom*, October 19, 1929.

34. Abba Achimeir, "Dostoyevsky Lifnei ha-Het ve-Onsho" (Dostoyevsky before *Crime and Punishment*), *Ha-Boker*, October 22, 1937.

35. Yevin, "Etika ve-Omanut" (Ethics and art), in *Ketavim* (Writings), 257.

36. Jabotinsky, "Al America" (On America), in *Al Sifrut ve-Omanut* (On literature and art), 187.

37. Ibid., 189.

38. The letter was republished in the literary journal *Siman Kria* 21 (December 1990): 300–1.

39. Ibid.

40. Jabotinsky, "Al Amerika" (On America), in *Al Sifrut ve-Omanut* (On literature and art), 191–92.

41. See Bowie, *Aesthetics and Subjectivity,* 241.

42. See David Ohana, "Zarathustra in Jerusalem: Nietzsche and the 'New Hebrews,'" in Wistrich and Ohana, *The Shaping of Israeli Identity,* 38–60.

43. Ibid., 44.

44. A. D. Gordon, "Our Tasks Ahead," in Hertzberg, *The Zionist Idea,* 379.

45. Ibid., 381.

46. Abba Achimeir, "Physiocracy ve Marxism" (Physiocracy and Marxism), JI P5/2/14.

47. Y. H. Yevin, "Matay Nechakem?" (Until when will we wait?), *Hazit ha-Am*, March 17, 1933.

48. Jabotinsky, "Al Amerika" (On America), in *Al Sifrut ve-Omanut* (On literature and art), 192.

49. Jabotinsky, "Prakim be-Philosophia ha-Sotzialit shel ha-Tanach" (Chapters in the social philosophy of the Bible), in *Umah ve-Hevrah* (Nation and society), 188.

50. Pound, "The City," in *Selected Prose,* 226.

51. See Abba Achimeir, "Ha-Golem ve Maharal" (The golem and Maharal), JI P5/2/9.

52. Abba Achimeir, "Washington," *Hazit ha-Am,* March 13, 1932.

53. Heidegger warned that culture should not be dominated by a technology that "threatens man with the possibility that it could be denied to him to enter into a more original revealing and hence to experience the call of a more primal truth" (Heidegger, "The Question Concerning Technology," 28).

54. See Greenberg, *Klapei Tish'im ve-Tish'ah* (Against ninety-nine), 36.

55. Jabotinsky, "Korah u-Mishak" (Necessity and play), in *Umah ve-Havera* (Nation and society), 197.

56. Jabotinsky, "Ha-Bourim" (The Boers), in *Reshimot* (Notes), 220.

57. See Shavit, *Merov la-Medinah* (From majority to a state), 299.

58. Quoted in Cinzia Sartini Blum, *The Other Modernism*, 34.

59. On the general view of the radical European Right on gender, see Neocleous, *Fascism*, 79. See also Mosse, *Nationalism and Sexuality*, 156.

60. Kafkafi, "The Psycho-Intellectual Aspect of Gender Inequality," 188–211, esp. 189.

61. Hazleton, *Israeli Women*, 17.

62. See Lucia Re, "Fascist Theories of 'Woman' and the Construction of Gender," 81–82. See also Hawthorne and Golsan, *Gender and Fascism in Modern France*, 7.

63. Abba Achimeir, "Be-Shetach Shiltonah shel ha-Askanut" (Under the rule of the functionaries), *Hazit ha-Am*, November 18, 1932.

64. Abba Achimeir, "Be-Eretz Poshtei ha-Yad ve-ha-Regel" (In the land of beggars) *Hazit ha-Am*, September 30, 1932.

65. Abba Achimeir, "Realismus Romanti o Romantica Realistit" (Romantic realism or realistic romanticism), *Hazit ha-Am*, September 30, 1932; and "Gorgolov," *Hazit ha-Am*, August 2 1932.

66. Y. H. Yevin, "Hayei Nesu'im" (Married life), *Doar ha-Yom*, February 28, 1930.

67. Y. H. Yevin, "Tarbut Asirim" (A culture of prisoners), in *Ketavim* (Writings), 248.

68. Ibid.

69. Avraham Meikovich, "Le-She'elat ha-Isha ha-Ivrit" (Regarding the Hebrew woman), *Madrich Beitar* 2 (1932): n.p.

70. Jabotinsky, "Ekronei Beitar" (The principles of Beitar), in *Ba-Derech la-Medinah* (On the way to the state), 328.

71. Ibid.

72. Jabotinsky, "Tristan Da Runha," in *Several Stories Mostly Reactionary*, 178–79.

73. Ibid., 180.

74. Jabotinsky, *Hamishtam* (The five), 222.

75. Ibid., 226.

76. Jabotinsky, "Ekronei Beitar" (The principles of Beitar), in *Ba-Derech la-Medinah* (On the way to the state), 329.

77. Ibid.

78. See Mosse, *The Image of Man*, 151.

79. See Laurence Silberstein's discussion of the role of masculinity in

Zionism in *The Postzionism Debates,* 198–99. See also Boyarin, "Massada or Yavneh?" 306.

80. Gluzman, "Ha-Kmiha le-Hetrosexualiut" (Longing for heterosexuality), 145–62.

81. Derrida, "Edmond Jabès and the Question of the Book," 65.

82. See Mosse, *The Image of Man,* 152.

83. Lyotard, *Heidegger and "the jews,"* 22.

84. Silverman, "Re-Figuring 'the Jew' in France," 201.

85. For a discussion of the postmodern essentialist view of Judaism, see Ben-Naftali, "Lyotard ve 'ha-yehudim'" (Lyotard and the Jews), 159–70, esp. 163.

86. Azoulay and Ophir, "One Hundred Years of Zionism," 68.

87. See Zerubavel, "New Beginning, Old Past," 73.

88. Z. E. Cohen, "Al Od She'ela Ahat" (About one more question), *Hazit ha-Am,* August 16, 1932.

89. Foucault, "Space, Knowledge, and Power," 245.

90. Y. H. Yevin, "Beitar ve-Hamahapecha ba-Tzionut" (Beitar and the revolution in Zionism), *Homesh Beitar,* January 3, 1932.

91. Hen Merhavia, "Ekronei Beitar" (The principles of Beitar), *Mishmar ha-Yarden,* March 1935.

92. "Ha-Macabia ha-Rishona" (The first Maccabi Games), *Avukah* 2 (March 1932): n.p.

93. Y. Cohen, "Biryonim" (Hoodlums), in *Kitvei Yaacov Cohen, Shirim* (The writings of Ya'acov Cohen, Poems), 292–95. This poem became the anthem of Brith ha-Byrionim (the Brotherhood of zealots), the radical revisionist group headed by Abba Achimeir that operated in Palestine in the early 1930s.

94. Haim Gouri, interview by Ari Shavit, "The Odysseus Complex," *Ha-aretz,* March 3, 2000.

95. Ben Gurion, "Halutziut" (Pioneering), in Becker, *Mishnato shel David Ben Gurion* (The teachings of David Ben Gurion), 249.

6. Neither East nor West

1. Ofir Ha-Ivry, "The New Prince," *Azure* (spring 1997): 104–46.

2. Jabotinsky, "Al Tochnit ha-Avukatzia" (On the evacuation plan), speech to the Warsaw Club of Physicians and Engineers, October 1936, in *Ne'umim, 1927–1940* (Speeches), 201.

3. Jabotinsky, "Edmee," in *On Several Stories Mostly Reactionary,* 127.

4. Jabotinsky, "Ofnat he-Arabesqot" (The Arabesque fashion), in *Al Sifrut ve-Omanut* (On literature and art), 222.

5. Jabotinsky, "Rochlei ha-Ru'ah" (On the hawkers of the spirit), in *Al Sifrut ve-Omanut* (On literature and art), 239.

6. Ibid., 220.

7. Ibid., 213 (emphasis added).

8. Assar, "Signon ha-Arabesqua" (The Arabesque style), *Ha-Yarden*, December 17, 18, 20, 1934.

9. See Whitelam, *The Invention of Ancient Israel*, 59.

10. David Ben Gurion, "Atzma'ut Tarbutit" (Cultural independence), in *Mishnato shel David Ben Gurion* (The teachings of David Ben Gurion), 634–35.

11. Abba Achimeir, "Ha-Yehudim be-Germania" (The Jews in Germany), JI P5/2/10.

12. Abba Achimeir, "Ha-Mahapecha ha-Israelit ha-Gedolah" (The great Israeli revolution), in *Ha-Tzionut ha-Mahapchanit* (Revolutionary Zionism), 240–44.

13. Hen Merhavia, "Al Ekronei Beitar" (On the principles of *Beitar*), *Mishmar ha-Yarden* 5 (1935): n.p.

14. Dov Chomsky, "Am ha-Sefer" (The people of the book), *Madrich Beitar* 5 (1933): n.p.

15. Jabotinsky, *Shimshon*, 166–67.

16. See Nakhimovsky, *Russian-Jewish Literature and Identity*, 55. Nakhimovsky attributes Jabotinsky's discontent to his position as an assimilated Jew who was torn between his Jewish and Russian identities. While the parallels between Samson and a modern assimilated Jewish intellectual are interesting, I contend that Samson represents the dilemma of an Israeli leader torn between his national urges and his commitment to a universalist doctrine.

17. Jabotinsky, *Shimshon*, 86.

18. Jabotinsky to Carpi, February 23, 1934, JI A1/2/22/2. Itamar Ben Avi argued that like many other names of places around the Mediterranean, *Italy* is a Hebrew name. According to Ben Avi, the name is composed of three Hebrew words (*I*—island in Hebrew, *Tal*—dew in Hebrew, and *Yam*—sea in Hebrew). Ben Avi suggested that the source of this name is pre-Latin, perhaps from the Etruscan period, hinting at possible links between the ancient Hebrew and Etruscan cultures. See Itamar Ben Avi, "Derech Yamenu ha-Ivry" (Through our Hebrew sea), *Doar ha-Yom*, October 16, 1929.

19. Jabotinsky, *Ha-Mivtah ha-Ivri* (The Hebrew accent), 8.

20. Ibid., 9.

21. Jabotinsky to Yitzhak Sciachi, February 26, 1932, Jabotinsky Institute, A1/2/22/1.

22. Ibid.

23. The revisionists' historiographical approach to the ancient East had a profound influence on the Canaanite movement, whose leaders came from Revisionist circles but eventually adopted an anti-Zionist stance. For the most complete analysis of the Revisionist roots of the Canaanites, see Diamond, *Homeland or Holy Land.*

24. M. A. Perlmutter, "Al Gdot ha-Yam ha-Tichon" (On the shores of the Mediterranean), *Ha-Yarden,* September 12, 1934.

25. "Goralo shel Am: ha-Am ha-Iri Beshe'ibudo ve-Shihruro" (The fate of a people: The Irish people in their oppression and liberation), *Mishmar ha-Yarden* 1 (1935): n.p.

26. The analogy in this article to the Jewish condition is not only cultural; it contains a clear political message as well. The article discusses in great detail the Irish struggle for independence from British rule and sees its success as proof that such a struggle, in which the Zionists must engage, is worthwhile.

27. Abba Achimeir, "Katalunia" (Catalonia), *Haaretz,* November 4, 1927.

28. Abba Achimeir, "Tzafon ve Darom be-Arhav" (North and South in the United States), JI P5/2/35.

29. *Ha-Yarden* published an article from an Italian newspaper that attacked French culture and French youth, who prefer abstraction and universalism to life itself, life that is one with the nation and the state. See *Ha-Yarden,* September 14, 1934.

30. A. Faran, "Orientazia Mizrahit ba-Medinyut ha-Ivrit" (An eastern orientation in the Hebrew policy), *Ha-Yarden,* September 7, 1934.

31. Abba Achimeir, "Sinn Fein," in *Ha-Tzionut ha-Mahapchanit* (Revolutionary Zionism), 18.

32. Weinbaum, "Jabotinsky and the Poles," in Polonsky, *Polin,* 5:158.

33. *Ha-Yarden,* August 25, 1935.

34. Jabotinsky, "On Adventurism," quoted in Katz, *Lone Wolf,* 1340.

35. Jabotinsky clearly laid out this shift in policy in a speech that he gave in Warsaw in 1936 when he criticized England's policies in Palestine and pointed to Italy as the rising power in the region, a strong country that could be a true supporter of the Zionist and Jewish cause. The speech from June 13, 1936, was published in an information bulletin issued by the South African branch of the Revisionist Party (JI G3/5/10).

36. Hen Merhavia, "Ha-Medinah ke-Matara Sofit" (The state as a final goal), *Mishmar ha-Yarden* 9 (1935): n.p.

37. Jabotinsky to Mussolini, July 16, 1922, in *Igrot 1918–1922* (Letters), 3:337–40.

38. See Stein-Ashkenazie, *Beitar be-Eretz Israel* (Beitar in Eretz Israel), 25.

39. Clearly, the movement was more popular among Milan's Zionists than Rome's, perhaps because Milan was a more popular destination for Jewish students from eastern Europe.

40. Quoted in "Italy," an internal publication of the Jabotinsky Institute, JI G14/1. On November 5, 1931, Leone Carpi wrote a letter to the Italian authorities in which he criticized the British policies in Palestine and called on the Italians to adopt a radical approach with regard to the eastern question (CZA A73/7).

41. Sciachi to the Italian Revisionists (1929, no specific date provided), JI G14/2.

42. Carpi, speech before the first New Zionist Organization Conference, Vienna, September 1935, JI G14/5.

43. See A. Revere, "Hitler e gli Ebrei" (Hitler and the Jews), *L'Idea Sionistica* no. 2–3 (1931): 3.

44. Abba Achimeir, "Realismus Romanti o Romantica Realistit" (Romantic realism or realistic romanticism?), *Hazit ha-Am,* September 30, 1932. On November 12, 1935, *Ha-Yarden* published an article written by an Italian minister in which he declared that racial theories were not part of the Italian worldview. On November 24 the Revisionist daily published an article about the patriotism of Italian Jewry and declared that anti-Semitism did not exist in Italy.

45. Daniel Carpi has pointed out that the Italians were frustrated by the ineffectiveness of their pan-Arabic policy and sought other alternatives (Zionism) to weaken the British position in the region (Carpi, "Ha-Maga'im shel Ze'ev Jabotinsky be-Italia ba-Shanim 1932–1935" (The negotiations of Jabotinsky in Italy) in Y. Achimeir, *Ha-Nasich ha-Shahor* (The black prince), 349.

46. Ibid., 350.

47. On Weitzmann's meetings with Mussolini see Daniel Carpi, "Pe'iluto shel Weitzmann be-Italia ba-Shanim 1923–1934" (Weitzmann's activities in Italy in the years 1923–1934), in *Ha-Tzionut* (Zionism), 2: 169–207.

48. Dr. Lante Lattes, note for members of the Palestine Executive of the Union of Zionist Revisionists regarding the article in the *Piccolo della Sera,* March 9, 1932, CZA S25-2088.

49. The memorandum was published in Renzo De Felice, *Storia degli Ebrei Italiani Sotto il Fascismo* (The history of Italian Jews under fascism), 196–97. De Felice viewed this memorandum as proof of the close relations that developed between the Revisionists and the Italian Foreign Ministry from 1932 to 1935.

50. The idea of opening a Beitar training school in Italy had already

been broached in a conversation between Jabotinsky and the businessman Angelo Donati; Jabotinsky conveyed the gist of that conversation to Leone Carpi in a letter in November 1931. The letter to Sciachi was intended for the Italian authorities, which was how Jabotinsky made contact with Raffaele Guariglia, who was the head of the Middle Eastern desk at the Italian Foreign Ministry. See Daniel Carpi, "Ha-Maga'im shel Ze'ev Jabotinsky be-Italia ba-Shanim 1932–1935" (The negotiations of Jabotinsky in Italy), in Y. Achimeir, *Ha-Nasikh ha-Shahor* (The black prince).

51. Jabotinsky to Beitar cadets in Civitavecchia, November 20, 1934, JI A1/2/24/3.

52. Yirmiyahu Halperin, "Toldot ha-Yamaut ha-Ivrit" (The history of Hebrew seamanship), typescript. See chap. 6, p. 24, JI H1/19.

53. "Civitavecchia, Un Tragico Bagno" (Civitavecchia, a tragic affair), *Il Popolo di Roma,* May 23, 1935.

54. "Allievi dell'Unione Sionisti Revisionisti" (The students of the Revisionist Zionist Union), in *Bollettino del Consorzio Scuole Profesionali per la Maestranza Maritima* (Bulletin of the professional schools of maritime workers), pamphlet, February 1935.

55. See "Ma Kara la-Sefina be-Tunis," (What happened to the boat in Tunis), *Haaretz,* February 25, 1938.

56. See "Gli Allievi-Ufficiali del Sara 1," *L'Italiano di Tunisi,* January 9, 1938. The article claimed that Zionism was a colonialist movement and that, while the majority of the movement served British interests in the region, the Revisionists acted in the service of Italian fascism. Similarly, the publication *Cial Tunisie* declared that in Tunis the Revisionist cadets, who were fascist in their ideological beliefs as well as in their public appearance (dress and salutes), carried out Mussolini's policy, which advanced the selfish interests of the Italian regime at the expense of both Jews and Arabs. See "Encore une Provocation Mussolienne" (Another Mussolini-like provocation), *Cial Tunisie,* January 5, 1938.

57. *Ha-Yarden,* August 13, 1937.

Epilogue

1. From 1984 to 1988 the Likud and Labor created a "national unity" government, and Shimon Peres, the leader of the Labor Party, was the prime minister from 1984 to 1986. On the territories see Shapiro, *The Road to Power,* 149. As Colin Shindler claimed in his study of the Israeli Right, Likud's policy was based on the belief that the Zionist leadership's acceptance of the partition plan was an original sin and that only a return to all the territories promised to the Jewish people (and since 1967 protection

of those territories) would bring true salvation to the Jewish nation. See Shindler, *The Land Beyond Promise,* xviii–xix.

2. Shapiro, *The Road to Power,* 168. The critic Yitzhak La'or has claimed that for the Eastern Jews, the leaders of the Likud have offered a simple way of identifying with the state: hating the Arabs. According to La'or, Jews who came from Muslim countries assumed an "eastern" identity in Ashkenazi-dominated Israel, and in order to escape this definition (the Arabs are also seen as part of the East) Jews from Arab nations tended to support the overtly anti-Arab ideology of the Likud. See Yitzhak La'or, "Who Shall We Blame It On?" *London Review of Books,* February 20, 2003.

3. The three intellectuals who headed the maximalist faction of revisionism, Achimeir, Greenberg, and Yevin, also were removed from any position of influence under Begin's leadership. In 1938 Abba Achimeir, fearing another arrest by the British authorities, escaped Israel and spent most of the next decade out of the country. Upon his return he continued to write about Jewish history and current affairs in different Revisionist publications, but he was not politically involved in the movement. Uri Zvi Greenberg spent most of the second half of the 1930s in Poland, escaping that country two weeks after the Nazi invasion. Though he was not active in the Irgun, Greenberg represented Herut in the first Knesset—but he was a poet lost in an institution run by functionaries and party operatives, and after he completed his term he left organized politics for good. Greenberg continued his artistic career, and he was recognized by the Israeli literary and academic establishment for his poetic greatness (he won the Israel Prize—the highest honor bestowed by the State of Israel on a public figure—in 1953), but like Achimeir he was no longer involved in the politics of the Revisionist movement. The third leader of the maximalist faction, Y. H. Yevin, also lost his central position in the Revisionist movement by the late 1930s, and in the decades that followed, he all but disappeared from the Zionist and Israeli public sphere. Only through the persistence of close friends was a collection of his writings published in 1969.

4. Menachem Begin, "Le-Zichro shel Ze'ev Jabotisnky—Pekudat Seder" (In memory of Ze'ev Jabotinsky—A call for order), in *Mori* (My teacher), 52.

5. See Shlaim, "The Likud in Power."

6. Jabotinsky, "Mah Rotzim ha-Tzionim ha-Revisionistim" (What the Zionist Revisionists want), in *Ba-Derech la-Medinah* (On the way to the state), 283.

7. Peleg, *Begin's Foreign Policy,* 53.

8. Ibid.

9. Ian Lustick has argued that the logic of Jabotinsky's iron wall—the

assumption that Israel's relations with its Arab neighbors should be predicated on creation of a powerful military barrier between Israel and its neighbors—was the basis of not only the Revisionist movement's ideological platform but of the entire Zionist and Israel leadership since the late 1930s. See Lustick, "To Build and to Be Built by," 196–223.

10. Begin, "Lo la-shav Amal" (Work that is not in vain), in *Mori* (My teacher), 58 (emphasis added).

11. Menachem Begin's speech before the Knesset, June 15, 1949, JI P20/11/7.

12. Israel (Scheib) Eldad (1910–1996), like Abba Achimeir, received a doctoral degree in philosophy from the University of Vienna. He was a Beitar activist and came to Palestine during the Second World War and joined the underground movement Lehi. After Avraham Stern, the founder and leader of Lehi, was captured and killed by the British in February 1942, a new power structure emerged in Lehi, and Eldad became one of its leaders. After the establishment of the State of Israel, Eldad launched a journal, *Sulam* (Ladder), which served as a platform for his attacks on the Israeli political establishment. He also published articles in different Israeli dailies, and he had a weekly column in *Yedioth Aharonot*. Eldad taught courses at various Israeli universities and translated the writings of Nietzsche to Hebrew.

13. Israel Eldad, "Tzva ha-Havlaga le-Yisrael" (The Israel restraint force), *Sulam* 19 (1951): n.p.

14. Israel Eldad, "Yom Zikaron le-Lohamei Herut Yisrael" (Memorial Day for fighters for the freedom of Israel), *Sulam* 46 (1953): n.p.

15. See Sprinzak, *The Ascendance of Israel's Radical Right*, 40–41.

16. Gertz, *Shvuya be-Haloma* (Caught in her dream), 67.

17. Quoted in Rowland, *The Rhetoric of Menachem Begin*, 52–53.

18. In July 1945 Begin already was claiming that only the Jewish struggle for national independence would bring redemption to an enslaved and decimated people. See Rowland, *The Rhetoric of Menachem Begin*, 53.

19. Begin, "Why We Must Stand Fast," *American Zionist*, January 1971, p. 11.

20. In 1979 Begin's government signed a peace agreement with Egypt and returned the Sinai Peninsula to the Egyptians. According to Ilan Peleg, Begin's government from 1977 to 1979 pursued a policy aimed at neutralizing Egypt as a member of the anti-Israeli Arab coalition, but this policy was part of an overall goal: Israeli control over the West Bank and Gaza. See Peleg, "The Right in Israeli Politics," 149–150.

21. See "Hosefet et ha-Kesher" (Uncovering the tie), in "Milhemet ha-Elitot" (War of the elites), special supplement to *Yedi'ot Aharonot*, September 24, 1998.

22. It is interesting to note here that shortly after he became prime minister, Netanyahu pushed Benny Begin—Menachem Begin's son—and Dan Meridor, the son of an Irgun leader, out of his government and eventually out of the Likud. Netanyahu's father, Ben-Zion, was an intellectual and academic who was close to Jabotinsky. With the ascendance of Menachem Begin and his group, Ben-Zion Netanyahu was left out of the movement's centers of power, and he eventually left Israel for the United States. The victory of Benjamin Netanyahu over the movement's "princes" (the second generation of Irgun leaders, as they were called) symbolized, then, the end of the era of Irgun leadership in the Revisionist movement.

23. Ofir Ha-Ivry, "In the Beginning," *Azure,* summer 1996.

24. Yoram Hazony, "Did Herzl Want a Jewish State?" *Azure* (spring 2000): 39.

25. *Hazit ha-Am,* February 16, 1934.

26. See S. Fischer, "Tenu'at Shas" (The Shas movement), in Ophir, *Hamishim le-Arbai'im ve-Shmoneh* (Fifty to forty-eight), 331.

27. See Silberstein, *The Postzionism Debates,* 170.

28. Ibid., 7.

29. Lyotard, "Universal History and Cultural Differences," in *The Lyotard Reader,* 321; Ram, "Zikaron ve Zehut" (Memory and identity), 11.

30. See Ilan Pappe, "Tzionut ke Parshanut Shel ha-Metsiut," (Zionism as an interpretation of reality) *Haaretz* May 26, 1995.

31. Silberstein, "Historiyonim Hadashim ve-Tzotziologim Bikorti'im" (New historians and critical sociologists), 105–22. See Foucault, *Remarks on Marx,* 150.

32. See Kimmerling, "Academic History Caught in the Cross-Fire," 57.

33. Azoulay and Ophir, "One Hundred Years of Zionism," 68.

34. See Ram, "Zikaron ve Zehut" (Memory and identity).

35. Sheves's statements were made in an interview to Israeli radio the day after the assassination. They were quoted extensively in the Israeli press in subsequent weeks.

36. See Azoulay, "Dlatot Ptuchot" (Open doors).

37. Pappe, "Critique and Agenda," 79.

38. On the changes that Israeli politics has undergone since Begin's rise to power, see Gertz, *Shvuia be-Haloma* (Caught in her dream), 12.

39. Amnon Raz-Krakotzkin, "Ha-Dat Shamra al ha-Am ha-Yehudi" (Religion protected the Jewish people), *Ha'ir,* April 1, 1994. Elsewhere, Raz-Krakotzkin wrote that "nationalism, which regarded itself among other things as the secularization of Jewish life, did not manifest itself in the creation of a Jewish identity that is separated from theology, but was an

interpretation of theology and the Messianic idea." For Raz-Krakotzkin only a separation of the political and the theological, and a definition of Jewish life in Israel according to theological and cultural parameters, not by national ones, would save the Jews in Israel from the catastrophe inherent in the messianic idea. See Raz-Krakotzkin, "Bein Brith Shalom u-bein Beit ha-Mikdash (Between Brith Shalom and the Temple), 92.

40. Michael Lerner, "Post-Zionism: Restoring Compassion, Overcoming Chauvinism," *Tikkun,* March–April 1998, p. 38.

41. Azoulay and Ophir, "One Hundred Years of Zionism," 69. Ophir and Azoulay have contended that in a postmodern and post-Zionist Israel, "The religious Jews, who will cease to sanctify the land with their blood and the blood of others, will be able to develop their religious culture and renew it according to the demands and possibilities of the postmodern world, free from the tyrannical power of the state. Secular Jews will be able to develop their Judaism without having to rely on the nationalist interpretation, which came from the separatist elements of religious Judaism, and without the chauvinist baggage that is required by their political alliance with the religious Jews. Traditional Jews will be able to cultivate their tradition without the chauvinist cover that nationalism provides." See Azoulay and Ophir, "Shayarim Shel Eropa" (Remains of Europe), in *Yamim Ra'im* (Bad days), 204.

42. See Danny Efraty, "Ve-Shuv Hadash Asur" (And again new is forbidden), *Meimad* 7 (1996): 26–27.

43. Jencks, "The Death of Modern Architecture," 23.

44. Silberstein, *The Postzionism Debates,* 22.

45. See Vittiello, "Desert, Ethos, Abandonment," 140–42.

46. Silverman, "Re-Figuring 'the Jew' in France," 201.

47. Surette, *Pound in Purgatory,* 166. As Derrida himself put it: "By a slow movement whose necessity is hardly perceptible, everything that for at least some twenty centuries tended toward and finally succeeded in being gathered under the name of language is beginning to let itself be transferred to, or at least summarized under, the name of writing." See Derrida, *Of Grammatology,* 6.

48. Silberstein, *The Postzionism Debates,* 8.

49. Lusky, "Sefer Zikaron le Hilmi Shusha" (A memory book for Hilmi Shusha), 23.

50. Tennenbaum, "Hilmi Shusha—Hesped Lelo Milim" (Hilmi Shusha—A eulogy without words), 43–44.

51. For a discussion of Tennenbaum's analysis of violence see Ilan Gur Ze'ev, "Zicaron, Tephila Hilonit" (Memory, A secular prayer), *Haaretz Sepharim,* March 26, 1998.

52. Morrison, *The Poetics of Fascism,* 9.

53. Gutwein, "Left and Right," 37.

54. Gutwein, "Zehut Neged Ma'amad" (Identity versus class), 242.

55. Žižek, *The Ticklish Subject,* 208.

56. Jabotinsky, "Al America" (On America), in *Al Sifrut ve-Omanut* (On literature and art), 187.

57. Gadi Taub, "Post Tzionut—Ha-Kesher ha-Tzarfati-Amerikai-Yisraeli," (Post-Zionism—The French-American-Israeli connection) in Tuvia Friling (ed.) *Teshuvah le-Amit Post Tzioni* (An Answer to a Post-Zionist colleague) (Tel Aviv: Yedi'ot aharonot: Sifre hemed: 2003), 224–42, esp. 230–32.

58. Ibid., 233.

Bibliography

Archival Sources

Jabotinsky Institute, Tel Aviv

A1   Personal Archive of Ze'ev Jabotinsky

B4   Archive of Beitar Youth Movement: Beitar Headquarters, Riga-Vienna, 1945 – 49

G2   Archive of the Union of Zionists-Revisionists and the New Zionist Organization: World Union of Zionists-Revisionists, Executive, London, 1928 – 35

G3   Archive of the Union of Zionists-Revisionists and the New Zionist Organization: World Union of Zionists-Revisionists, Executive, Paris-London, 1930 – 46

G14   Archive of the Union of Zionists-Revisionists and the New Zionist Organization: Union of Zionist Revisionists, Italy, 1928 – 48

D1   Archives of Organizations and Institutions of the National Workers' Movement: The Revisionist Workers' Bloc, 1925 – 34

H1   Archives of Institutions of the Herut Movement, Herut-Liberal Bloc (Gahal), The Liberal Party, the Likud: The Herut Movement, The Likud, 1948 – 94

K14   Archives and Collections of Documents, Miscellaneous: Brith Ha-Biryonim (Collection), 1930 – 34

K20   Archives of British Colonial Office, Public Records Office (PRO), Photostats, 1917 – 48

P5   Personal Archives and Collections: Abba Achimeir

P20   Personal Archives and Collections: Menachim Begin

Central Zionist Archives, Jerusalem

A73   Personal Archive: Leone Carpi

Labor Party Archive, Beit Berl
2-23-1934   Labor Party, Meetings of the Executive, 1934
2-25-1934   Labor Party, Meetings of the Executive, 1934
2-22-1935   Labor Party, Meetings of the Executive, 1935
Labor Movement Archive, Lavon Institute, Tel Aviv
Abba Achimeir Archive, Ramat Gan
Abba Gaissinowitsch, "Bemerkungen zu Spenglers Auffassung Russlands" (Remarks on Spengler's concept of Russia), Ph.D. diss.

Printed Sources

Daily Newspapers, Periodicals, and Journals
Avukah (Tel Aviv, 1931–32, 1935, 1939)
Beitar (Tel Aviv, 1933–34)
Bollettino del Consorzio Scuole Profesionali per la Maestranza Maritima (Rome, 1935)
Cial Tunisie (Tunis, 1938)
Do'ar ha-Yom (Jerusalem, 1928–31)
Ezor Magen (Tel Aviv, 1934)
Haaretz (Tel Aviv, 1920–37)
Ha-Mashkif (Tel Aviv, 1938–40)
Ha-Tzafon (Haifa, 1926–27)
Ha-Umah (Tel Aviv, first published in 1962)
Ha-Yarden (Jerusalem and Tel Aviv, 1934–41)
Hazit ha-Am (Jerusalem and Tel Aviv, 1932–35)
Homesh Beitar (Tel Aviv, 1932)
Il Popolo di Roma (Rome, 1935)
Kuntras (Tel Aviv, 1924).
L'Idea Sionistica (Milan, 1930–38)
L'Italiano di Tunisi (Tunis, 1938)
Madrich Beitar (Warsaw, 1932–35)
Mishmar ha-Yarden (Jerusalem and Tel Aviv, 1934–35)
Mozna'im (Tel Aviv, 1931)
Rassvet (Paris, 1924–34)
Sadan (Tel Aviv, 1925–27)

Published Sources

Achimeir, Abba. *Brith ha-Biryonim* (The brotherhood of zealots). Tel Aviv, 1972. First published 1953.

———. *Ha-Tziunut ha-Mahapchanit* (Revolutionary Zionism). Tel Aviv, 1966.

———. *Hinenu Sikrikim* (We are Sikrikis). Tel Aviv, 1978.

———. *Moto shel Yosef Katsenelson* (The death of Yoseph Katsenelson). Tel Aviv, 1974.

———. *Yuda'ikah* (Judaica). Tel Aviv, 1960.

Achimeir, Yoseph, ed. *Ha-Nasich ha-Shahor: Yosef Katsenelson ve-ha-Tenuah he-Leumit bi-Shnot he-Sheloshim* (The black prince: Yoseph Katsenelson and the national movement in the 1930s). Tel Aviv, 1983.

Aronoff, Myron J. "Myths, Symbols, and Rituals of the Emerging State." In Silberstein, *New Perspectives on Israeli History.*

Avineri , Shlomo. *The Making of Modern Zionism.* New York, 1981.

Avital, Moshe. *Ze'ev Jabotinsky: Moreh, Manhig, Medina'i, Lohem, No'em, Balshan, Sofer u-Meshorer* (Ze'ev Jabotinsky: Teacher, leader, politician, warrior, orator, linguist, writer, and poet). New York, 1980.

Azoulay, Ariella. "Dlatot Petuchot: Museonim Histori'im be-Halal ha-Tziburi ha-Israeli" (Open doors: Museums of history in Israeli public space). *Teoria ve-Bikoret* 4 (summer 1993): 79 – 95.

Azoulay, Ariella, and Haim Dauel Lusky, eds. *Hilmi Shusha—Magash ha-Keseph* (Hilmi Shusha—The Silver Platter). Tel Aviv, 1997.

Azoulay, Ariella, and Adi Ophir. "One Hundred Years of Zionism, Fifty Years of a Jewish State." *Tikkun,* March–April, 1998, pp. 68 –70.

———. *Yamim Ra'im: Bein Ason le-Utopia* (Bad days: Between disaster and utopia). Tel Aviv, 2002.

Barzel, Hillel. "Uri Zvi Greenberg: ha-Gvanim she-ba-Mikhol" (Uri Zvi Greenberg: The shades of a brush). In *Uri Zvi Greenberg: Bibliograpia,* ed. Yohanan Arnon. Tel Aviv, 1980.

Becker, Ya'acov, ed. *Mishnato shel David Ben Gurion* (The teachings of David Ben Gurion). Tel Aviv, 1958.

Begin, Menachem. "Jabotinsky Set Us upon the Path of Freedom." In Schechtman, *Rebel and a Statesman.*

———. *Mori: Ze'ev Jabotisnky* (My teacher: Ze'ev Jabotisnky). Jerusalem, 2001.

Beit-Hallahmi, Benjamin. *Original Sins: Reflections on the History of Zionism and Israel.* New York, 1993.

Ben-Ghiat, Ruth. "Fascism, Writing, and Memory: The Realist Aesthetic in Italy, 1930–1950." *Journal of Modern History* 67 (September 1995): 630–56.

Ben Gurion, David. "Avodah Ivrit" (Hebrew labor), and "Matan Aretz"

(Giving a land). In Becker, *Mishnato shel David Ben Gurion* (The teachings of David Ben Gurion).

———. *Mi-Ma'amad le-Am* (From class to nation). Tel Aviv, 1933.

———. *Mishmarot* (Watches). Tel Aviv, 1935.

———. *Tnuat ha-Poalim ve ha-Revisionismus* (The Labor movement and revisionism). Tel Aviv, 1933.

Benjamin, Walter. "The Work of Art in the Age of Mechanical Reproduction." In *Illuminations*. New York, 1969.

Ben-Naftali, Michal. "Lyotard ve "ha-yehudim" (Lyotard and the Jews). *Teoria ve-Bikoret* 8 (summer 1996): 159–70.

Berman, Russel. "The Wandering Z: Reflection's on Kaplan's *Reproductions of Banality*." In Kaplan, *Reproductions of Banality*.

Bilski Ben-Hur, Raphaella. *Kol Yahid hu Melech* (Each individual a king). Tel Aviv, 1988.

Blum, Cinzia Sartini. *The Other Side of Modernism: F. T. Marinetti's Futurist Fiction of Power*. Berkeley, Calif., 1996.

Bowie, Andrew. *Aesthetics and Subjectivity: From Kant to Nietzsche*. Manchester, England, 1990.

Boyarin, Daniel. "Massada or Yavneh? Gender and the Arts of Jewish Renaissance." In *Jews and Other Differences: The New Jewish Cultural Studies,* ed. Jonathan Boyarin and Daniel Boyarin. Minneapolis, Minn., 1997.

Bullock, Marcus, and Michael W. Jennings, eds. *Walter Benjamin: Selected Writings, 1913–1926*. Vol. 1. Cambridge, 1996.

Carpi, Daniel. "Pe'iluto shel Weitzmann be-Italia ba-Shanim 1923–1934" (Weitzmann's activities in Italy in the Years 1923–1934). In *Ha-Tzionut: Ma'asef le-Toldot ha-Tenuah ha-Tzionit ve-ha-Yishuv be-Eretz-Israel* (Zionism: A collection of the history of the Zionist movement and the Jewish settlement in Israel). Vol. 2. Tel Aviv, 1971.

Carroll, David. *French Literary Fascism: Nationalism, Anti-Semitism, and the Ideology of Culture*. Princeton, N.J., 1995.

Cassirer, Ernst. *Language and Myth*. New York, 1946.

Cohen, Erik. "Israel as a Post-Zionist Society." In Wistrich and Ohana, *The Shaping of Israeli Identity*.

Cohen, Ya'acov. *Kitvei Ya'acov Cohen, Shirim* (The writings of Ya'acov Cohen, Poems). Tel Aviv, 1938.

De Felice, Renzo. *Storia degli Ebrei Italiani Sotto il Fascismo* (The History of Italian Jews under Fascism. Turin, Italy, 1961.

Delzell, Charles F. *Mediterranean Fascism, 1919–1945*. New York, 1970.

Derrida, Jacques. "Edmond Jabes and the Question of the Book." In *Writing and Difference*. Chicago, 1978.

———. *Of Grammatology*. Baltimore, Md., 1976.

Diamond, James. *Homeland or Holy Land? The "Canaanite" Critique of Israel*. Bloomington, Indiana, 1986.

Eagleton, Terry. "Ideology and Its Vicissitudes in Western Marxism." In *Mapping Ideology*, ed. Slavoj Žižek. London, 2000.

Eldad, Israel. "Jabotinsky Distorted." *Jerusalem Quarterly* 16 (summer 1980): 25–30.

Even, Ephraim. *Ha-Pilug ba-Tzionut: Madu'a Hekim Jabotinsky et ha-Histadrut ha-Tzionit ha-Hadasha* (The schism in Zionism: Why did Jabotisnky create the New Zionist Organization?). Jerusalem, 1992.

Ferri, Enrico. *Socialism and Modern Science*. Chicago, 1909.

Fischer, Klaus P. *History and Prophecy: Oswald Spengler and the Decline of the West*. New York, 1989.

Fischer, Shlomo. "Tenu'at Shas" (The Shas movement). In *Hamishim le-Arbai'im ve-Shmoneh: Momentim Bikorti'im be-Toldot Medinat Israel* (Fifty to forty-eight: Critical moments in the history of the State of Israel), ed. Adi Ophir. Tel Aviv, 1999.

Fishlov, David. *Michlafot Shimshon: Gilgulay Demuto shel Shimshon ha-Mikra'i* (Samson's locks: The transformation of biblical Samson). Haifa, 2000.

Foucault, Michel. "Power and Strategies." In *Power/Knowledge: Selected Interviews and Other Writings, 1972–1977*. Edited by Colin Gordon. New York, 1980.

———. *Remarks on Marx*. New York, 1991.

———. "Space, Knowledge and Power." In *The Foucault Reader*. Edited by Paul Rabinow. New York, 1991.

Gasman, Daniel. *Haeckel's Monism and the Birth of Fascist Ideology*. New York, 1998.

Gepstein, S. *Ze'ev Jabotisnky: Hayav, Milhamto, Hesegav* (Ze'ev Jabotinsky: His life, war, achievements). Tel Aviv, 1941.

Gertz, Nurith. *Shvuia be-Haloma* (Caught in her dream). Tel Aviv, 1995.

Ginosar, Pinhas, and Avi Bareli, eds. *Tzionut: Pulmus Ben Zmanenu* (Zionism: A contemporary debate). Be'er Sheva, Israel, 1996.

Gluzman, Michael. "Ha-Kmiha le-Hetrosexualiut: Tziunut ve-Mini'ut be'Altneuland." (Longing for heterosexuality: Zionism and sexuality in Herzl's *Altneuland*). *Teoria ve-Bikoret* 11 (fall 1997): 145–62.

Gordon, A. D. *A. D. Gordon, Selected Essays*. New York, 1938.

———. "Our Tasks Ahead." In Hertzberg, *The Zionist Idea.*

Goren, Ya'acov. *Ha-Imut ha-Kove'a: Bein Tenu'at ha-Avodah la-Tenu'a ha-Revisionistit* (The determining dispute: Between the Labor and Revisionist movements). Tel Aviv, 1986.

Goux, Jean-Joseph. *Symbolic Economies, After Marx and Freud.* Ithaca, N.Y., 1990.

Graur, Mina. *Ha-Itonut shel ha-Tenu'ah ha-Revisionistit ba-Shanim 1925–1948* (The press of the Revisionist movement, 1925–1948). Tel Aviv, 2000.

Greenberg, Uri Zvi. *Clapei Tishiim ve-Tisha'ah* (Against ninety-nine). Tel Aviv, 1928.

———. *Ezor Magen u-Ne'um Ben ha-Dam* (Defense sphere and the speech of the mortal one). Tel Aviv, 1930.

———. *Kelev Bait* (House Dog). Tel Aviv, 1929.

Gross, Nathan, and Ya'acov Gross. *Ha-Seret ha-Ivry* (The Hebrew movie). Jerusalem, 1991.

Gur-Ze'ev, Ilan. *Ascolat Frankfurt ve-ha-Historia shel ha-Pesimism* (The Frankfurt school and the history of pessimism). Jerusalem, 1996.

Gutwein, Daniel. "Left and Right: Post Zionism and the Privatization of Israeli Collective Memory." In *Israeli Historical Revisionism: From Left to Right,* ed. Anita Shapira and Derek Penslar. London, 2003.

———. "Zehut Neged Ma'amad: Rav-Tarbutiyut ke-Ideologia Neo-Liberalit" (Identity versus class: Multiculturalism as a neoliberal ideology). *Teoria ve-Bikoret* 19 (fall 2001): 241–58.

Ha-Ivry, Ofir. "The New Prince." *Azure* 2 (spring 1997): 104–46.

Halevi, H. S. "Pan-Basilia." In Wirnik, Rubin, and Ramba, *Manhig ha-Dor* (The leader of the generation).

Haramaty, Shlomo. *Ha-Hinuch ha-Ivry be-Mishnat Jabotinsky* (The Hebrew education in Jabotinsky's teachings). Jerusalem, 1981.

Hawthorne, Melanie, and Richard J. Golsan. *Gender and Fascism in Modern France.* Hanover, N.H., 1997.

Hazleton, Lesley. *Israeli Women: The Reality Behind the Myths.* New York, 1977.

Heidegger, Martin. "The Question Concerning Technology." In *The Question Concerning Technology and Other Essays.* New York, 1977.

Heller, Yoseph. "Ha-Monism shel ha-Matarh o ha-Monism shel ha-Emtzaim? Ha-Mahloket ha-Ra'ayonit ve-ha-Politit bein Ze'ev Jabotinsky lebein Abba Achimeir, 1928–1933." (The Monism of the goal and the monism of means? The ideological debate between Ze'ev Jabotinsky and Abba Achimeir). *Zion* 52, no. 2 (1987): 315–69.

———. *Lehi: Ideologia ve-Politica 1940–1949* (Lehi: Ideology and politics). Jerusalem, 1989.

———. "Ze'ev Jabotinsky and the Revisionist Revolt against Materialism— In Search of a World View." *Jewish History* 12 (fall 1998): 51–67.

Hertzberg, Arthur. *The Zionist Idea: A Historical Analysis and Reader*. New York, 1970.

Hever, Hanan. *Bi-Shvi ha-Utopia: Masa al Meshihiyut ve-Politika ba-Shira ha-Ivrit bein Shtei Milhamot ha-Olam* (Captives of Utopia: An essay on messianism and politics in Eretz Israel between the two world wars). Jerusalem, 1995.

Jabotinsky, Ze'ev. *Al Sifrut ve-Omanut* (On literature and art). Jerusalem, 1958.

———. *Autobiographia*. Jerusalem, 1947.

———. *Ba-Derech la-Medinah* (On the way to the state). Jerusalem, 1959.

———. *Ba-Sa'ar* (In the storm). Jerusalem, 1959.

———. *Filitonim* (Feuilleton). Jerusalem, 1949.

———. *Hamishtam* (The five). Tel Aviv. 1957.

———. *Ha-Mivtah ha-Ivri* (The Hebrew accent). Tel Aviv, 1930.

———. *Ha-Revisionism ha-Tziony Likrat Mifne: Kovetz Ma'amarim be-Rassvyet le-Shanim 1932–1934* (Zionist revisionism approaching a turning point: A collection of articles from Rassvyet). Tel Aviv, 1986.

———. *Igrot 1898–1914* (Letters). Edited by Daniel Carpi. Jerusalem, 1992.

———. *Igrot 1914–1918* (Letters). Edited by Daniel Carpi. Jerusalem, 1995.

———. *Igrot 1918–1922* (Letters). Edited by Daniel Carpi. Jerusalem, 1997.

———. *Igrot 1922–1925* (Letters). Edited by Daniel Carpi. Jerusalem, 1998.

———. *Igrot 1926–1927* (Letters). Edited by Daniel Carpi. Jerusalem, 2000

———. *Ketavim Tzioni'im Rishonim* 1903–1906 (Early Zionist writings). Tel Aviv, 1949

———. *Megillat ha-Gedud* (The story of the Jewish legion). Tel Aviv, 1957.

———. *Michtavim* (Letters). Tel Aviv, 1959.

———. *Ne'umim* 1905–1925 (Speeches). Jerusalem, 1958.

———. *Ne'umim* 1927–1940 (Speeches). Tel Aviv, 1957.

———. *Reshimot* (Notes). Tel Aviv, 1959.

———. *Several Stories Mostly Reactionary*. Pocket ed. Paris, 1925.

———. *Shimshon* (Samson the Nazarite). Jerusalem, 1959.

———. *Shirim* (Poems). Jerusalem, 1958.

———. *Sipurim* (Stories). Tel Aviv, 1949.

———. *Sippur Yamai* (The story of my life). Tel Aviv, 1957.

———. *Umah ve-Havrah* (Nation and society). Tel Aviv, 1959.

———. *Zichronot Ben-Dori* (Contemporary recollections). Tel Aviv, 1950.

Jencks, Charles. "The Death of Modern Architecture." In *The Language of Post-Modern Architecture*. New York, 1991.

Kafkafi, Eyal. "The Psycho-Intellectual Aspect of Gender Inequality in Israel's Labor Movement." *Israel Studies* 4 (spring 1999): 188–211.

Kaplan, Alice Y. *Reproductions of Banality: Fascism, Literature and French Intellectual Life*. Minneapolis, Minn., 1986.

Katz, Shmuel. *Lone Wolf: A Biography of Ze'ev Jabotisnky*. 2 vols. New York, 1996.

Kimmerling, Baruch. "Academic History Caught in the Cross-Fire." *History and Memory* 7, no. 4 (1995): 57.

Kister, Yoseph. *Etzel* (The Irgun). Tel Aviv, 1994.

Koepnick, Lutz. *Walter Benjamin and the Aesthetics of Power*. Lincoln, Neb., 1999.

Liebman, Charles S. and Eliezer Don-Yehiya. *Civil Religion in Israel*. Berkeley, Calif., 1993.

Lusky, Haim Da'uel. "Sefer Zikaron le Hilmi Shusha" (A memory book for Hilmi Shusha). In Azoulay and Lusky, *Hilmi Shusha*.

Lustick, Ian. *Arabs in the Jewish State*. Austin, Texas, 1980.

———. "To Build and to Be Built By: Israel and the Hidden Logic of the Iron Wall." *Israel Studies* 1 (spring 1996): 196–223.

Lyotard, Jean-François. *Heidegger and "the jews."* Minneapolis, Minn., 1990.

———. *The Lyotard Reader*. Edited by Andrew Benjamin. Oxford, 1989.

Marsh, Alec. *Money and Modernity: Pound, Williams and the Spirit of Jefferson*. Tuscaloosa, Ala., 1998.

Marx, Karl. *Early Writings*. New York, 1964.

Massey, Doreen. *Space, Place and Gender*. Minneapolis, Minn., 1994.

Medoff, Rafael. *Militant Zionism in America: The Rise and Impact of the Jabotinsky Movement in the United States, 1926–1948*. Tuscaloosa, Ala., 2002.

Moriarty, Michael. *Roland Barthes*. Stanford, Calif., 1991.

Morris, Benny. "The New Historiography: Israel Confronts Its Past." *Tikkun* (November–December 1988): 19–23.

———. "Origins of the Palestinian Refugee Problem." In Silberstein, *New Perspectives on Israeli History*.

———. *Righteous Victims: A History of the Zionist-Arab Conflict 1881–1999* New York, 1999.

———. *1948 and After: Israel and the Palestinians*. Oxford, 1994.

Morrison, Paul. *The Poetics of Fascism*. Oxford, 1996.

Mosse, George. *The Image of Man: The Creation of Modern Masculinity*. Oxford, 1996.

————. *Nationalism and Sexuality: Middle-class morality and sexual norms in modern Europe.* Madison, Wis., 1985.

Mussolini, Benito. *The Political and Social Doctrine of Fascism.* Rome, 1935.

Nakhimovsky, Alice Stone. *Russian-Jewish Literature and Identity.* Baltimore, Md., 1992.

Neocleous, Mark. *Fascism.* Minneapolis, Minn., 1997.

Nolte, Ernst. *Three Faces of Fascism.* New York, 1965.

Ohana, David. "Zarathustra in Jerusalem: Nietzsche and the 'New Hebrews.'" In Wistrich and Ohana, *The Shaping of Israeli Identity.*

Ornstein, Ya'acov. *Be-Kvalim* (In bondage). Tel Aviv, 1973.

Pappe, Ilan. "Critique and Agenda: The Post-Zionist Scholars in Israel." *History and Memory* 7 (1995).

————. "Seder Yom Hadash la Historia ha-Hadasha" (A new agenda for the new history). *Teoria ve-Bikoret* 8 (summer 1996): 123–38.

Payne, Stanley G. *Fascism: Comparison and Definition.* Madison, Wis., 1980.

Peleg, Ilan. *Begin's Foreign Policy, 1977–1983: Israel's Move to the Right.* Westport, Conn., 1987.

————. "The Right in Israeli Politics: The Nationalist Ethos in the Jewish Democracy." In *Israel's First Fifty Years,* ed. Robert O. Freedman. Gainesville, Fla., 2000.

Penslar, Derek J. *Zionism and Technocracy: The Engineering of Jewish Settlement in Palestine, 1870–1918.* Bloomington, Ind., 1991.

Poleskin-Ya'ari, Ya'acov. *Ze'ev Jabotinsky: Hayav ve-Pe'ulato* (Ze'ev Jabotinsky: His life and his acts). Tel Aviv, 1930.

Pound, Ezra. *Selected Prose, 1909–1965.* New York, 1973.

Ram, Uri. "Zikaron ve Zehut: Sotsiologia Shel Vikuah ha-Historyonim be-Yisrael" (Memory and identity: A sociology of the historians' debate in Israel). *Teoria ve-Bikoret* 8 (summer 1996): 9–32.

Raz-Krakotzkin, Amnon. "Bein Brith Shalom u-bein Beit ha-Mikdash: Ha-Dialectica shel Ge'ulah u-Meshihiut be-Icvot Gershom Shalom" (Between Brith Shalom and the temple: Redemption and messianism in the Zionist discourse through the writings of Gershom Scholem). *Teoria ve-Bikoret* 20 (winter 2002): 87–112.

Re, Lucia. "Fascist Theories of 'Woman' and the Construction of Gender." In *Mothers of Invention: Women, Italian Fascism, and Culture,* ed. Robin Pickering-Iazzi. Minneapolis, Minn., 1995.

Reinharz, Jehudah. *Chaim Weitzmann: The Making of a Statesman.* New York, 1993.

Rowland, Robert C. *The Rhetoric of Menachem Begin: The Myth of Redemption Through Return.* Lanham, Md., 1985.

Schechtman, Joseph B. *Rebel and a Statesman: The Life and Times of Vladimir Jabotinsky.* 2 vols. Silver Spring, Md., 1986.

Schiller, Friedrich. *On the Aesthetic Education of Man: In a Series of Letters.* New York, 1965.

Schwartz, Shalom. *Jabotinsky Lohem ha-Umah* (Jabotinsky, the nation's warrior). Jerusalem, 1943.

Segev, Tom. *1949: The First Israelis.* New York, 1986.

――――. *The Seventh Million: The Israelis and the Holocaust.* New York, 1993.

――――. *Yemey ha-Kalaniyot* (Two Palestines). Jerusalem, 1999.

Shapira, Anita. *Ha-Ma'avak ha-Nichzav: Avodah Ivrit, 1929–1939* (The lost struggle: Hebrew Labor, 1929–1939). Tel Aviv, 1977.

――――. *Herev ha-Yonah* (The sword of the dove). Tel Aviv, 1992.

――――. *Land and Power: The Zionist Resort to Force, 1881–1948.* New York, 1992.

Shapira, Anita, and Daniel Carpi, eds. *Avodah Ivrit ve Ba'aya Aravit* (Hebrew Labor and an Arab problem). Tel Aviv, 1974.

Shapiro, Yonathan. *The Road to Power.* New York, 1991.

Shavit, Ya'acov. *Ha-Mitologiot shel ha-Yamin* (The mythologies of the right). Beit Berl, Israel, 1986.

――――. *Ha-Yahadut be-Rei ha-Yevanut ve-Hofa'at ha-Yehudi ha-Helenisti ha-Moderni* (Judaism in the Greek mirror and the emergence of the modern Hellenized Jew). Tel Aviv, 1992.

――――. *Jabotinsky and the Revisionist Movement.* London, 1988.

――――. "Le'umiyut, Historiographia ve-Revisia Historit" (Nationalism, historiography, and historical revision). In Ginosar and Bareli, *Tzionut.*

――――. *Merov le-Medinah: Ha-Tenuah ha-Revisionistit—ha-Tochnit ha-Hityashvutit ve-ha-Ra'ayon ha-Hevrati 1925–1935* (From majority to a state: The Revisionist movement—The colonization program and the social idea, 1925–1935). Tel Aviv, 1978.

――――. *The New Hebrew Nation: A Study in Israeli Heresy and Fantasy.* London, 1987.

Shimoni, Gideon. *The Zionist Ideology.* Hanover, N.H., 1995.

Shindler, Colin. *The Land Beyond Promise: Israel, Likud and the Zionist Dream* New York, 2002.

Shlaim, Avi. "The Likud in Power: The Historiography of Revisionist Zionism" *Israel Studies* 1 (fall 1996): 278–93.

Shoham, Reuven. *Sneh Basar ve-Dam: Poetica ve-Retorica be-Shirato ha-Modernistit ve-ha-Architipit shel Uri Zvi Greenberg* (A living burning bush: Poetics and rhetoric in the modernist and archetypic poetry of Uri Zvi Greenberg). Be'er Shevah, Israel, 1997.

Shohat, Ella. *Israeli Cinema: East/West and the Politics of Representation.* Austin, Texas, 1989.

Shoshani, Reuven. "Ha-Basis ha-Metodologi shel Heker Ideologiot: Mishnato ha-Medinit ve-ha-Hevratit shel Ze'ev Jabotisnky" (The methodological study of ideologies: The political and social doctrine of Ze'ev Jabotisnky). Doctoral diss., Hebrew University, Jerusalem, 1990.

Silberstein, Laurence J. "Historiyonim Hadashim ve-Tzotziologim Bikorti'im: Bein Post Tzionut le Post Modernism" (New Historians and critical sociologists: Between post-Zionism and postmodernism). *Teoria ve-Bikoret* 8 (summer 1996): 105–22.

———. *The Postzionism Debates: Knowledge and Power in Israeli Culture.* New York, 1999.

———, ed. *New Perspectives on Israeli History: The Early Years of the State.* New York, 1991.

Silverman, Max. "Re-Figuring 'the Jew' in France." In *Modernity, Culture, and "the Jew,"* ed. Bryan Cheyette and Laura Marcus. Stanford, Calif., 1998.

Sirkin, Nachman. "Kriah la-Noar ha-Yehudy" (A call to Hebrew youth). In Slutsky, *Tenuat ha-Avodah ha-Erets Yisraelit* (The Israeli Labor movement).

Slutsky, Yehuda, ed. *Tenuat Ha-Avodah Ha-Erets Yisraelit* (The Israeli Labor movement). Tel Aviv, 1966.

Sorel, Georges. *Reflections on Violence.* New York, 1941.

Spengler, Oswald. *The Decline of the West.* 2 vols. New York, 1939.

Sprinzak, Ehud. *The Ascendance of Israel's Radical Right.* Oxford, 1991.

Stanislawski, Michael. *Zionism and the Fin de Siecle: Cosmopolitanism and Nationalism from Nordau to Jabotinsky.* Berkeley, Calif., 2001.

Stein, Kenneth W. "One Hundred Years of Social Change." In Silberstein, *New Perspectives on Israeli History.*

Stein-Ashkenazy, Esther. *Beitar be-Eretz-Israel, 1925–1947* (Beitar in Eretz Israel). Jerusalem, 1997.

Sternhell, Ze'ev. *Ha-Mahshava ha-Fashistit le-Gevanei'a* (The fascist thought and its variations). Tel Aviv, 1988.

———. *Neither Right nor Left: Fascist Ideology in France.* Berkeley, 1986.

———. *Yesodot ha-Fashism* (The birth of fascist ideology). Tel Aviv, 1996.

Surette, Leon. *Pound in Purgatory: From Economic Radicalism to Anti-Semitism.* Urbana, Il., 1999.

Sychreva, Juliet. *Schiller to Derrida: Idealism in Aesthetics.* Cambridge, England, 1989.

Tennenbaum, Adam. "Hilmi Shusha—Hesped Lelo Milim" (Hilmi Shusha—A eulogy without words). In Azoulay and Lusky, *Hilmi Shusha.*

Thompson, Doug. *State Control in Fascist Italy.* New York, 1991.

Trevor-Roper, H. R. "The Phenomenon of Fascism." In *Fascism in Europe,* ed. S. J. Woolf, London, 1981.

Triush, Y. "Jabotinsky on Art." In Wirnik, Rubin, and Ramba, *Manhig ha-Dor* (The leader of the generation).

Tzahor, Ze'ev. "Ben Gurion's Mythopoetics." In Wistrich and Ohanna, *The Shaping of Israeli Identity.*

Vittiello, Vincenzo. "Desert, Ethos, Abandonment: Towards a Topology of the Religious." In *Religion,* ed. Jacques Derrida and Gianni Vattimo. Stanford, Calif., 1998.

Weinbaum, Laurence. "Jabotinsky and the Poles." *Polin* 5 (1990): 156–72.

Weingrod, Alex. "How Israeli Culture Was Constructed: Memory, History and the Israeli Past." *Israel Studies* 2 (spring 1997): 228–39.

Whitelam, Keith W. *The Invention of Ancient Israel: The Silencing of Palestinian History.* London, 1997.

Wirnik, Yerahmiel, Y. Rubin, and Aizik Ramba, eds. *Manhig ha-Dor* (The leader of the generation). Tel Aviv, 1946.

Wistrich, Robert S. and David Ohana, eds. *The Shaping of Israeli Identity: Myth, Memory and Trauma.* London, 1995.

Wyman, David S., and Rafael Medoff. *A Race against Death: Peter Bergson, America, and the Holocaust.* New York, 2002.

Yevin, Y. H. *Ketavim* (Writings). Tel Aviv, 1969.

———. *Meshorer Mehokek* (Poet legislator). Tel Aviv, 1938.

Zarthal, Idith. *From Catastrophe to Power: Holocaust Survivors and the Emergence of Israel.* Berkeley, Calif., 1998.

Zemach, Shlomo. *Al ha-Yafe* (On the beautiful). Tel Aviv, 1939.

———. *Avodah ve-Adama* (Labor and land). Jerusalem, 1950.

Zerubavel, Yael. "New Beginning, Old Past: The Collective Memory of Pioneering in Israeli Culture." In Silberstein, *New Perspectives on Israeli History.*

———. *Recovered Roots: Collective Memory and the Making of Israeli National Tradition.* Chicago, 1995.

Žižek, Slavoj. *The Ticklish Subject: The Absent Centre of Political Ontology.* London, 1999.

Index

Achimeir, Abba: aesthetics and, 84; Arlozoroff murder case and, 12, 39; Begin's leadership and, 208n3; Beitarists and, *xiii;* biblical heroes and, 37; biographical information, 16–17, 208n3; on colonization, 114; on communism, 19; on cultural decline, 188n20 *(see also* Spengler *under this heading);* on Diaspora, 143, 188n21; on economic roles of the state, 59; on Italy, 152; Jabotinsky on, 20–21; on Jewish soul, 35–36; Marxism and, 19, 185n46; as maximalist, 15; Mediterranian culture and, 148–49; on modernism, 119; pictured, 106; "Raskolnikov in the Central Jail," 38–39; on revisionism's legacy, *xviii–xix;* on revolution, 18–19; on socialism, 19, 58, 114, 127; Spengler and, 17–18, 35–38, 58; theology as symptomatic of decline, 143–44; on U.S. politics and north/south dichotomy, 149; on war and national identity, 40–41; on Western philosophy, 84

aesthetics: the banal or mundane rejected, 87, 127–28; as escape from conventional rules, 85; freedom and, 85; futurist aesthetics, 102; Jabotinsky as author, 6; Jabotinsky on, 42, 82–83, 87–91, 94; Labor Zionist perspective on, 103; life as aesthetic experience, 119; politics, aesthetization of, 77–83, 100–103; rationality rejected in Revisionist aesthetics, 76–77; realism and, 87, 197n37; rejection of Western culture and, 83–84, 96; representation and, 75–76, 80; Revisionist critique of Hebrew culture and, 83; Schiller's concept of play, 68; spiritual space and, 118–19; war as aesthetic experience, 80–81; Yevin on, 127–28

Allenby, Edmund, 4–5

Amalekites, Arabs as modern-day, 165

American culture: Achimeir on, 149, 188n20; black culture as example of racial consciousness, 119–21; frontier and, 116; Jabotinsky's admiration for aspects of, 89, 116; Revisionists and, 119–20

anti-Semitism: Anglo-Saxon heritage linked to, 153–54; Haeckel and, 44; in Poland, 182n16; revisionism and, *xviii;* socialism as anti-Semitic, 40

Arabs: agricultural tradition and, 113; "Arab revival," 140–41; Beitar cadets clashes with, 157–58; as enemies of the Jewish people, 165, 168; Great Arab revolt and partition